# THE FOLK HANDBOOK

## Working with songs from the English tradition

**A BACKBEAT BOOK**

First edition 2007

Published by Backbeat Books (an imprint of Hal Leonard Corporation)

19 West 21st Street, New York, NY 10010, USA

www.backbeatbooks.com


Devised and produced for Backbeat Books by Outline Press Ltd

2A Union Court, 20-22 Union Road, London SW4 6JP, England

www.backbeatuk.com


ISBN: 978-0-87930-901-5

There is a website to accompany this book
at www.folkhandbook.com.

Creative Director: NIGEL OSBORNE

Editor: JOHN MORRISH

Design: PAUL COOPER

Music editor: ROD FOGG

Transcriptions of CD tracks: JULIAN ELLOWAY


Origination and print by Colorprint (Hong Kong)


07 08 09 10 11  5 4 3 2 1

# Contents

COVER PICTURES: Martin Carthy (background);
Kate Rusby (inset).

# Foreword

## BY SHIRLEY COLLINS

The question "What is folk music and is it a revival or a survival?" has been exercising us for quite a while. Alan Lomax wrote in 1958: "The first function of... folk music is to produce a feeling of security for the listener, by voicing the particular quality of a land and the life of its people... Folk song calls the native back to his roots..." And some 50 years later, in 2007, our champion of English music, John Kirkpatrick, echoed that, saying: "It reinforced your identity – it was community cement, and you knew exactly who you were."

Traditional music by its very definition springs from the past. It has a history, some songs and ballads evolving over centuries, some over mere generations. But in our time, the approach of some people attempting to update this music can be inappropriate, sometimes lacking in understanding, and failing to pay sufficient attention to the value of what we have. Certainly the tradition belongs to everyone, but we are the stewards of it for future generations, and should cherish, nurture and respect it.

The best of the English songs have graceful tunes, a melancholy without sentimentality, a subtlety of decoration and rhythm. Occasionally there's an age-old mystery or darkness at their heart. There's a fascination too in the way the songs changed over time, and the forms in which they've come down to us, where verses have been re-ordered or lost, smudged away, where sometimes you just catch a glimpse of what was meant. This is not to say that every song is profoundly beautiful, though. After all, they cover every aspect of life, and words and tunes are appropriate to their subject.

The move to save this tradition has been going on for longer than you might suppose. John Broadwood, for instance, had been collecting 'from the lower orders' in Sussex and Surrey in the early 1800s, publishing his first book in 1843. However, the major part of folk-song collecting was done on the cusp of the 19th and 20th centuries. As concern grew that these old songs might be lost if not noted down, people like Cecil Sharp, Ralph Vaughan Williams, and Hammond and Gardiner came to the fore as collectors in the early 1900s. Vaughan Williams wrote: "Whatever is done in the way of preserving traditional music must be done quickly; it must be remembered that the tunes of true folksongs exists only in the oral tradition, so that if they are soon noted down they will be lost forever." Recorded sound was in its infancy, and only a very few cylinder recordings exist from that time, so the songs had to be learned off the page. The crucial difference, and the great advantage of the second major English collection made for the BBC, notably by Peter Kennedy, Alan Lomax, and Bob Copper in the 1950s, was that the recordings allowed us to hear the singing style as well as the songs. Then, in the 1970s, Mike Yates made one of the most important and fascinating collections, that of English gypsies.

The tradition was tenacious; it had survived two World Wars, the drift of the labouring classes from the land because of the changes in our agricultural system, and the rapid rise of pop culture.

Bob Copper understood the continuity of the songs and the singers he collected from. In his book *A Song for Every Season* he wrote: "These people were the last of an old school and they clung on to singing the old songs as one of the few things that remained constant in a rapidly changing world. And it's not only the songs, it's the life they stand for that matters."

Past generations of singers, their knowledge, their experience, and their lives inhabit these songs, and if we allow them, speak directly to us.

**Shirley Collins,** LEWES, ENGLAND, 2007

THE **FOLK**
**STORY**

# An introduction to folk

BY **VIC GAMMON**, NEWCASTLE UNIVERSITY, UK

The folk song movement in England began with the collection of traditional songs in the field. Here Cecil Sharp, the great collector of the early 20th century, notes down a song called 'The Golden Glove' from Edwin Clay of Brailes, Warwickshire, in April 1910.

THERE ARE MANY MYTHS AND MISUNDERSTANDINGS about folk music, particularly associated with ideas about what is genuine, pure, and authentic. One of the most useful ways of thinking about folk music is as the popular music of the past. There are important differences between modern pop and traditional music but equally there are significant similarities.

Obvious differences between modern pop and modern forms of popular music include the fact that modern pop is commercially produced, whereas folk music is often seen as home-produced, home-made music. Such a view is substantially correct but should not obscure the fact that people made a living (or part of a living) from folk music as far back as we have written records. In the context of today, 'folk' is a minority interest within popular music.

The idea of oral tradition is often invoked to explore what is distinctive in folk music. To people like the collector Cecil Sharp, oral tradition, the passing on of material by ear and mouth, gave folk music its particular characteristics and made it different from other types of music. But in the past, traditional songs and dance music circulated widely in written form, both print and manuscript, as well as by oral means. And many modern pop bands work in totally aural ways, yet what they produce is not considered folk music.

Folk music is often said to belong to a specific people, to have characteristics that make it particularly English, Irish, Appalachian, Gypsy, or whatever culture or group is being discussed. Again, there is an element of truth in this idea – different musics exhibit different stylistic elements – but this should not obscure the fact that tunes and songs move about and have a remarkable ability to cross borders and crop up in surprising places. Sometimes, in the case of songs, they even cross into different languages in the process.

To return to the original point, a good way to start thinking about folk music is as the popular music in the past. It is a music that was actively used and performed in a society that had none of the modern means of musical communication available to us today. Before the 20th century, to hear sung or instrumental music, you either had to make it yourself or listen to other human beings making it. In describing folk music in these terms we have to think that popular can mean *of* the people as well as *for* the people.

## The subject-matter of traditional song

Traditional songs cover a wide range of human experience. The categories used to group songs in this anthology give a good idea of that range. The relationship of the sexes is the

PREVIOUS PAGE Cecil Sharp created piano accompaniments for the songs and dance tunes he collected, and gave many public demonstrations of folk dance.

most common subject area for traditional songs. They range from the most tender of love songs to the crudest of bawdy material. Often the treatment is serious, sometimes funny. Love can be unkind and sometimes the outcome of a love affair can be hatred, deception, cruelty or murder.

Crime, more generally, is a popular subject and the exploits of highwaymen, pirates and pickpockets feature in some songs, often ending with punishments such as hanging or transportation. Separation and death are common themes, and crop up in songs about the military, emigration, and the sea. Work itself is also a subject as, for example, in songs about mining and the cloth industry. Some songs accept the world as it is, others have a distinctly political flavour and make a protest against perceived injustice. Songs were often sung in social gatherings, and some songs take conviviality and drinking as their subjects. Some traditional calendar customs have particular songs performed as part of the custom, as, for example, at the Hobby Horse celebration performed in Padstow, Cornwall, in May. The various calling-on songs associated with traditional plays, where the characters are introduced, provide further examples. Christmas carols and wassail songs are clearly associated with the calendar customs of the winter season.

## The role of traditional instrumental music

Traditional instrumental music, whether played on fiddle, dulcimer, whistle or, in the 19th century, concertina or melodeon, had a number of different functions. First of all, people played instrumental music because it was enjoyable to do so. It may well be dance music but it was not necessarily played for dancing. In order to learn an instrument to a reasonable standard of proficiency it is necessary to put in hours of practice, learning technique and pieces totally disconnected from the act of dancing.

When instrumental music was played for dancing it ranged from the informal to the public. There was a widespread tradition of solo and sometimes duet step dancing where the dancer would improvise or draw on a set of known steps to instrumental accompaniment. This was often done as part of a pub session, although step dancing contests were known in various parts of England. Clog dancing is step dancing performed in clogs and was widely practised in the north of England.

Social dancing, where couples danced often as part of a set of dancers, has a long history in England. Such dancers were accompanied by either a solo instrumentalist or a small band and sometimes directed by someone calling the 'figures' of the dance (who often doubled as an instrumentalist). 'Country dances' (set dances with a particular programme of figures) were increasingly fashionable among the social elite from the 17th century and were a particular feature at the assembly rooms of spa towns from the 18th century. There is evidence that these elite country dances were performed in a rather different style to the dances at harvest homes, on village greens, and in the commercial dancing booths that were a feature of travelling fairs, although there may have been an element of acting the country bumpkin when members of fashionable society did them.

Display dancing (sometimes inappropriately called 'ritual dancing' or 'ceremonial dancing') was usually associated with calendar customs. Surviving dance customs such as the Padstow Hobby Horse and The Helston Furry Dance, both from Cornwall, and Cotswold morris dancing, from Gloucestershire and Oxfordshire, were associated with the spring whereas East Anglian molly dancing and north-of-England sword dancing were associated with mid-winter customs. At Bacup, in industrial Lancashire, the face-blackened and clogged coconut dancers perform in the streets of the town at Easter.

Morris dancing remains one of the best-known aspects of folk music. The tradition of Bampton in Oxfordshire, pictured here in 1911, is first mentioned in print in 1847 but seems likely to have started in the 18th century or earlier. The village's morris 'side' continues today.

Sometimes dance customs are associated with folk plays. Nowadays such dances are often performed for entertainment purposes, severed from their associated customs by both traditional (those with something like a continuous history of performance over a number of years) and revival dancers. This practice can give cause for concern from some devotees.

The instrumental accompaniment of dance traditions varies from a solo instrumentalist to a full band. Some Cotswold morris dancers hold that this style is best performed by a solo instrumentalist fully in time with the varying speed of the dance. In particular the 'capers' sections of some dances require the instrumentalist to watch for the dancer landing after a high leap to bring in the next strong beat. In other traditions, where dancers use more of a set tempo, bands can be used. In the case of Helston it is the town band, while in Bacup it is a small brass band that provides the music. Other ensembles can be fairly ad-hoc, as in the tradition of north-west morris dancing. Here an ensemble might include free-reed instruments such as concertina, melodeon, and accordion, and occasionally brass, and sometimes fiddle and drum in assorted numbers.

## The varieties of traditional songs and dance music

Traditional songs come in a wide variety of shapes and sizes. In England a song can range from a few lines to dozens of verses in length. Some have choruses, repeated elements or refrains, other do not.

Broadly speaking, English traditional songs can be thought of as belonging to one of three types: ballad, lyric, and catalogue.

### Ballads

In a ballad, the narrative or story-telling aspect is dominant in the song text. Narrative involves change – the situation at the end of the song is different from that at the start and one or more events have taken place. In traditional versions of 'The House Carpenter' (also known as 'The Daemon Lover', p125) a woman leaves her family to go off with a lover who turns out to be the devil (or something similar). At the start of the song she is living with her family and alive. At the end of the song she is separated from her family and implicitly going to die. A significant transformation has taken place. In 'Barbara Allen', Barbara's disdain for the male character hastens his death. She then dies of sorrow. In many traditional versions there is a symbolic unification in death as the rose and briar intertwine. We could summarise the transformation in the song as from alive/disunited to dead/united.

Scholars of earlier generations have tended to reserve the term ballad for longer, older songs that display certain stylistic features (notably the 305 songs and variants included in Francis Child's *The English And Scottish Popular Ballads*). In contrast, in popular usage a *ballad* or *ballet* was any song printed on a ballad sheet. I use the term for any song with a relatively strong narrative element. Used this way, the majority of traditional songs are ballads in that they tell some sort of story.

### Lyric songs

In a lyric song the storytelling element is much weaker. Rather, the prime task of the song is to express a particular mood, feeling, or relationship. There is sometimes an element of story in lyric songs but it is often quite vague and outweighed by the feelings the song expresses. In 'My Husband's Got No Courage In Him' (p204), for instance, although the situation of the impotent husband is explored and some of the tactics of the wife to help him are detailed, the situation at the end of the song remains the same as it is at the outset. Thus the song expresses a state of being without narrative development (although the wish that he be dead at the end of the song hints at the possibility of narrative action). 'Good Ale' (p101) is a song in which the singer praises drink in terms of a relationship of love.

### Catalogue songs

Sometimes related to the lyrical song is my final category, the catalogue song. A catalogue is a list of things; the dominant feature of such songs is the enumeration of a list. 'The Barley Mow' (p94) is a catalogue of drinking vessels. In this case the song is both cumulative and convivial, and something of a game, in that it could be used to test sobriety or to make the unsuccessful contestant give a forfeit. 'All For Me Grog' (p92) is a catalogue of the things the drinker has given up to spend his money on having a good time. Catalogue songs are often quite formulaic; each verse can start with the same phrase or the same grammatical construction. 'The Keys Of Canterbury' (p140), for instance, has a list of what the wooer will give the woman if he will accept her.

If the ballad, the lyric and the catalogue are three broad types that help us understand how songs are put together and what they do, they are not watertight categories and some songs mix elements of two or even three of the types. Some ballads are very formulaic and develop the story through a catalogue. 'The Mermaid' (p187), for instance, tells the story of a shipwreck but its central passage is a catalogue of crew members making final statements.

Description of a more elaborate kind is not a very significant feature of traditional songs but narrative songs can contain lyrical passage that express a particular view. In 'The Bonny Labouring Boy' (p119), for instance, the girl gives a description of the young working man she loves. Such lyrical descriptions are relatively rare – action and narrative are the main concern of English traditional songs.

## The elements and forms of traditional songs

English traditional songs use a few common metres, or rhythmical patterns, in their words, but there is also quite a lot of variety. Many of the older songs (for example those in Child's collection, including songs like 'The Unquiet Grave',) are set in 'common ballad metre', which is described as 8.6.8.6 (in which the numbers refer to the usual number of syllables per line). This form was not only used for secular songs but was also very extensively used for metrical psalms, which are biblical texts, often from the Old Testament *Book of Psalms*, translated in a regular pattern so they can be set to music. These were the mainstay of congregation singing in English churches between the 16th and 19th centuries.

Another commonly encountered metre is the so-called 'come-all-ye' form. The name comes from a commonplace opening used for songs particularly originating in the 18th and 19th centuries. The syllable pattern of these songs is 14.14.14.14. This use of a longer line allows for extended phrases both in terms of words and music (although it will be noticed that 14 equals 8 + 6, so this longer line can be thought of as related to common ballad metre). A good example of the use of this type of metre is 'Van Dieman's Land' (p272).

Choruses can be added to these basic forms, either interleaved or at the end of each verse. These can be short tags or as long as a whole verse, as in 'What Is The Life of a Man' (p88) or 'Spanish Ladies' (p189). Choruses can further the meaning of the song, as in these cases, or they can be a nonsense interlude, as in the chorus of 'Seventeen Come Sunday' (p145). Even nonsense can contribute to sense, either in terms of giving a breathing space in the narrative or because there is suggestive sense within the nonsense. Choruses also contribute to singing as a social act, as audiences can contribute to the performance of a song through its chorus without necessarily having to know the words.

There are many variations on these older forms. Some early ballads, carols, and work songs incorporate a chorus line after each verse line. A famous example of this is 'Scarborough Fair' (p236); a number of the early ballads in Child's collection have this characteristic including 'Riddles Wisely Expounded'. Sea shanties and other work songs are structured in a very similar way.

Repetition is used in some songs, and this works in certain ways like a chorus. In the south of England it was very common to repeat the last two lines of a four-line verse. If the audiences were to join in with this a degree of concentration on the text of the song is required. I have heard 'The Banks Of Sweet Primroses' (p110) performed this way. In some versions, 'Come Write Me Down' (p123) repeats the last line only but it is not simply a repeat of the melody used when the line is sung for the first time. Here the repeat of the text allows the music to come to a satisfying completion. Sometimes the first as well as last parts of a song are repeated.

All this use of choruses, refrains and repeated elements points to the fact that traditional song has a strong social aspect. Solo performer and audience are united in the act of performance through the social elements built-in to the structure and performance of songs. The solo singer may take the lead but the song is only fully consummated when the audience joins and supports his or her efforts. Thus the social nature of the music is, in certain ways, built-in to the structures of the music.

A song is a complex unity of different elements brought together in performance. A text, set in a particular form is 'carried' by a tune or melody. The performance may or may not have an accompaniment. As it has been recorded (both on paper and in audio) English traditional song has mostly been an unaccompanied idiom, but there are examples of accompaniment and it may have been more common than has generally been thought.

The unaccompanied character of English traditional song may be a result of when collecting took place (only in significant amounts after about 1890). Accompaniment, when it has been present, has taken various forms including free-reed instruments and fiddles. The Copper Family's form of harmony singing can be considered a form of vocal accompaniment.

Some songs certainly show signs of unaccompanied performance in their relative rhythmic freedom and use of rhythmic variation. Songs that use this type of technique can look very complex on the page but sound absolutely fine in performance. Common times for English traditional songs are 4/4 and 6/8. Less commonly represented time signatures include 5/4 (a significant number of good examples of this), 6/4, and 9/8.

English traditional song tunes are often described as 'modal'. A mode is simply a particular scale, an arrangement of tones (whole-steps) and semitones (half-steps). A major scale can be described by the pitch gaps or intervals between each note as tone-tone-semitone-tone-tone-tone-semitone or for short TTSTTTS. We can show the modes most commonly used in English traditional song in this way:

| Mode name | White piano keys | Intervals | Comments |
|---|---|---|---|
| Ionian | C to C | TTSTTTS | Major scale: major third, sixth and seventh |
| Mixolydian | G to G | TTSTTST | Major scale but with a flattened seventh |
| Dorian | D to D | TSTTTST | Minor scale but with a major sixth and a minor seventh |
| Aeolian | A to A | TSTTSTT | 'Natural minor': minor third, sixth and seventh |

The majority of English tunes are in the Ionian mode or major scale – this is just as true for dance tunes as it is for song airs. Some English tunes show distinct pentatonic characteristics. That means they use a scale containing intervals of whole tones and one-and-a-half tones, for instance CDEGAC or GACDEG. But such scales are not used in England as commonly as they are in Scotland.

A different and important way of thinking about folk song scales was pioneered by the collector and composer, Percy Grainger. Grainger thought that classification by mode put too much of a straight jacket on tunes. He noticed that tunes would seem to move from mode to mode rather freely. He argued that really there was but one rather loosely knit folk-song scale with certain intervals being prone to variability. If we show our four modes built on the note C we can easily see their similarities and differences.

| Ionian | C | D | E | F | G | A | B | C |
|---|---|---|---|---|---|---|---|---|
| Mixolydian | C | D | E | F | G | A | Bb | C |
| Dorian | C | D | Eb | F | G | A | Bb | C |
| Aeolian | C | D | Eb | F | G | Ab | Bb | C |

The shading shows the note that is different in this mode compared to the previously listed example. The difference between one mode and another is simply a one note change. Grainger noted that some singers changed the intervals they sang during a performance. This can be clearly heard on many recordings.

It follows from this that a tune can exist in different forms and in different modes. Compare the traditional 'The Woodcutter' with 'The Miller Of Dee' (a song first recorded in the 18th century) and with two tunes entitled 'Highland Mary', the one a song tune and the other a morris dance tune (see over).

Although these examples 'feel' quite different, having different time signatures and being set in different modes or scales, the similarities will be easily apparent. The contours of the melodies are very similar; in short, they are identifiably the same tune in variant forms.

A US scholar, Samuel Bayard, initiated a whole set of theories around the idea of

## The Woodcutter
From John Broadwood, *Old English Songs* (London, 1843)

## The Miller of Dee
From W Chappell, *Popular Music Of The Olden Time* (London, 1859)

## Highland Mary
From Frank Kidson, *Traditional Tunes* (Oxford, 1891)

# Highland Mary

From Vic Gammon, aural memory of morris dance musicians, 2006

'tune families', and this sort of work was developed by Bertrand Bronson. There are problems with this area of study – it is sometimes very difficult to tell where one tune family ends and another starts – but the fact that tune families exist is incontestable. To give just one example, the tune most people know as 'God Rest Ye Merry, Gentlemen' exists in a number of different versions (often to texts integral to the custom of wassailing). Some versions are in 4/4 time, some in 6/8; some are in modes with minor thirds, some in modes with major thirds. What is consistent is the general outline of the melody.

Prior to Bayard, some German scholars, notably Wilhelm Tappert, had developed ideas about 'wandering melodies'. By comparing many examples it became clear that some tunes had the ability to travel vast distances, cross natural and cultural boundaries, and remain fairly stable for long periods of time.

Wandering tunes can be both song tunes and dance tunes and there is a lot of wandering between these two genres as songs are adapted to dance tunes and dance tunes are made to carry words.

## Oral traditions, song making and dance music

We have a paradox with oral tradition. Variation is inevitably part of it, but so is retention and conservation. Some folk song scholars of earlier generations, and their supporters today, saw and see oral tradition as an essential part of the making of folk music. Oral tradition (or if you want to stress the ears rather than the mouth, aural tradition) is not simply the passing on of material by hearing and memory. An aspect of that process stamps the characteristic qualities of diction and musicality that many critics have admired in folk song. In part, this is a function of how the human brain works and the ways it memorises. An image often invoked, in relation to material shaped by oral tradition, is that of a pebble in a stream, worn smooth and perfected by the constant action of the water over a long period of time. This image is often linked with the idea that oral tradition is a pure and good thing and anything to do with print is corrupting and bad. An extension of this view is that illiteracy is seen as a positively good thing as it saves people from such corruption. In certain ways these sorts of view were held by Francis Child, the US ballad scholar, and Cecil Sharp, the English collector.

One problem with this is that no pure oral tradition has existed in England, or the English-speaking world, since the development of printing in the 16th century and

The same basic folk tune can occur in several different versions and different modes. Nonetheless, the general outline of the melody remains.

perhaps before then. Songs were circulated in manuscript form in the middle ages. The circulation of song texts on ballad sheets and in song books followed quickly on the development of printing in the 16th century. The practice of keeping notebooks of songs has been widespread. The first printed collections of popular dance music in musical notation date from the 17th century, as do the earliest instrumentalists' manuscript books containing such material. Though many people were linguistically and musically illiterate in pre-industrial England, significant numbers were not. The singing and music-making of those not able to use printed or handwritten media could still be influenced by material in written form, even though they may have been at several stages of separation from the printed or manuscript original.

It is best not to think of literacy and orality as opposed to each other but rather as interacting ways of communicating. There is plenty of evidence that songs circulated orally were picked up by broadside printers who issued them on song sheets. Some manuscript tune books look as if they are copied from printed originals but others record variants of tunes that are most likely to have developed orally.

Oral tradition can be dominantly a creative or a degenerative process. At any moment both tendencies are probably at work, the outcome depending somewhat on the culture and strength of a tradition. The processes by which a song or tune mutates from one version into another remain quite mysterious but that such a process takes place is irrefutable even if its lines of transmission are inevitably obscure. One can observe both creativity and degeneration by looking at any collection that brings together different versions of songs, for example Bronson's *The Traditional Tunes Of The Child Ballads*.

Where the processes of singing and instrumental music-making are well practised in places where a musical tradition is flourishing, we can reasonably infer that creativity can also flourish (although in a number of musical cultures a high value is placed on getting the performance absolutely right and unchanged – even if in reality significant change takes place). One can also observe degeneration. In a decaying tradition, except in the mouths of a few remaining singers of the first order, degeneration is bound to dominate. Creativity can even emerge out of degeneration when a talented performer repairs or fills out what he or she perceives to be an incomplete or corrupt text or a poor section of melody. Traditional performers also vary in their talent, aptitude, and interest; some will decay and limit a tradition, others will foster and develop it.

### Print culture, broadsides and tune books

Some writers have gone as far as to assert that print is a stabilising influence on oral tradition. It is impossible to know what English traditional song and instrumental music would have been like without the influence of print so it is hard to decide whether such an assertion is right. What we do know is that many of the songs that were written down and recorded by folk song collectors had circulated on printed sheets, some as far back as the Tudor and Stuart periods.

The songs represented in this book seem to have originated between about 1600 and 1850. (I am tempted to call this the 'folk song period'.) 'John Barleycorn' (p103) was in print in the 1620s, although later versions greatly reduced the length of the song. The modifications of 'The Daemon Lover' (p125) in oral tradition make a fascinating study. Whole elements were added to the story and the focus changed completely. 'The Barley Mow' (p94) has an early version preserved in a 16th-century manuscript which is not cumulative; and the address is to 'bell amy' (beautiful friend) rather than 'barley mow' (the harvest). Clearly oral recreation has done its work on this song.

Other songs have later origins, although dating is never easy and a song may be much older than the earliest copy we have of it. The collector-scholars Frank Kidson and Anne Gilchrist were particularly good at finding early versions of songs and tunes that were recovered from oral tradition. Some songs can easily be dated, at least in terms of their earliest possible date. 'Admiral Benbow' (p170) is a historical figure who died following action in 1702 – though some historians would think the song more legend than fact. Songs about Marlborough (d1722), Wolfe (d1859), Nelson (d1805) and Napoleon (d1821) can all be dated with a degree of accuracy. In the case of Napoleon it is interesting that the songs that seem to have stuck are those that portray him as a romantic hero rather than the vile swine of some of the ballads pumped out by the British during the French Wars. Songs about battles such as the Nile (1798) and Alma (1854) can also be dated with some ease.

'Maria Marten' dates from 1828 when her murderer, William Corder, was executed. Many of the songs mentioned were products of writers for the broadside ballad trade trying to cash in on topical sensations and in the process producing songs that stuck in the popular imagination. 'Maria Marten' dates from the period of the final flourish of the broadside ballad trade, although song sheets were produced into the 20th century. The concentration of a market in the expanding urban centres meant than broadside ballads were a profitable line for printers until new forms of popular entertainment and changes in fashion sounded their death knell in the second half of the 19th century.

Other songs are much more difficult to date, a problem increased by printers' willingness to rehash old material when they thought it would be profitable to do so. Songs were produced, distributed, and sung throughout the period, and I have been surprised many times to find a song is much older than I had previously thought. For example, 'The Wild Rover' and 'Old MacDonald Had A Farm' both exist in versions from the 17th century.

## The origins and dissemination of traditional songs and dance tunes

We, therefore, have to think of the traditional song repertory as a dynamic and changing thing. It contains old songs but incorporates new ones. It sometimes rediscovers old songs and treats them as if they are new songs. The evidence suggests that the popular repertory is essentially eclectic – it will take song and tune material from wherever it finds it. If the material suits then it will last and be performed, although it might get altered substantially along the way and be adapted to prevailing stylistic norms.

There have been two theories in the past that have tried to explain the origin of folk song. For brevity, I will call them the rising theory and the sinking theory.

The rising theory states that everything comes originally from the people or 'the folk' (however defined). Such a view is linked to the ideas of the Romantic Movement. The sinking theory states the opposite. Here it is argued that the people make nothing. All folk culture, including song and instrumental music, originates with elite groups, and then, by some sort of cultural filtering down, ends up, often in mangled form, as the possession of the people.

Both theories have elements of truth, but neither will do. When we look carefully at the elements that make up traditional songs and dance music, what is most impressive is the complexity of where the material comes from. Take the example of 'Bruton Town' (p150) or 'The Famous Farmer'. The story told by the song is essentially that of 'Lisabetta and the Pot of Basil', which is in *Decameron*, by the medieval Italian writer Boccaccio. This was in print as a book in English by the 17th century. It's the story of love between the daughter of a house and a servant, the servant's killing by the woman's brothers, the dead lover's appearance in a dream in which he tells her where his body is, and her finding the body. Thus far the two plots, story and songs, are very similar but they have different endings. The Italian story has the shocking but picturesque ending of the woman decapitating the dead lover and planting his head in a pot of basil before dying herself. The English song versions have different endings. In one strand the woman simply dies. In another she returns to accuse her brothers who are then hung; there is no mention of her death.

Is this an example of the sinking theory, a piece of medieval Italian art become a street ballad? On one level this would seem to be the case. But everything has to start somewhere, and it seems the story is perfectly adapted to the idiom of English traditional song. The existence of the alternative endings in English song versions, the one simply tragic, the other with an element of just revenge, suggests that this story was not settled within English culture. We might compare the hanging scene of the Punch and Judy show – regularly performed as recently as the 1950s but little seen today, no doubt as a response to changing sensibilities.

Another example of the sinking theory might be the cropping up of 'classical' music in the tune books and repertories of traditional fiddle players. We find examples of Mozart, Haydn, and Pleyel in village musicians' tune books, alongside popular country dance music. In recent years I have heard a melodeon player performing a 6/8 version of the 'Ode To Joy' tune from the climax of Beethoven's Ninth Symphony as if it were a morris dance tune. This is perhaps a knowing musical joke but also is an example of how melodic material can be recontextualised.

There are examples of 'elite' poetry being circulated on broadsides, and in some cases there is evidence that such songs were popularly sung. There are also examples of educated individuals purposely writing material for the broadside press. Nevertheless, it seems clear that the bulk of song material of the past was made for a popular audience by people who belonged to the same social group. A related view would be to argue that, whatever the origins of the material, it passed through the filters of a selection of printers and ballad sellers who knew their markets and were trying to make a living. It then passed through the filter of being remembered and passing into oral tradition or being discarded. Here we are close to Sharp's idea of 'selection' by the community.

Let us consider the rising theory. According to this idea, everything originates with the people, who are the source of creativity. Sometimes this idea is linked to a belief in the revitalising nature of folk material which, it is asserted, can have a beneficial effect on the wider culture. Whether you believe everything worthwhile originates from the people depends, in part, on how 'the people' are defined. Through the ages, composers and writers have made use of 'folk' material for various purposes, be it the elaborate sets of variations of Elizabethan and Jacobean composers, John Gay's *Beggar's Opera*, some of the compositions of Vaughan Williams, or some of the poetry that W.H. Auden modelled on ballads. Popular material has long provided writers and composers with material to bounce off and work into their creations. Other composers and writers have made fun of popular material, as Henry Purcell does in *King Arthur*. Folk music certainly contains most of the basic elements of art, but all art reflects the conditions of its production. It seems to me a damaging relic of Romantic thought to have a mystical view of the power of folk art.

Folk music is often said to be communal in authorship, and for a long time this idea held sway in folk music circles. What does this mean? It does not mean that songs were written by committee – although examples of this have been known. It is more that in the transmission of songs and music, these are reshaped by individuals; a line reworked here, a grace note added there, so that by the end of the process the song or tune is transformed. It cannot mean that generally most songs did not at one stage have an individual author. There are some exceptions to this – I'm thinking here of things such as wassail songs and sea shanties, which often consist of nothing more than so many known and interchangeable parts. Similarly in the process of, mainly oral, transmission, commonplace phrases and whole sections of other songs can be grafted in if the use is appropriate. There is an element of oral recreation in most folk song performance, and this itself can result in characteristic patterns of melodic and verbal material such as incremental repetition (patterns such as "The first to come by... The second... The third..."). Nevertheless, I would assert that the overwhelming majority of songs in this book had an individual author, even if the end result of transmission and reshaping is a song very different from the form in which it started. Song and tune makers worked within the cultural forms and convention they knew, and there is a strong case for thinking of these as collective and social in character. As A. L. Lloyd pointed out, the anonymity of folk song may represent nothing more than an accident of history.

Sharp argued that folk music was communal in another sense "in that it reflects the mind of the community". I would not want to suggest there is one such mind, but if we were to rephrase that as something along the lines of "songs tend to deal with important issues of the society that produces them", then I think this is clearly the case. I do not see that this makes song or music communal, any more than contemporary soap operas are communal. It is better to say songs address issues that are significant to their audiences; that have some sort of cultural purchase; they produce a significant meaning. A fascinating point is that they can still produce significant meanings for us even though we live in a very changed society.

English folk song and dance music (whether defined in the restrictive way of Sharp and some other early collectors, or in a wider and more inclusive way) throughout its history interacted with itself and with the products of other media. Broadside ballads provided the material for songs that became traditional and in turn printers re-collected songs from tradition to put on to ballad sheets. 'Barbara Allen' (p112), one of the most widely collected songs of the English-speaking world, was first heard as a stage song by Samuel Pepys and was being performed on the stage a century later. Ballad operas of the 18th century incorporated many traditional songs and tunes. Many traditional songs such as 'The Sweet Nightingale' and 'Poor Sally Sits A-Weeping' would appear to have originated as stage songs. The early music hall in the 19th century drew off the vernacular song tradition for much of its material before it became secure in its own creativity. That well known patter song of the early halls, 'Villikins And His Dinah', was nothing more than a burlesque version of an older broadside ballad, 'William and Dinah'. In turn, music hall songs were put on song sheets and in cheap songbooks, only to turn up in the repertories of traditional singers visited by collectors.

We see similar processes at work in dance music. 'Flowers of Edinburgh', printed many times since the mid 18th century, may have been by James Oswald, the genteel composer who helped create the 18th-century Scottish drawing room style of music. The tune travelled to colonial America, and also ended up as a favourite tune of English morris dancers. 'Black Joke' was a filthy song of the 18th century that became a favourite dance tune and spawned other 'joke' tunes with their odd but interesting 6 +10 bar formats. It was also used by morris dancers. 'The Fall Of Paris' has a surprising history; starting as a song of the French revolution, 'Ça Ira!' was played as a march by the British army, became a popular piano piece in England but was also played by traditional musicians in Britain and Ireland. It still exists as an old-time fiddle tune in the USA, 'The Mississippi Sawyer'.

The traffic goes in all directions, up, down, and sideways. Some material sinks, some rises. Take the tune and song 'Greensleeves' (sometimes wrongly attributed to Henry VIII). We know it today through the pastoralism of Vaughan Williams' *Fantasia*, as an easy musical reference to invoke the Tudor period in films, and as the tune for a Christmas carol, as well as being in many musical instrument tutors. Edwardian collectors found it as a song tune (carrying a risqué text invoking a shepherd to come home for his 'breakfast') and as a morris jig. It occurs in a number of different forms in Francis O'Neill's collection of Irish dance music (compiled in the USA). Thomas Moore used it as a tune for one of his *Irish Melodies* – one of the most popular songbooks in 19th century USA. It is in *The Beggar's Opera* (1728) and in the 17th and 18th centuries it was used to carry a number of bawdy texts, often with the jeering refrain 'Which Nobody Can Deny', which became an alternative title for the tune. The song was first recorded in the Stations Register in Elizabethan times, but could be older. This seemingly most English of tunes is based on the *passamezzo antico*, a chord progression widely used in Italian music of the early modern period. It is a heroic survivor.

I can only sketch some examples that give a glimpse of the complexity of origins of that body of material we glibly refer to as folk songs and folk tunes. Folk music has complex and varied origins. Its material comes from many places but, crucially, it has been assimilated to the musical conventions of ordinary people, who performed it in the manner they had learnt, largely orally but influenced by print, for their own pleasure and entertainment and sometimes for income and reward. The folk music repertory is therefore heterogeneous; it is a bringing together of various things of quite different origins and usually changing them in the process. From such a perspective, ideas of the 'purity' of folk music are profoundly unhelpful.

People took songs and tunes with them wherever they went. Instrumental music required the money to devote to the acquisition and maintenance of instruments, so the poorest in society were usually excluded from their possession. Some showed great ingenuity, however, in making instruments for themselves, such as fiddles, cellos, dulcimers, and flutes.

With trade, colonisation, and migration, "wherever they went" could mean anywhere in the world. Through emigration, English songs and tunes ended up in the four corners of the globe. Sometimes they remained much in the form that they had left England; some of the best-preserved examples of some English traditional songs have been collected in former colonies. Sometimes songs and tunes blended with musical elements provided by fellow settlers from other countries, including Africa in the case of the USA. Sometimes new songs were made in the settled countries, based on the ones that had been brought from England.

Older ideas of folk music were often racially based. Echoes of this persist in notions such as 'Celtic music'. One of the interesting elements in the more recent revival of instrumental folk music in Ireland and Scotland, and among those elsewhere who identify with those countries, is that the repertory has been shaped to eliminate what are perceived as alien English elements. Listening to Irish and Scots recordings made in the 1920s, I am often struck by how 'English' the music sounds to my ears. Under the influence of nationalism, there seems to have been an effort to make Irish and Scots music a more pure emblem of their countries. In stark contrast, many English people seem to be somewhat embarrassed that England has any traditional music at all!

I have tried in these pages to provide a sketch of a type of music that is of its essence hybrid, adaptable, and dynamic. Can a music so characterised be described as having any integrity? Can it be described as English?

The music has integrity because the different elements are pulled together and unified by the people who have made and perpetuated it. It is English because English people made it. On close inspection it is clear that English music had much repertory and many musical elements in common with Scots, Irish and Welsh music. The differences are also important.

The best analogy is with language and accent. We may use the same words but accent them differently. We may use different words that are particular to the dialect we speak. We may have a way of constructing a phrase that is largely confined to the region from which we come. Consider some examples.

In the period of the first folk revival, some writers got hot under the collar as to whether a tune, 'Brighton Camp', also known as 'The Girl I Left Behind Me', was English or Irish. In 1913, Frank Kidson and W.H. Gratton Flood, of England and Ireland respectively, exchanged erudite information on sources to support their country's claims to the tune. As people of their time, it clearly mattered to them, but should it have done? The tune and song were obviously very popular in both countries; they obviously accorded to popular taste, which is attested by the vigorous survival of the tune to the present day.

'The Bonny Bunch of Roses' (p242) is a song about Napoleon. It probably dates from the mid 19th century. It portrays Napoleon as a failed hero. It has been collected in England, Wales, Scotland, Ireland, Canada, and the USA. We have traced ballad sheet printings of it to most of these countries. Unusually for 19th century ballad sheets, many sets of 'The Bonny Bunch of Roses' carry a tune indication: 'The Bunch of Rushes, O'. We know this as both an erotic song and a dance tune, and see that the 'Roses' song has some elements of parody, or at least a similar sounding end line. As an instrumental tune, 'Rushes' is a lively hornpipe. As a song, 'Rushes' has been collected in England, Ireland, and Canada and I know of printings of it from London, Liverpool, Brighton, and Birmingham. 'The Bonny Bunch of Roses' has some qualities of diction that suggest it might have been written by an Irishman, but the song was popular in both countries.

One final example: 'Morgan Rattler' is a great three-part Irish jig. It crops up a lot in English musicians' manuscripts as well as Irish collections. We also know it is a common English song tune that carried a number of texts (including one of the grossest lyrics I have ever read) in the early 19th century. If it is an Irish tune, then it was one much liked by English musicians and widely played by them. Ultimately, I come to the view that, in music, use is much more important than origins, and origins are often unknowable in any case.

## Collecting, revivals and research

Modern interest in what came to be known as folk music can be dated from the 1760s and the publication of two flawed but seminal works, Percy's *Reliques* and MacPherson's *Ossian*. The latter was a translation and amalgamation of Gaelic songs, made in an attempt to create a Scottish epic. The *Reliques* was a publication of a 17th-century ballad manuscript, somewhat 'improved' by the editor and with the rude examples left out. In a sense these books shifted some elements of informed opinion away from classicism and Enlightenment thinking and laid the foundations for what would become the Romantic movement. This movement laid stress on irrationalism, inspiration, the variety in human existence, and wildness rather than order.

A number of important developments ensued. In England, Joseph Ritson founded critical song scholarship, partly in reaction to Percy's liberties with texts. On the Scottish borders, Sir Walter Scott and James Hogg started something resembling a modern folk song collection. In Germany, where Percy and MacPherson had considerable influence, Romanticism took its next major step forward.

J.C. Herder was a clergyman who became the most important Romantic thinker in terms of our subject. In particular, Herder elaborated the idea of 'Das Volk', the people, nation or folk; none of these English words really captures the connotations of the German word. They were the custodians of the 'nation's soul' which was manifested in their culture, particularly in their stories, customs, and songs. Herder produced a collection of songs in 1774, *Alte Volksleider*, and another in 1778–9, *Volksleider*; the term 'folk song' did not come into use in English until about a century later. Significant followers of Herder were the Grimm brothers, who developed some of his ideas and produced their famous collections of stories in the first decades of the 19th century. In some ways the folksong and folklore movements of the 19th century represent a response to the stimulus provided by the work of Herder and the Grimms.

In England things did not move very fast. The years around the French Wars (1793–1815) saw significant publication of sometimes highly edited and 'improved' folk music material in Scotland and Ireland; nothing really comparable happened in England. Interest picked up a little in first half of the 19th century, with a number of small collections (notably those of Gilbert, Sandys, and John Broadwood). More was going on beneath the surface, as is witnessed by the manuscript collections of John Bell and John Clare. Folklore established itself as a field of study by mid century and other important work was under way.

In London, William Chappell, spurred by an early attack of musical nationalism, was working on what became his *Popular Music Of The Olden Time* (1859). Simultaneously, the American scholar Francis Child was producing the first edition of his ballad collection, which was published in 1860. Child went on to extend his work into his five-volume collection, *The English And Scottish Popular Ballads* (1882–1898). Both these works are still important in this field, but by the time Child published the last of his volumes a movement to collect English traditional songs from oral tradition had already begun.

The years from the late 1880s to the early 1890s saw the publication of significant collections of songs taken from oral tradition and originating in different parts of the country. W.A. Barrett and Lucy Broadwood worked mainly in Sussex and Surrey, and Broadwood and J.A. Fuller Maitland attempted to draw together a collection of songs representing all the counties of England. Sabine Baring-Gould worked with colleagues in the south-west, Frank Kidson in Yorkshire and the Borders. In 1898, the Folk Song Society was formed and publication of its journal began the following year. The *Journal of the Folk Song Society* provided an outlet for material being obtained from oral sources as well as a place for scholarly papers and commentaries.

The work of the Society languished rather in the early years of the new century. In 1903, both Cecil Sharp and Ralph Vaughan Williams commenced their collecting and publication of traditional songs and a new energy was injected into the movement. The years before World War I form something of a high point in English folk song collection. It was never a vast movement, but the work of those two men, plus people such as W. Percy Merrick, George Gardiner, and H.E.D. Hammond, ensured the rescue of a great deal of song material we might otherwise never have known about. We are still exploring a lot of the material they left us. The most important motivation for these collectors was usually musical nationalism – they wished to found a national school of composition, a project that bore most fruit in the work of Vaughan Williams. They also tended to believe that folk music in its recontextualised form, often in choral settings or with piano accompaniments, would have a beneficial effect on education and the culture of the country. In developing these ideas they drew deeply on Romanticism and racial ideas that ultimately derived from Herder and other German thinkers.

World War I took the wind out of the sails of the folk song movement. Some of its leading lights, such as George Butterworth, were killed in action. Many of the leading collectors died in the 1920s and the Folk Song Society shrank in active membership. In 1932 the dwindling Folk Song Society 'merged' with the English Folk Dance Society and lived on as an active minority interest within the English Folk Dance and Song Society.

There were some interesting developments, however. Alfred Williams published his words-only anthology, *Folk Songs Of The Upper Thames*, which put the emphasis on song texts and their role in people's lives. E.J. Moeran began to record traditional singers and make the records available. James Madison Carpenter, a somewhat reclusive American, made a significant collection of material in various parts of Britain, publication of which is progressing but not yet complete.

By the 1940s it might have seemed that the folk music movement had run its course in England, but it was not so. In retrospect we can see small things happening that were to have important consequences. A.L. Lloyd published his pamphlet *The Singing Englishman* in 1944, a flawed but important work later to be reworked into *Folk Song In England* (1967). People at the BBC had started taking an interest in folk music, notably Francis Collinson and later Peter Kennedy. In the early 1950s, the American collector Alan Lomax came to England and acted as a catalyst that accelerated developments already in place. By the 1960s what some refer to as 'the second folk song revival' was in full swing.

A.L. Lloyd (left), seen performing with Ewan MacColl in a typical folk club of the late 1950s.

During the 1960s and 1970s the nation was covered by a network of folk clubs, and a scene emerged in which considerable numbers of people could make some sort of a living by performing at them. The club scene was supplemented and ultimately surpassed by the development of festivals. The music performed at both clubs and festivals varied greatly; some of it had some relationship with traditional folk music – a lot of it did not. The movement was complex and never had one single idea or approach, although alliances of convenience were common and a left-wing impetus was present in some aspects. The music performed varied from revived traditional music to political and protest songs, to comedy, to pure self-indulgence. The open and democratic ethos of the movement gave space to performers of varied capability and some of the clubs simply sank under the weight of the mediocrity of their performers.

The movement did give a platform to people who performed a revived version of English folk music. Leading lights of this genre included Martin Carthy, Shirley Collins, The Watersons, and John Kirkpatrick. It also gave a platform to some traditional singers and instrumentalists, including The Copper Family, Fred Jordan, Willie Scott, George Spicer, and others. It also produced some unexpected spin-offs, including a whole group of comedians who honed their craft in folk clubs, as well as various forms of experimentation, including the folk-rock movement, which attempted to present a synthesis of traditional music and rock within the context of pop music performance.

A movement to collect, make available, and understand traditional music was part a stimulus for the second revival and an element of it. Collectors such as Peter Kennedy, Mike Yates, John and Katie Howson, and Keith Summers all showed there was still material to be collected, and some of it was of a very good quality. Roy Palmer and others made a lot of material available in popular anthologies of songs. Record companies, most notably Topic Records, found they could survive by publishing

21 THE FOLK HANDBOOK

The Watersons, consisting of sisters Lal (left) and Norma Waterson (right), brother Mike (back), and cousin John Harrison (front) were one of the most important vocal groups in the English folk revival of the mid 1960s. Lal died in 1998, but Mike and Norma Waterson continue to perform, often with Norma's husband Martin Carthy and their daughter Eliza.

recordings of revival performers and some traditional performers. From the 1970s a new interest in traditional dance and its accompanying music was evident, though its roots were older. The publication of manuscript music of dance musicians was one aspect of this interest.

In the wake of this activity, a new scholarship developed, largely but not entirely based around the revitalised *Folk Music Journal* (the descendant of the *Journal Of The Folk Song Society*) under the editorship of Ian Russell. The new scholarship was characterised by a questioning of received interpretations and a re-examination of evidence in the light of new concerns. One of the key issues to emerge was a questioning of the ideas, motivations, and methods of the earlier collectors, most significantly Cecil Sharp. This caused bitter controversy, and is likely to continue to do so. Now, with the increasing resources available (such as the Roud Index and the Bodleian Broadside Ballads on the web) and the ability to study folk music in various ways at British universities such as Newcastle and Sheffield, it is to be hoped that even better folk music scholarship will emerge in the future.

One of the constants of the folk music revival in England since the 1930s has been the Vaughan Williams Memorial Library. Founded by Cecil Sharp's bequest of books and papers, the Library is a repository of the key publications of the English folk song movement, and has many of the important manuscript and sound recording collections. Anyone seriously interested in English traditional music will make use of this Library at some stage and in some way. It is a wonderful resource that we need to support and cherish.

The Library is important because in many ways it provides the basis for the future of English folk music. Does folk music have a future? It certainly has a past, and it has repeatedly shown resilience. Interest in the subject does seem to come and go in waves, with troughs in between. Inevitably, folk music is different when it re-emerges in a changed social, political, economic, and aesthetic set of circumstances. A casual search shows me that there have been a couple of recordings of 'Barbara Allen' issued this year – not bad for a song that is about 350 years old. The recordings may be good or they may be terrible, but the interesting thing is that the song goes on being re-recorded. English folk music does seem to have an ability to speak to us across time and through space. We seem to be able to take from it something that is satisfying and stimulating. Yes, I think it has a future.

# Folk portraits

BY **JOHN MORRISH**

### F.J. Child (1825–96)

FRANCIS CHILD WAS AN AMERICAN ACADEMIC (he rose to become professor of English at Harvard) whose pioneering work in collecting the ballads of England and Scotland remains influential to this day. In creating the five-volume *English And Scottish Popular Ballads*, published between 1882 and 1898, he went back to original manuscripts and printings, creating an invaluable source for both scholars and performers. His main failing, which sets him apart from later folk song collectors and scholars, was that he did not collect the music. Although a small number of extra songs have been added to the canon in the years since his death, the so-called 'Child ballads' remain at the centre of our understanding of the ballad tradition.

### Sabine Baring-Gould (1834–1924)

THE REVEREND SABINE BARING-GOULD was a pioneer of folk song collection. As 'squarson' – both squire and parson – of the village of Lew Trenchard (now Lewtrenchard), in Devon, he was in a good position to seek out singers in Devon and Cornwall. The result was *Songs And Ballads Of The West*, published between 1888 and 1891, one of the very first collections of song that claimed to be "made from the mouths of the people". Baring-Gould often rewrote the words of the songs he and his associates collected, on the grounds of indecency or because he thought them too 'modern'. Although he considered it his most important achievement, collecting folk song was only one of Baring-Gould's interests. He also wrote more than 40 novels, many of them best-sellers, and the words to 'Onward Christian Soldiers', the well known hymn. As a young priest in the industrial North of England, he had met an illiterate factory girl of 16, arranged for her to be educated, and then married her. They had 16 children. Notably eccentric, Baring-Gould is once said to have asked a small child, "And whose little girl are you?" "Yours, daddy," came the reply.

Sabine Baring-Gould

### George Gardiner (c1852–1910)

GEORGE GARDINER, WHO WAS BORN IN KINCARDINE-ON-FORTH, in Scotland, became one of the most important early collectors of English folk song. Starting work in 1904, and concentrating largely on Hampshire, he recorded more than 1,000 songs, although he did not copy them all out from his field notebooks. His method was to write down the lyrics and then send out one of his musical collaborators, H. Balfour Gardiner, Charles Gamblin, or C.F. Guyer, to note the tune. This inevitably led to a certain amount of confusion. He last collected in 1909, a year before his death.

George Gardiner

### Frank Kidson (1855–1926),

FRANK KIDSON, WHO CALLED HIMSELF "a journalist and a bit of an author", was a member of the first committee of the Folk-Song Society and an important authority in the early history of the movement. Starting as an artist and collector of printed material, particularly songs and ballads, he began writing about them in the *Leeds Mercury*, concentrating on their histories. As time went on he turned increasingly to songs he collected on trips around Scotland and the north of England. His method was unusual: he took with him his niece, Ethel Kidson, who memorised the tunes until they could find a piano to assist in the process of writing them down. In 1891, he published a collection, *Traditional Tunes*, and Ethel published more after his death. He left a huge collection of printed material and manuscripts, which is held at the Mitchell Library in Glasgow, one of the largest public reference libraries in Europe.

Frank Kidson

### Lucy Broadwood (1858–1929)

LUCY BROADWOOD WAS THE GRANDDAUGHTER of John Broadwood, founder of the celebrated firm of piano-makers. In the 1840s, her uncle, also John Broadwood, had published a book of folk songs, entitled *Old English Songs*. In the 1880s, she began collecting songs, publishing a selection in *English County Songs* (1893). By that time she was singing in private and charitable concerts and, in 1898, she became one of the founders of the Folk-Song Society. She went on to hold all the important posts in the organisation, while continuing to collect material. As editor of the Society's journal, she upheld high standards of accuracy.

Lucy Broadwood

### Kate Lee (1859–1904)

KATE LEE WAS CHRISTENED CATHERINE SPOONER; one of her cousins was the academic William Spooner, whose supposedly eccentric way of speaking gave us the word 'Spoonerism'. After marrying barrister Arthur Lee and having two children, she became determined to make a career as an opera singer. This she did with considerable success, adding to her performances traditional material from Lucy Broadwood's *English County Songs*. In the mid 1890s she began to collect songs on her own account, mainly in Norfolk, but also in Sussex, where she encountered the Copper family. In 1898, she organised the inaugural meeting of the Folk-Song Society, becoming its first secretary. In that role, she wrote the Society's *Hints To Collectors Of Folk Music*, a short document full of excellent advice that was not always followed: "Just as it is desirable that the words of a ballad should be given exactly as they are sung or spoken, so it is essential that the tunes should represent, as nearly as may be, what the collector hears." In 1900, Mrs Lee, as she was always known, fell ill with the cancer that was to kill her, depriving the infant society of its driving force. She was persuaded to hand over control to Lucy Broadwood, whose academic emphasis she had strongly opposed.

### Cecil Sharp (1859–1924)

CECIL SHARP WAS THE DOMINANT FIGURE in the English folk song revival, a prolific collector and writer whose attitudes and practices left their mark on the movement.

Born in London, Sharp spent several years in Australia as a young man before returning to Britain and trying to make a living as a musician, becoming a music teacher and choirmaster. In 1899, he first saw a morris dance, at Headington in Oxfordshire, and noted down the tunes. In 1903, having already published a book of British songs based on other people's collections, he began collecting songs himself. The first one he took down was 'The Seeds Of Love', from John England, gardener to his friend Charles Marson, a Somerset vicar. It is often said that he overheard England singing as he mowed the lawn, but in fact he seems to have sought him out on Marson's recommendation. Sharp collected 41 further songs on the same visit, and went on to collect nearly 5,000 songs in England and North America over the course of his career.

In 1904 he joined the committee of the Folk-Song Society (later the EFDSS) and began promoting the cause of folk song in schools; his aim was not merely to collect and study songs but to revive the practice of singing them. In 1907 he published *English Folk Song: Some Conclusions,* which first expressed his essentially Darwinian ideas about songs improving through the survival of the fittest, as well as his concern with folk song as a force for reviving and 'purifying' English culture, removing commercial and cosmopolitan influences. In both these respects, he was a product of his times.

Sharp was a powerful networker and committee man who was involved in a number of bitter disputes throughout his life. In 1905, a clash with the education authorities over the authenticity of some of the supposed folk songs they recommended for use in schools spilled over into the Society. The same year, he began working with Mary Neal, a social worker, to revive and teach morris dancing. But their approaches soon began to diverge, over the way the dances were taught and performed, and after a ferocious clash, played out in the newspapers, the folk dance movement split into two separate organizations, Neal's Espérance Guild Of Morris Dancers and Sharp's English Folk Dance Society, founded in 1911. Both groups went into abeyance during the First World War (several of Sharp's dancers were killed in action) and Neal's was never revived. In 1914, Sharp sailed to America to choreograph folk dances for a Shakespeare production, and to lecture. On a subsequent trip, two years later, he began collecting songs in the

After more than 10 years as a collector of folk song in England, Cecil Sharp went to America with his assistant Maud Karpeles (right) and began again there, amassing some 1,500 songs in the Appalachian mountains.

Appalachians, where he believed he had found a preserved English tradition of song unspoilt by commercial and contemporary influences. He was to collect some 1,500 songs in America, often in very harsh conditions.

Sharp was a controversial figure in life and has been ever since, both for his views and his collecting practice. Although he was punctilious in writing down the words of the songs, he was obliged by the standards of the time to tone down sexual references and tidy up the songs for publication. He also had to provide piano accompaniments to make the songs acceptable to the music-buying public. His views on what constituted 'pure' folk song were narrow. Nonetheless, he dominated folk music in England for two decades and remains a powerful force to this day.

## Phil Tanner (1862–1937)

PHIL TANNER, OF LLANGENNITH ON THE GOWER peninsula in Wales, was the only Welsh singer to have come to prominence in the folk song revival, although he considered himself a Gowerian rather than a Welshman. Born in Glamorgan, he was a millhand and farm labourer who sang at weddings and country dances, and took part in the custom of wassailing, which took place on Old Christmas Day (January 6th). Tanner had a huge repertoire, learned from his family and local people. In the 1930s, he recorded some 78 rpm records for Columbia, then went on to sing at Cecil Sharp House and be recorded by the BBC. He too can be heard on Topic's *The Voice Of The People* series.

## Anne Gilchrist (1863–1954)

Anne Gilchrist

ANNE GILCHRIST WAS A CLASSICALLY TRAINED musician whose professional involvement with folk music began when she was asked to sing at a lecture by Frank Kidson. From 1906 she began to produce scholarly articles and annotations for the journal of the Folk-Song Society. In that year she also published the first fruits of several years of collecting songs in Scotland and Lancashire. She soon became an expert on folk music, dance and folklore, especially in the north of England, an area that had previously been neglected by early collectors. But her particular scholarly and personal enthusiasm was for tunes. An obituary in *The Times* described her as "a living encyclopaedia of tunes and their history", something she demonstrated in countless articles for the journals of the Folk-Song Society and later the English Folk Dance and Song Society. Miss Gilchrist's last scholarly article appeared when she was 79 years old. Sadly, her vast contribution to folk music studies has often been overlooked, mainly because she did not publish a book.

## The Hammond brothers

The Hammond brothers (centre and right)

HENRY AND ROBERT HAMMOND WERE TIRELESS collectors in the first folk song revival. Henry was born in Priston, Somerset, in 1866. His brother Robert was two years younger. Henry became a classics teacher at the Edinburgh Academy, where he met George Gardiner and began collecting songs with him. In 1905, he began working with his brother, first in Somerset and then in Dorset. Henry would note the tunes, while Robert took down the words. By 1907, they had collected some 900 songs in six counties, including more than 100 from a single singer, Mrs Russell of Upway in Dorset. A selection of the songs appeared in the Folk-Song Society's journal in 1907, and 16, arranged for piano by Cecil Sharp, appeared as the first volume of *Folk Songs Of England, Book 1*, which Sharp edited and published in 1908. Henry Hammond died in 1910. The life of his brother remains a mystery.

## Alfred Williams (1877–1930)

ALFRED WILLIAMS, BORN NEAR SWINDON in Wiltshire, was one of the few song collectors to be primarily concerned with the words. His book *Folk-Songs Of The Upper Thames* (1923) included texts, but no tunes, gathered in Oxfordshire, Gloucestershire, Wiltshire, and Berkshire. After leaving school at 11 to work on a farm, Williams took a job at the Great Western Railway works in Swindon at 15. He would remain there for 23 years, during which time he educated himself, rising at 4am to learn Latin and Greek and taking a correspondence course at Ruskin Hall, Oxford. By 1907 he was writing poetry and published several volumes before leaving the factory due to ill health in 1914. A year later he published his most famous book, *Life In A Railway Factory*, which he had written in 1911 but was unable to publish because of its criticisms of working conditions. After serving in India during World War I, he returned to a life of poverty in Wiltshire, while continuing to write and study, even teaching himself Sanskrit.

Alfred Williams

## Sam Larner (1878–1965)

SAM LARNER OF WINTERTON, NORFOLK, was an important traditional singer who spent most of his working life at sea as a herring fisherman. He began singing early; at nine years old he would earn small change by singing to coach parties that stopped in the village. He learned most of his repertory of 60 or more songs at sea and sang them in fishing ports around the coast of Britain. In 1933, when he was 55, ill health forced him to seek a livelihood on land; he was a road-mender and labourer until he was 65. When he was 78 years old he first came to the attention of the wider world, having been recorded by a BBC producer who was in his village looking for folk singers. Ewan MacColl and Peggy Seeger recorded him and invited him to London to perform. He subsequently featured in a number of radio and television programmes. An ebullient performer, he can be heard on Topic's *Voice Of The People* series of CDs.

## Percy Grainger (1882–1961)

PERCY GRAINGER ARRIVED IN LONDON in 1901 from Australia, hoping to make a living as a concert pianist and jobbing musician. Fascinated by folk song, he began collecting in Lincolnshire in 1905. Unlike his peers in the Folk-Song Society, he was an enthusiastic user of the new Edison phonograph, invented 20 years earlier, with which he recorded the celebrated Lincolnshire singer Joseph Taylor. The use of the phonograph demonstrated that singers would sing a melody differently each time they sang it. He became sceptical of the prevailing idea that folk songs were based around ancient modes, and argued that they used a loose scale in which thirds, sixths and sevenths could be major or minor. His views, published in the society's journal, came in for strong criticism. In 1914 he moved to New York, where he composed and

Percy Grainger

performed. His best-known piece was a setting of 'Country Garden', a morris tune collected by Cecil Sharp at Headington in Oxfordshire. Grainger was a man of eccentric views. He believed in the superiority of the 'Nordic' race, shunned Italian words in his musical notation, but disliked all things German.

### Clive Carey (1883–1968)

CLIVE CAREY ENTERED THE FOLK MOVEMENT as a collector of songs and dances in Sussex, Essex, and Oxfordshire. He assisted Mary Neal with her Espérance Morris Guild dance group, and sided with her in her bitter dispute with Cecil Sharp. In 1915, he published *Ten English Folk Songs*. After World War I, he became a celebrated opera singer and director, and subsequently professor of singing at the Royal College of Music in London.

### Maud Karpeles (1885–1976)

Maud Karpeles

MAUD KARPELES WAS BORN IN LONDON to a family of German Jewish descent. With her sister Helen she first encountered folk dance and song in 1909, at the Stratford-on-Avon Festival. The pair then attended Cecil Sharp's dance classes so that they could teach them to poor children they were helping in Canning Town, in London. The dance club they founded became the nucleus of the English Folk Dance Society, which Sharp founded in 1911, and the sisters demonstrated the dances when he lectured around Britain. Thereafter Maud Karpeles became Sharp's close colleague and amanuensis, living in his house for 20 years and accompanying him on collecting trips, most notably to the Appalachian mountains during World War I. After Sharp's death, in 1924, she went on to publish the American material, co-write his biography and, as his literary executor, fight to protect his legacy and his copyrights. She also played a leading role in the institutions of the folk world, most notably as one of the founders of the International Folk Music Council. And she completed work that Sharp had planned in North America, collecting extensively in Newfoundland. Having edited posthumous editions of Sharp's *English Folk-Song: Some Conclusions*, she went on to write her own theoretical work, *An Introduction To English Folk Song*, in 1973. This was essentially a restatement of Sharp's ideas about the 'purity' of folk music, and was out of step with modern scholarship by the time it was published.

### Harry Cox (1885–1971)

Harry Cox

HARRY COX WAS ONE OF THE MOST IMPORTANT traditional singers of the 20th century. A farm worker who spent his entire life in Norfolk, except for a spell in the Royal Navy during the First World War, he began singing in local pubs as a child, accompanying his father, who was himself a noted singer. Harry also learned the fiddle, the melodeon and the tin whistle. He learned most of his songs from his father, but he also had a large collection of broadsides, bought by his mother as a young woman, and he sang many of those. In 1921, E. J. Moeran, the composer and folk collector, heard him sing, noted down ten of his songs and arranged for him to travel to London to make a record at Decca's studios. Later he would be recorded by the BBC and would perform for many of the luminaries of the folk song movement, including Ewan MacColl, Alan Lomax, and Peter Kennedy. His broad repertoire, including some 140 songs, and his technique and phrasing, captured in numerous recordings, made him a huge influence on the art of traditional song.

## George Butterworth (1885–1916)

AFTER REJECTING THE LEGAL CAREER HIS FATHER had planned for him, George Butterworth struggled to make his way in music. After spells as a music critic and a teacher, he started but did not finish a course at the Royal College Of Music. He found more inspiration in his long friendship with Ralph Vaughan Williams and in folk music. He began collecting in 1906, amassing more than 450 songs, dances, and dance tunes. In 1911, he joined Cecil Sharp in founding the English Folk Dance Society, and was one of the six dancers in Sharp's original morris 'side'. He once declared "I'm not a musician, I'm a professional dancer", but in the years just before 1914 he produced a small number of fine compositions drawing on his folk background, many still played and heard today, including 'Banks Of Green Willow', an orchestral piece based on the folk song of the same name (p148). On the outbreak of World War I, he joined up, destroying much of his youthful music shortly afterwards. In 1916, while serving in the Somme, he was shot through the head and buried in an unmarked grave.

George Butterworth

## The Copper Family

THE COPPER FAMILY HAVE A UNIQUE PLACE in the history of folk music in England. In 1899, songs collected from farming brothers Thomas and James 'Brasser' Copper, of Rottingdean in Sussex, were published in the first annual journal of the Folk-Song Society, formed the previous year. There had long been a family tradition of singing, and the brothers claimed to be able to trace some of their songs back to their 18th-century forebears. In the 1950s, the family was rediscovered, with Brasser's son Jim and grandsons Bob and Ron being recorded by the BBC and others. In 1952, the family appeared at the Albert Hall in London, which led to public performances around the world. Bob Copper became a song collector and author, publishing *A Song For Every Season*, a history of the family and its times that also included 47 songs from Jim Copper's handwritten family songbook. Bob Copper died in 2004, but the tradition continues through six of his grandchildren. Aside from the strength of their repertoire and the continuity of their tradition, the Coppers are particularly interesting because they sing in harmony, which is unusual in English folk song.

## A.L. Lloyd (1908–1992)

A.L. LLOYD, KNOWN AS BERT, was a leading figure in the post-war revival of folk song in England. As well as producing two studies of the subject, *The Singing Englishman* and *Folk Song In England*, he was a considerable performer. A loyal Communist from the 1930s, he attacked the EFDSS tradition as middle-class, and sought to introduce Marxist ideas on class struggle into folk scholarship. At the same time, he did valuable work in bringing what he called 'industrial folk song', the music of miners and other industrial workers, into the main stream of the folk movement. He did, however, accept Cecil Sharp's ideas about the evolution of folk song through oral transmission; later, there was a rapprochement with the EFDSS. As co-editor of *The Penguin Book Of English Folk*

A.L. Lloyd

*Songs* (1959) with Ralph Vaughan Williams, he was to form a bridge between the first and second folk revivals. The book was a key source for the English folk-rock boom of the early 1960s. As a performer, Lloyd was known for his forceful and dramatic – if not always perfectly pitched – style.

### Ralph Vaughan Williams (1872–1958)

RALPH VAUGHAN WILLIAMS WAS ONE OF THE GREATEST British composers of the 20th century. He had long been familiar with both John and Lucy Broadwood's published collections of folk songs when, in December 1903, he collected his first song. Over the next 10 years, he collected some 800 songs and carols. He borrowed some folk tunes for his *English Hymnal* of 1906. Although World War I put an end to his collecting, folk song had had a powerful influence on his efforts to create a distinctively English musical style. When he died in 1958, he was president of the English Folk Dance and Song Society, which subsequently renamed its library in his honour. In 1959, his *Penguin Book Of English Folk Songs* was published. Co-edited with A.L. Lloyd, it formed a bridge between the first and second folk revivals in England. It would prove a key source for the folk enthusiasts of the 1960s.

Ralph Vaughan Williams

### Walter Pardon (1914-1996)

WALTER PARDON, WHO SPENT HIS ENTIRE LIFE in Knapton, Norfolk, was one of the greatest of traditional singers. A carpenter by trade, he learned his songs and his style from members of his family, particularly his uncle, Billy Gee. As a child, he sang at family parties and church events. In adulthood, he did not sing publicly, there being no pub or tradition of singing in his village. Instead, he would sit quietly at home – he was a lifelong bachelor – playing the old songs on his melodeon or button accordion and recalling them for his own enjoyment. A cousin, Roger Dixon, was fascinated by the songs and persuaded Pardon to record some on a small tape recorder. He passed the tapes to Peter Bellamy, a singer and collector, which led to the recording and release in 1976 of an LP record, *A Proper Sort*. Aside from recording several more albums, Pardon now began to sing at folk festivals and clubs, and was invited to sing in Washington DC as part of the US bicentennial celebrations. He had a repertoire of some 180 songs – not all of them strictly 'folk' – and sang them in a distinctively gentle and thoughtful style. A fine performance of his favourite song, 'The Rambling Blade', is featured on the CD accompanying this book.

### Alan Lomax (1915–2002)

ALAN LOMAX WAS BORN INTO FOLK MUSIC scholarship. His father, John Lomax, was a collector of American song and later the curator of the Library of Congress's folk song archive. From the age of 18, Alan accompanied his father on collecting trips in the South, using primitive recording equipment to record singers, black and white. A left-winger and dedicated anti-racist, Alan Lomax fled to Britain in 1950 to escape McCarthyism. In London, he became a regular broadcaster on folk matters, as well as joining the BBC's early efforts to record folk song. He wrote on the subject, and was responsible for bringing together A.L. Lloyd and Ewan MacColl. He also found time to

Alan Lomax

start a skiffle group. In 1958, he returned to the US, taking with him the English singer Shirley Collins. Together they spent two months making new recordings around the States. Later, he adopted a more theoretical approach, devising Cantometrics, an ambitious attempt to use statistical methods to establish correlations between musical styles and their social and cultural conditions. He was, in that way, a pioneer of what is now called 'world music'. Anyone who has seen the film *O Brother Where Art Thou?*, or heard Moby's albums, will have heard examples of Alan Lomax's field recordings. But his influence and importance in the world of folk music, both in the US and the UK, went far beyond that.

## Ewan MacColl (1915–1989)

EWAN MACCOLL WAS ONE OF THE DRIVING FORCES behind the 1950s revival of folk music in Britain. Born to Scots parents living in Salford, in the north of England, he changed his name from Jimmy Miller while working in radical theatre as a writer, director and actor. He had been brought up singing traditional songs, and after the war moved away from theatre towards music. In 1953, he established the Ballads And Blues Club in London, along with Alan Lomax, Bert Lloyd, and others. In 1956, he met American singer Peggy Seeger, forming a partnership and later marriage that lasted the rest of his life. They introduced a policy that singers at the club, whether British or American, should only sing songs from their own tradition. This proved controversial. Later MacColl and Seeger established the Critics Group, a repertory company trained in their particular style and techniques of folk singing. MacColl was a fiercely political figure, a member of the Communist party for most of his life, who alienated many in the folk world. Nonetheless, as singer, collector, and writer he influenced a generation of folk performers. To the wider world he is better known as the writer of 'Dirty Old Town' and 'The First Time Ever I Saw Your Face'.

Ewan MacColl and Peggy Seeger

## Peter Kennedy (1922–2006)

PETER KENNEDY WAS BORN INTO THE TRADITIONAL music world. His father, Douglas Kennedy, followed Cecil Sharp as head of the English Folk Dance Society, and his mother, Helen Kennedy (née Karpeles), had been the first secretary of the organisation. Maud Karpeles was his aunt. In the late 1940s, he joined the staff of the English Folk Dance and Song Society, working first in the north-east of England and then in the west of England, where he developed the idea of using local performers and dancers and created his own dance band. Shortly afterwards he joined the BBC and began using early portable tape recorders to document traditional singers and players. When Alan Lomax came to England, Peter Kennedy worked extensively with him. By the time of his death he had amassed a catalogue of some 450 CDs and DVDs on his own Folktrax label.

Peter Kennedy (left)

## Fred Jordan (1922–2002)

FRED JORDAN, WHO WAS BORN AND BROUGHT UP in rural Shropshire, was a farmhand who performed his first song in public at the age of seven. In later life he sang regularly in pubs, and later in old people's homes. His songs came from his mother and

Fred Jordan

father and from workmates and gypsies he encountered. He came to prominence during the folk revival of the 1950s, after Peter Kennedy had recorded him for the BBC, and went on to travel widely to folk clubs and festivals. His singing was based on the repertoire of English traditional song, but in later years he was influenced by the revival and learned new material. He was known as an accomplished performer who always put across the story in a song.

# Folk and the English

BY JOHN MORRISH

ANYONE WHO HAS TRAVELLED WILL HAVE ENCOUNTERED the folk cultures of other nations. Even in western Europe, it is not uncommon for young people to set aside their skateboards, baseball caps, and mp3 players to don traditional costume and perform the songs and dances of their region. That they do this without either self-consciousness or coercion is astonishing to visitors from England, where traditional music is often the subject of amused condescension or scorn.

The low level of interest in folk music in England – temporary media-driven revivals excepted – would have dismayed Cecil Sharp, but it would not have been unfamiliar to him. At the start of his collecting career, in 1903, the existence of English folk song was largely unknown to educated people of his social class. Those who sang for the collectors were likely to be elderly people working in the countryside. The Folk-Song Society recommended its members seek out "gardeners, artizans, gamekeepers, shepherds, rustic labourers, gipsies, sailors, fishermen, workers at old-fashioned trades, such as weaving, lacemaking, and the like, as well as domestic servants of the old school, especially nurses". These people were asked for songs they remembered hearing sung, but nothing they had learned at school or at a concert. They were invited to recall a time, in their own youth, when most people sang.

To the city-dweller, all this was remote and irrelevant. English culture has been dominated by the life of the city since the time of Shakespeare. Every Frenchman is a countryman at heart, longing to return to his ancestral village like Marcel Pagnol's Jean de Florette, but in England the rural life is often a matter for disdain. As early as Shakespeare and his contemporaries, country people are already the butt of humour. Partly this was due to the rise of a class of professional comic actors, whose performances parodied the speech, mannerisms, and clothing of country people. The greatest Elizabethan comic, Richard Tarlton, dressed as a stereotype countryman and muddled his words for humorous effect.

It is no coincidence that the word 'clown' originally meant a country-dweller or peasant, before becoming associated with stage buffoonery. Samuel Pepys, writing in the second half of the 17th century, appreciated the humour in seeing rustics represented on stage. The bumpkin was a standard character in restoration drama. What is more, ballads purporting to be written by lovestruck country folk began to appear, representing them as ignorant and uncouth. This was not all caricature: education, literacy, and the ownership of books were all phenomena of the towns rather than the countryside. Singing, though, was a popular entertainment for all classes. Pepys was an enthusiastic singer of songs in all traditions: Italian, French, Elizabethan, ballads, and the bawdy.

The collectors who formed the Folk-Song Society were, on the contrary, interested only in songs they considered to be old and genuinely rural in origin, believing the illiterate peasantry to have inherited the musical riches of an earlier, pre-industrial age. They scorned the new, believing that true folk song had been destroyed by commercial music in the form of the music hall, but also by railway travel, the growth of the towns and even by education itself.

Thomas Hardy, writing just before song collection began, set his novels in the early part of the 19th century, when the elderly singers lionised by Sharp and his colleagues would have been children and when they considered the singing tradition still to be healthy. But Hardy's singers are old men, and their efforts are mocked by younger villagers. At the shearing supper in *Far From The Madding Crowd*, a farmhand called Joseph Poorgrass sings 'The Seeds Of Love' (which he claims as his own composition, although it would be the first song Cecil Sharp collected, only eight years after publication of the novel) and is ridiculed.

This, coupled perhaps with the diffidence that has long been associated with the English character, meant that the singers made no effort to present their songs to a wider world. Singing was just a fact of rural life: everyone did it, at school, at work, on the way to work, while doing their domestic chores, in the fields, and in the pub. When the collectors came knocking, the singers were happy to oblige them, but the transaction did not, in most cases, change their lives. For the collectors, on the other hand, the act of collection seems to have been filled with significance. They felt it would put them in touch with an older England, reviving not just the nation's music but its national spirit.

That reverence, and the weight of expectations, immediately placed the collectors at a distance from the singers and the material. That they were mostly representatives of the highest strata of middle class society served also to make them first alien and then faintly ridiculous both to their rural sources and the urban population. In any case, a love of tradition was more common among observers than those living the rural life. When they got the chance, country people enjoyed mass entertainment, including the music hall songs and popular dances that the intelligentsia despised on their behalf.

Nevertheless, Sharp and his associates were extremely influential in education. The songs they had collected were sung in English schools well into the second half of the 20th century. But official culture is ripe for satire in a less reverent age. Kingsley Amis's hugely popular first novel, *Lucky Jim* (1954), is a comedy of academic life in the provinces. It includes a sustained and very funny attack on a professor with an interest in madrigals, recorder playing, and folk culture. Aside from being a wicked lampoon of Amis's own father-in-law, a retired civil servant and morris dancer called Leonard Bardwell, it reflected a genuine tension in English life. The arrival of Queen Elizabeth II, coupled with state culture's tendency to romanticise the past, had led to the short-lived and self-aggrandising fantasy that modern Britons were "New Elizabethans". The result was a heady cocktail of nonsense, destined to be ridiculed.

Satire of a broader kind came in 1965, when the writers Barry Took and Marty Feldman invented a character called Rambling Sid Rumpo for the BBC radio series *Round The Horne*. Portrayed by Kenneth Williams, Rumpo sang cod folk songs in which parodies of the formulae of folk song ("Fare thee well, my apple-cheeked Betty-o") were mixed with outrageous double entendres. Clearly, something was in the air. The character's debut just preceded the earnest attempt by Fairport Convention and others to create a synthesis of traditional music and rock'n'roll and make it popular. In retrospect, that was doomed. Folk song still had a whiff of the schoolroom about it, and for good reason: as late as the 1970s school music largely consisted of listening to classical music and singing traditional songs.

That is not the case in English schools today. The English are, as many commentators have noted, uncertain about their identity. And the romantic nationalism that drove the work of Sharp and his colleagues has had little appeal in recent decades. The current national curriculum for music calls only for children to be taught "knowledge, skills and understanding" through "a range of live and recorded music from different times and cultures including music from the British Isles, the 'Western classical' tradition, folk, jazz, and popular genres, and by well-known composers and performers". This ragbag of styles is an uneasy compromise intended to mollify everyone from the dedicated multiculturalist to the upholder of the Western classical canon: the likely result is that traditional English song will be extremely lucky to get any sort of hearing.

There is an instructive contrast to be made with the music curriculum for Wales, which is openly nationalistic: chlidren are required to know "the music of Wales", something that can be fostered by "singing traditional Welsh folk songs". The language factor has, of course, helped Welsh music retain its identity in a way that has not been possible for English-language popular music in a century. But in some ways, the Welsh are re-running the history of English traditional song in the Sharp era. Whether such an approach will lead to appreciation – or apathy – remains to be seen.

# English folk song in America

## BY STEPHANIE SMITH, SMITHSONIAN INSTITUTION, US

ENGLISH FOLK SONG HAS HAD A PROFOUND, though often subtle, influence on America and American folk song. The historical connections are clear. Ballads and song were brought across to America by English, Scots and Ulster Scots settlers, many of whom made their way into the large region known as Appalachia, which stretches along the line of the Appalachian Mountains from Alabama to Quebec.

Cecil Sharp collected folk songs in Appalachia (which includes Eastern Kentucky, Southwest Virginia, East Tennessee, Western North Carolina, North Georgia, and the entire state of West Virginia) during several trips to America between 1916 and 1918. His avowed purpose was to find survivals of English folk song, and he was delighted to discover multiple pockets of thriving folk song traditions in Kentucky, Tennessee, North Carolina, and Virginia. This was clearly a discovery beyond his wildest dreams. Given Sharp's poor health and the difficulties of travel he and his assistant Maud Karpeles encountered as they made their way through predominantly rural and largely undeveloped country, his collection of Appalachian folk songs still stands as a significant achievement in the documentation of English song tradition. He came to Appalachia at the invitation of Olive Dame Campbell, who had already done some song collecting. Sharp's visits and his collecting in a real sense validated the English folk song heritage in America.

While in America, Sharp also actively taught folk dance, and founded the American Branch of the English Folk Dance Society (EFDS) in 1915. It eventually became the Country Dance and Song Society of America (CDSS), and has actively promoted Anglo-American song and dance traditions through its programs and publications to the present day. CDSS has sponsored week-long programs of English, and then more inclusively American dance and song, at Pinewoods Camp near Plymouth, Massachusetts, since the 1930s. Other weeks, such as Berea College Christmas Country Dance School in Kentucky, founded in 1938 by Englishman Frank Smith, also feature English dance and song. English folk song has thus been linked programmatically with English dance for the majority of the 20th century, and the trend continues. Through his pupils and the organisation he founded in America, Sharp's influence can be felt through the generations.

The Weavers, one of the most important and influential American folk groups of the mid 20th century, played and sang traditional music from around the world.

The mid 20th century folk revival in America helped in a large way to spark the revival in Britain. The influences also went the other direction. As the late Scottish singer Hamish Imlach commented to me, speaking about the late 1950s and early 1960s, the Americans "were all frantically trying to sing 'Greensleeves' and ignore American music, and we were all frantically trying to learn Woody Guthrie songs and sound like Lead Belly over here". The seriousness of the American political songs sung

Pete Seeger, who left The Weavers in 1952 to pursue his solo interests as performer, songwriter, and political activist.

35

by The Weavers, Woody Guthrie, Pete Seeger, and others attracted British audiences, and also helped pave the way for a newfound appreciation of the traditional songs and music in America, as evidenced by groups such as The New Lost City Ramblers who learned their music from the Southern sources. The interest in traditional music was a form of political statement.

In the 1960s, English folk revival performers made appearances in America, including The Young Tradition, Bob Davenport, Lou Killen, and scholar A.L. Lloyd, who performed at the Newport and Philadelphia Folk Festivals. The early American folk song popularisers – including The Kingston Trio, Peter, Paul and Mary, Joan Baez, and Judy Collins – led many to investigate the roots and sources of the songs, which were often English. Simon and Garfunkel recorded 'Scarborough Fair', which was hugely influential, and Bob Dylan also flirted with traditional songs and tunes. These performers, to varying degrees, undoubtedly created a greater receptivity not only for traditional English folk song and English artists who made appearances at Newport and other festivals, but also for folk-rock recordings by Fairport Convention, Steeleye Span, and Pentangle that came out in the late 1960s and the 1970s. Though jokes are often made about the number of verses in ballads, these recordings pushed the envelope with their versions of the multi-verse ballads such as 'Matty Groves' and 'Tam Lin'. Earlier, in the 1950s and early 1960s, Folkways Records in New York had put out the brilliant *Anthology of American Folk Music* compiled by Harry Smith (1952), as well as other seminal releases such as Jean Ritchie's *British Traditional Ballads In The Southern Mountains* (1960). The Folkways treasure trove of traditional song lay undiscovered by some until later in the folk revival years.

I have long been fascinated by the British ballads that have been most popular in America and the way the ballad stories have changed in oral tradition. Like 'The Gypsy Laddie' (p136), 'The House Carpenter' (also known as 'The Daemon Lover', p125) has enjoyed a considerable popularity in America, as evidenced by Sharp's and other 20th century American collections. Both ballads involve a wife and mother enticed away from her home by a man (or men, in the case of the gypsies,) with a mysterious allure. Harry Smith included a 1930 recording of Clarence Ashley singing 'The House Carpenter' in the *Anthology of American Folk Music*, which is one of five Child Ballads in the *Anthology*. Interestingly, the American versions indicate that the supernatural aspect of the original ballad – 'The Daemon Lover' – which portrays the lover as a demon or the Devil, has been played down or eliminated, so that the ballad becomes, as North Carolina collector Frank C. Brown described, "a merely domestic tragedy". Americans have always had a great fondness for cautionary tales in their songs.

Once transplanted to America, the English ballads and songs were reshaped, and some dropped out of the tradition. There is a distinct tendency toward the lyric form in America, dealing with emotions, and the longer narrative songs have become shorter. The locations in many songs have been changed to American settings. The supernatural plot elements in the British originals have been rationalised in the American versions in many instances, although this is not true across the board; there are popular forms of the supernatural in American versions. Ghosts are quite common, as in 'Barbara Allen' (p112), 'Fair Margaret And Sweet William', and 'The Unquiet Grave' (p86). The figure of the Devil, particularly in a comic framework, is also popular, as in 'The Farmer's Curst Wife' (p220). The American versions have retained their references to kings, lords, and ladies, and in many songs there is a notable democratic thread. Love, in all its manifestations – tragic, romantic, and comic - is a predominant theme in American songs from the English tradition. It is thus not surprising that many singers from whom Sharp collected referred to their songs as "love songs".

In the 1960s, British folk-rock groups like Fairport Convention benefited from the renewed interest in traditional song among American performers and audiences.

Sharp collected songs from a number of outstanding women singers; in some of the songs collected then, and which persist in popularity, women are active, rather than passive, as in 'Lady Isabel and the Elf Knight'. One can imagine the appeal to female singers of a song in which the heroine hurls her would-be murderer over the edge of a cliff into the sea, after she has cunningly requested him to look away while she removes her "fine and costly" clothing. Although the American endings of 'The Gypsy Laddie' vary in outcome, the lady can be seen as making a choice to run away; one interpreter sees the ballad as an expression of the American frontier spirit. Explicitly sexual ballads from the English tradition have either dropped out of tradition or have been altered to suit the religious morality of the American people; but songs concerning husbands and wives – especially humorous examples such as 'Our Goodman' and 'Get Up And Bar the Door' have had a broad appeal. The dialogue form of these songs is well-liked by American singers. Songs of rape, common in the British tradition, appear less frequently in America, although songs in which a man kills his pregnant sweetheart are widespread, perhaps because they serve as moral warnings.

At various times in American history, the Anglo-American heritage has had its problematic aspects. One outgrowth of the 1960s Civil Rights movement and other socio-political movements, and more recently the world music explosion, has been an emphasis on multiculturalism. Anglo-American culture has sometimes been viewed as disproportionately dominant even as America becomes more multicultural. Newspaper articles from 1908 to the 1960s describe English traditions, particularly May Day – described as those of "Merrie England" in some cases – being celebrated in various American cities, including Los Angeles, Washington DC, and New York.

From the 21st century perspective, revivals of interest in traditional song occur in cycles, given a boost by references in popular media such as the release of the films *Songcatcher* and *O Brother, Where Art Thou?*. English folk song is a vital part of the American song landscape, and has had enormous cultural influences that will continue to be felt as younger generations discover it, just as previous ones have.

# The folk revivals

BY **MARK BREND**

THE TERM 'FOLK REVIVAL' TENDS TO PROVOKE a series of knee-jerk responses. Traditionalists fret about the integrity of folk song as an authentic art threatened by commercialism. Others see the use of folk song in contemporary musical settings as a natural part of the folk process, with songs finding new meaning and resonance with successive audiences, sustaining and refreshing the tradition. And a third group will imagine either a bunch of earnest Arran-sweatered beardies singing archaic nonsense in nasal voices – the musical equivalent of re-enacting ancient battles – or cleanly scrubbed youths in work-shirts joining hands for a rousing civil rights anthem. We need to look beyond these stereotypes to get to the heart of the idea of a folk revival.

The term 'folk revival' is itself something of a misnomer. What happens is not the resurrection of a dead cultural form; the music being revived is not moribund or extinct. Rather, its performance and appreciation are limited to a small community, separate from the popular music mainstream. The revival introduces the music to a much wider audience.

Since most of the songs in this book date from between 1600 and the mid 19th century, any interest in them much after that could be termed a revival. The collecting activities of Cecil Sharp and others were a revival; and folk revivals of one sort or another have become a reasonably regular phenomenon since the early 20th century. But it was the US and UK revivals of the 1950s and 1960s, more than any others, that introduced folk song to a mass international audience.

Actually, the two movements – although distinct from each other – are closely related. Key figures and songs criss-crossed the Atlantic, and the resultant cross-pollination did much to define the character of both scenes. In a sense, that mirrored the historical relationship between British (and specifically English) folk song and its American counterpart. The two traditions often overlap, and the interest of late 19th century and early 20th century collectors reflected this. Francis J. Child, whose *English And Scottish Popular Ballads* remains a key text, was an American, a Harvard scholar. And Cecil Sharp not only collected songs across England, he travelled to the Appalachian mountains to do the same. Long before this, many English songs had found their way across the Atlantic, nurtured in the minds and hearts of émigrés, to be absorbed into the emerging culture of the New World.

Some characteristics are common to all the folk revivals. The first of these is an adaptation of folk styles to fit other – usually more popular – music structures, which helps bring folk to bigger audiences. Before the 1950s/1960s revivals, English folk song had been adapted for performance in music halls. Its reconfiguration for an audience raised on rock'n'roll was much the same process at work.

One lasting outcome of the 1950s/1960s revivals was the rise of various strands of folk-influenced popular music that the pop audience has come to view as *being* folk music. Take a performer like Martin Carthy. To the broad pop audience, he is a typical English folkie, singing in a voice that defiantly rejects the American vocal mannerisms that normally pervade rock and pop. But to some in the traditional folk audience he is at best a moderniser, at worst someone who has meddled with the tradition. He is undeniably a product of a folk revival.

In most folk revivals, contemporary performers and writers produce new songs that incorporate some of the themes or traits – musical or lyrical – of folk. Bob Dylan started off performing only traditional folk and blues songs before he began writing his own material. But in the 40 years or so since then he has repeatedly drawn on folk tunes and turns of phrase for his own songs.

Again, this is nothing new. Although the initial composer's credit for most traditional songs is impossible to trace, it seems likely that many would have been originated not by some archetypal farm hand as he tilled the fields, but rather by professional or semi-professional performers – the pop singers of the day – using the language and concerns of working people.

The leading figures in folk revivals – whether performers, collectors, or writers – are often culturally far removed from the music they are reviving. From the 1950s onwards, revivals have typically been driven by the educated middle classes. Critics have pointed at the essential contradiction of predominantly urban, young, educated, middle-class performers celebrating the authenticity of the music of rural cultures that had ceased to exist decades or even centuries previously.

The American folk revival of the mid 20th century pre-dated the British example; its roots went back to the 1940s, when folk music had a brief period of major US commercial success with the odd career of The Weavers. Formed in 1947, this vocal/instrumental group scored a series of enormous hits before its members' communist sympathies – not conducive to a high-profile career in the McCarthy era – forced it to disband in 1952; there was literally nowhere for the group to play, and it was impossible for their label, Decca, to get their albums into the stores. The Weavers reformed when the grip of the McCarthy blacklist weakened as the decade wore on, but never repeated their earlier commercial success. Nonetheless, they'd proved that folk songs could be million-sellers, and a clutch of commercial folk bands followed them who matched their commercial – if not artistic – achievements. With The Kingston Trio's two-million-selling 1958 hit, 'Tom Dooley', a folk revival was in full swing.

Bob Dylan was deeply influenced by folk song in his early days. He is pictured performing at the 1962 Christmas party of the Singers' Club in London. It was his first visit to Britain.

The most prominent member of The Weavers was singer, guitarist, and banjo player Pete Seeger, who started a solo career in 1958 after briefly joining the reformed group. By that stage he was already seen as something of a benign patriarch of the American folk movement, a position he still holds nearly 50 years later.

Another key figure of the American folk revival was Harry Smith, a 29-year-old music lover, poet, and filmmaker, who was living in New York City when, in 1952, he compiled *The Anthology Of American Folk Music*. Although it wasn't a particularly big seller, it profoundly influenced a generation of musicians that included Bob Dylan and Joan Baez. The 84-track *Anthology* was originally issued by Folkways in three volumes – *Ballads*, *Social Music*, and *Songs* – each on two LPs. The songs were predominantly acoustic blues, gospel, and cowboy tunes, yet the *Anthology* begins with Dick Justice singing 'Henry Lee', closely related to the traditional

British ballad 'Young Hunting', as recorded in Child (Child 68). It is a case study in how far a song can travel. From its obscure roots in Britain centuries ago, it was originally recorded by Justice in 1929, and variants have since been cut by artists including Bob Dylan, Peggy Seeger, and more recently Nick Cave and The Bad Seeds on the album *Murder Ballads*. Four other Child ballads feature on the first volume of the *Anthology*, and many American singers of the period rummaged through Child for inspiration. For example, 'The Unquiet Grave' (p86) was recorded by Joan Baez, while variants of 'The Gypsy Laddie' (p136) have been released by dozens of US artists, including Pete Seeger and Jean Ritchie.

Another American song collector who delved into the English tradition, and forged a link between the US and UK revivals, was Alan Lomax. He travelled America with his father, the folklorist John Lomax, from the 1930s, recording people singing many of the Child ballads, and the songs of cowboys and cotton pickers, farmers and hobos. Their worked shaped the Archive of American Folk Song in the Library of Congress, a resource that did much to tell America about its own folk traditions. This archive, too, was fuel for the subsequent revival.

In the 1950s Alan Lomax extended his range, travelling throughout Great Britain (and Ireland, Spain, and Italy) recording indigenous folk music on a portable tape recorder. He instigated a number of British radio and television programmes during this time, including a 1952 TV documentary, *Folk Music Of Britain*, produced by David Attenborough. During these visits he forged links with the inner circle of London-based folk singers who would provide much of the energy for the British folk revival, among them Ewan MacColl and his wife, expatriate American Peggy Seeger (half-sister of Pete Seeger). At a party hosted by MacColl, Lomax met the young Shirley Collins – a prominent figure in the British folk scene to this day – the pair eventually spending a year together collecting songs in the American South.

Guitarists John Renbourn and Bert Jansch were two of the stars to emerge from the London folk clubs of the early 1960s.

Although by the late 1950s there was a thriving British folk scene, it did not yet have the far-reaching commercial consequences of its American counterpart. Although some of the American commercial folk groups – such as The Kingston Trio – had British hits, home-grown folk music had little impact on the wider popular music scene. A curious exception to this was skiffle, a peculiarly British phenomenon that was very popular between 1956 and 1958. Skiffle actually had its roots in traditional 'trad' jazz, but its biggest hits – such as Lonnie Donegan's 'Rock Island Line' – were souped-up, home-made takes on American folk tunes. It was a short-lived craze, but many pop and folk musicians who later rose to prominence strummed their first chords in skiffle bands.

By the early 1960s, both the British and American folk revivals were in full swing, and receiving a great deal of press. The difference between them was that, while the American had mainstream commercial clout, the British one remained a minority interest. In London it was sufficient to maintain a number of small but thriving clubs, including Bunjies and Les Cousins. These tiny rooms hosted up-and-coming British performers such as Davy Graham, Bert Jansch, John Renbourn, and Martin Carthy, and visiting Americans including Paul Simon, Richard Farina, Jackson C. Frank, and Bob Dylan. With hindsight, that's an impressive roll-call of talent, but at that time these people were known only to a discerning cabal of enthusiasts. It might have been a crucible forging raw talent, but the British folk music scene was not, at this stage, widely appreciated outside its own circle.

The London folk scene provided the stage for an episode that poses uncomfortable questions about the relationship between folk music and commerce. Martin Carthy's repertoire included an arrangement of the traditional song 'Scarborough Fair'. Paul Simon picked it up from him and included it on Simon and Garfunkel's third album, *Parsley, Sage, Rosemary And Thyme* (1966), in the process copyrighting the arrangement – which included a counter-melody from one of Simon's own songs – to himself. The song was a great success, and we can only assume that Simon – whatever the terms of his publishing deal – made a lot of money out of it. Should Carthy, and by extension all performers who adapt traditional songs, have copyrighted his arrangement? If so, is something lost from the tradition? Do the songs somehow belong to the people, and should that set them beyond publishers and their percentages? That is still Carthy's view today (see Working With Folk Song, p61).

To explain why the two folk revivals took root in the late 1950s, and why the American revival achieved more commercial success, we need to look at the broader popular music scene of the time. The US folk boom coincided with a lull in the energy of rock'n'roll. By 1960, the first generation of rockers were out of action. Buddy Holly and Eddie Cochran had been killed in accidents; Elvis Presley was in the army; Chuck Berry had problems with the law; Jerry Lee Lewis had incurred public and media wrath when he married his teenage cousin; Little Richard had found God; and Gene Vincent had turned to drink. And the revitalising British invasion was still a few years away. Into this vacuum were propelled manufactured teen idols – Frankie Avalon, Fabian, and the like – who had little of rock'n'roll's danger, energy, or power. American teenagers who had been so excited by Elvis in 1956 were now looking elsewhere for substance, authenticity, and a way to hit out at convention. Many found those things in folk.

The folk revival fostered a sense of beleaguered community. A particular attraction to youthful malcontents was the sense of 'us' (liberal, left-leaning pacifists) against 'them' (Republicans and bland, middle-class materialists). Folk was 'of the people'. It had intellectual pretensions. It was serious. It was critical of comfortable Middle America. It was anti-establishment.

Bert Jansch (above) was one of the British guitarists who met and played with Paul Simon (below) during his period touring the English folk clubs in 1964 and 1965.

Over the water the picture was subtly different. A quick glance at the late 1950s charts reveal that rock'n'roll's impact on the British music scene was more limited, certainly as compared with events in the US. The big-selling albums were soundtracks from musicals, and Mantovani, Jimmy Young, and Perry Como clogged up the singles charts. While it's true that Elvis had big hits, people such as Gene Vincent remained relatively obscure, and home-grown British rock rarely passed muster. Perhaps folk was less attractive to British youth because rock'n'roll remained comparatively rare and exotic, and retained its outlaw status?

The folk revival might at first have appeared liberating to disaffected American youth, but after a few years it began to feel like a prison. For all its apparent political liberalism, the US folk scene was musically conservative. Strict rules emerged about what was and what was not acceptable. It was often unclear what the rules were, and who had made them, but they tended to centre on notions of authenticity, community and anti-commercialism. For a young iconoclast such as Bob Dylan, initially drawn to the movement because of its authenticity, these rules would come to seem like restrictive narrow-mindedness dressed up as idealism. Dylan loved rock'n'roll too, and in this he was not alone. When The Beatles and The Rolling Stones spearheaded the first wave of authentic English rock'n'roll, Dylan and many of other young American folkies were captivated.

With her folk club background, Sandy Denny was central to Fairport Convention's move into traditional music.

Take Roger McGuinn and David Crosby, future members of The Byrds. Both had considerable previous form on the US folk circuit, yet by 1964 had grown tired of its strictures. McGuinn has since explicitly stated that The Byrds were formed to marry the chords and tunes of folk with the beat, harmonies, and instrumentation of The Beatles. Their 1965 breakthrough hit was a Dylan song, 'Mr Tambourine Man', that in its original form was an obtuse solo narrative stretching over many verses. The Byrds stripped it down to just two verses and a repeated chorus of soaring harmonies, alongside leader Roger McGuinn's chiming electric 12-string Rickenbacker guitar. It gave an indication of what an electric band could do to an acoustic song.

The marriage of folk and rock was consummated a few months later when The Byrds took Pete Seeger's 'Turn, Turn, Turn' into the charts with a similar electric treatment. In doing so they sent a clear message to the folk movement and the music business: folk songs played by young pop bands with electric guitars sold more records than folk songs strummed on acoustic guitars by earnest folk singers. Folk-rock was born. Folk music – as a style, an idea, a movement – never again had such commercial influence or such a foothold in US youth culture.

Dylan himself was quick to notice what was happening. It seems incredible and comical now, that his brief electric set at the Newport folk festival in 1965 should have caused such upheaval among folk fans and players. Did the gentle, avuncular Pete Seeger really try to cut the power cables as Dylan's electric band rocked through 'Maggie's Farm'? Probably not, but witnesses say he was pretty angry (although he has since claimed that this was simple annoyance that he couldn't hear what Dylan was singing).

Dave Swarbrick has been a stalwart of the British folk scene for nearly half a century. He is admired especially for his work with Martin Carthy.

The esteemed folk organ *Sing Out* reviewed the performance with barely concealed contempt. "Dylan emerged from his cult-imposed aura of mystery to demonstrate the new 'folk-rock', an expression that has already begun to find its way into the 'Top Forty' charts by which musical success is measured. To many it seemed that it was not very good 'rock', while other disappointed legions did not think it was very good Dylan."

Newport was the end of the folk revival as a meaningful force in American popular culture, a symbolic marker of a transition that had taken place in Dylan's career, and a culmination of the long-running rift between folk purists and innovators. Dylan had outgrown the movement that had spawned him. He was moving on, developing as an artist and alienating traditionalists. Many others would follow.

As a musical craze, American folk-rock had a short life, and it was over before a uniquely English variant emerged. The Byrds had pioneered psychedelia and were about to invent country rock before the world had even heard of Fairport Convention. The band now generally considered the quintessential English folk-rock group started as part of the psychedelic rock scene. Early in their career they were described as "the British Jefferson Airplane" on account of their female singer and a fondness for elongated acid rock guitar solos. Their repertoire was drawn from contemporary US folk-influenced performers such as Dylan and Joni Mitchell, alongside band originals and – very occasionally – electric arrangements of traditional songs.

Folk influences became gradually more prominent as personnel changed, first with the arrival of new singer Sandy Denny for The Fairports' second album, *What We Did On Our Holidays* (1968), and then with a guest appearance by folk fiddler Dave Swarbrick for its follow-up, *Unhalfbricking* (1969). Following that album's release, the band retired to a rented mansion in the west of England to recover from a car crash that had killed their drummer Martin Lamble. It was at this time that bassist Ashley Hutchings began researching traditional English songs at Cecil Sharp House, often presenting his latest discovery to the band only to find that Denny, a seasoned folk performer, already knew it. Indeed, it was Denny who had introduced the band to the traditional 'A Sailor's Life', which featured on *Unhalfbricking*. From these exchanges came the band's forth album, *Liege & Lief* (1969), on which, for the first time, the track-listing was dominated by variants on the credit "trad. arranged Fairport Convention".

After this watershed recording, band member Ashley Hutchings left to form Steeleye Span and The Albion Band, further exploring electric interpretations of traditional English songs. It is in this lineage where we can identify, finally, a distinctive English brand of folk-rock. It is a powerful comment on the impact and the influence of the folk revival that the wider pop/rock audience now equates this English-folk rock with folk music, a point underlined when *Liege and Lief* was voted the 'Best Folk Album Ever' by BBC Radio 2 listeners in 2002, and 'Most Influential Folk Album Of All Time' in BBC Radio 2's 2006 Folk Awards.

# Folk in Britain today

BY **NIGEL WILLIAMSON**

"IT'S COOL, IT'S HIP ... IT'S, ER, FOLK," ran a headline in the *Observer* newspaper in London last year, hailing the 'new' sound that was apparently sweeping the nation. There are two things you can guarantee about folk song. One is that, ever since the collector Cecil Sharp complained that music hall was destroying traditional music, there will always be voices of doom telling us that it is under threat of extinction. The other is that someone somewhere is always rediscovering it.

That *Observer* headline was heralding the latest so-called 'folk revival' to be discovered by the media. The brief attention given to a form of music that is normally ignored by the mainstream is welcome, of course. But all it really means is that another generation of performers has stumbled upon the rich wellspring of traditional British folk song. They are hardly 'reviving' folk music, for, as the traditional singer Bob Copper memorably put it, "this was the music before music was invented" – and it has never gone away. There are inevitably peaks and troughs of interest and vitality. But with reassuring regularity, successive generations have come along to sustain the tradition and rejuvenate it, ensuring that folk music remains a vibrant, living form rather than an ossified part of the English heritage industry, along with fake mediaeval banquets and mock jousting tournaments on a public holiday.

Yet every time we get one of these revivals, the same questions tend to arise. Perhaps the central one is this: why, in the 21st century, are we still signing songs about comely milkmaids and jolly ploughboys, wild gipsy rovers, and bold Lincolnshire poachers?

The Yorkshire-born singer Kate Rusby deals with the question in a down-to-earth and uncomplicated manner. "Of course the old ballads are still relevant. Completely! They're songs about people," she says simply. "That's what folk music is – the music of the people. They're about people's feelings and emotions and what happens to them in their lives: being born, falling in and out of love, growing old and dying. That doesn't change whether you're a ploughboy or a computer programmer. The songs might be 200 years old but we're still the same human beings. And it's never dull. Death, destruction, jealousy, drowning – it's all there. I like to call them castle-knocking-down songs, but I've never thought of them as old-fashioned. They've always seemed totally new to me and I get very emotionally involved in them."

Essentially, Rusby is saying that the values and experiences that remain unchanging in the human condition are far more profound than the superficial changes brought about by what we like to call progress. Once you've accepted that, then questions about the relevance of traditional folk song in a digital age become irrelevant. For a specific example, take the masterful version of 'Turpin Hero' created by singer and fiddler Eliza Carthy. The song is an 18th-century piece of gangsta-style myth-making on behalf of the notorious highwayman Dick Turpin, first performed some 40 years after his death. She says it reminds her of Superman, painting a picture of male braggadacio, as swaggering and outrageous as anything dreamed up by the bling-festooned rappers of today.

Carthy's mother Norma Waterson is another who subscribes to the 'all human life is there' approach. "War, death, incest, murder, unhappiness – folk music is just songs about the basic things that keep the world going round," she says. Perhaps that's why folk song also takes on a fresh and fundamental importance in a modern world obsessed with celebrity, glamour, and fashion. In a more innocent age, pop singers reflected the hopes, dreams, and disappointments of the people who bought their records, and shared a broadly similar lifestyle. Think of early Cliff Richard and The Shadows in the film *Summer Holiday*. They were simply working-class lads who got lucky; the expectation was that they would make a few records and a film or two, earn a few bob, and then, when it was all over, go back to driving a bus or working on the factory floor. Today, pop stars are remote icons who have as much to do with real life as royalty. Folk music is one of the few remaining forms of creative expression in which performers and audience still inhabit the same planet.

Eliza Carthy makes the point. "Folk music is just stories, stuff that people have done, and as it's part of life it means that it can never be boring," she says. "But more importantly, we really need it more than ever. Too much of the pop music you hear on the radio puts a sheen on your brain. If the only people who could make music are pop stars who go on diets to keep slim and have a stylist on 24-hour call to keep their hair in place at all times, the world would be very boring.

"Of course I want to make good CDs and it's great if the records get played on the radio. But at its most basic level, music is still about going into a pub or a club and hearing someone singing. That's where the connection comes from – and probably only folk music still works like that."

It's a point well made. Justin Timberlake might have millions of fans. But ask yourself this. When was the last time any of them really felt *connected* to their hero in

Eliza Carthy, backed by her father, Martin Carthy, on guitar.

any meaningful way? His remoteness and riches and his fame and fortune militate against it. Hip-hop, it can be argued, started as a kind of modern urban folk music, reflecting life on the street as lived by both performers and those who bought the records. Yet it quickly lost that connection. When he started out, no doubt Eminem did genuinely represent the voice of Detroit's dispossessed. Once he'd made his first million and moved to a gated community with a coterie of servants and security guards, by definition he no longer could.

On the other hand, a folk performer like Eliza Carthy seeks to create that sense of connection every night. Punk was another modern form that briefly emerged as a music of the people, and some, such as Norma Waterson, believe that folk music should have embraced it and regret its failure to do so. "When punk came about it should have happened in the folk clubs," she argues. "But the punks weren't allowed in and that's why folk music stagnated for a time during the 1980s."

Whether she's right or not, it was inevitable that punk would burn itself out, once it ceased to be a street movement and became a saleable product for major record companies such as EMI and Virgin. Before long, it had produced its own stars, who became a part of the system punk had tried to overthrow. Somehow, folk music, despite its various revivals, and the occasional comet bursting across its firmament, such as Bob Dylan or Paul Simon, remains immune to the superstar syndrome. Martin Carthy – perhaps the most revered name in British folk for the last 30 years – can still be found playing to a few dozen people in tiny pubs and folk clubs, travelling to his gigs on public transport.

In other words, folk music is not merely a repertoire of old songs but it is also an attitude of mind. Nobody ever became a folk musician to become rich and famous. Even in one of folk's upturns, nobody could be that deluded – and perhaps that is what has enabled it to remain a genuine music of the people, while rap and punk have just become further cogs in the pop machine.

Of course, folk performers still aspire to selling lots of records, filling concert halls, and enjoying the trappings of their success. Eliza Carthy sees no problem with that. "If you don't want to sell loads of albums and be on TV and reach a wider audience and you prefer to sit around in an Arran sweater, then that's fine," she says. "But I can't do that because I am a contemporary person. I approve of dragging folk music into a contemporary context. I like the records to look good, and it's about time folk was made more stylish. You have to sell records if you want to make a living out of folk music. I've never seen any conflict there."

Folk music has many ways to reach a wider audience in the modern world. One is the route that, for want of a better name, we might term 'folk fusion'. This can mean anything from a dub version of 'Tam Lin' by Benjamin Zephaniah and Transglobal Underground which "turns the story of a Scottish knight abducted by the Queen of the Faeries into a dark tale of modern clubland" to the post-millenial beats Jim Moray adds to such traditional tunes as 'Early One Morning' and 'Lord Bateman'. We shall return to the subject of fusion later.

Another route is to refresh folk song with an injection of youthful energy and vigour, while remaining unswervingly true to its roots and traditions. Eliza Carthy has journeyed down both paths – often at the same time – and points out that they do not have to be mutually exclusive. Interestingly, she has found non-traditional folk audiences can be extremely receptive to the most uncompromisingly traditional approach. "I find audiences very open-minded," she says. "When I sing an unaccompanied trad song it always touches people, but often they don't know what to call it. They ask you what it is, and when you tell them it's folk music, people will often say, 'Oh, but I don't like folk music.' Yet they've just given it a rousing ovation."

Many traditional folk performers have sought a wider audience by absorbing contemporary compositions into their traditional repertoire and claiming them as 'modern folk songs', or writing their own material in a traditional style. In 1999 Kate Rusby told me, "I'd rather bare my bum on the town-hall steps than make a pop record." Her approach has been to create a new repertoire based firmly on traditional models, so that it is virtually impossible when listening to her records to tell which are old songs and which are new.

Kate Rusby: "I'm dead proud to be a folk singer, me."

Her 1999 album *Sleepless* (which won her a Mercury Music Prize nomination and found her announcing "I'm dead proud to be a folk singer, me" to the great and the good of the British music industry at the awards ceremony) opens with a song called 'The Cobbler's Daughter'. The title suggests a piece that could have been written at almost any time in the past 200 years. Yet it's her own composition. She also regularly slips into the language of an 18th-century ballad in her lyrics. For example, her song 'All God's Angels', which appears on the same album, contains the lines:

"Will you walk hand in hand with me,/For I do carry a child by thee."

She has been criticised for such archaisms, which is far removed from the speech of modern Britain. But she is unrepentant. "The language is timeless and so is the subject," she says. "It's about unmarried motherhood, and what could be more contemporary than that? Most modern songwriters write about their own personal experience in a confessional kind of way, and I've always felt a bit cheated by that because they are in their own little world. I don't want to bore people with my problems. I want to tell a story that everyone can relate to and that's all that songs like 'All God's Angels' or 'The Cobbler's Daughter' are trying to do."

Another who mixes traditional songs with his own take on the British folk heritage is Seth Lakeman, the singer, fiddler and guitarist who was once part of the so-called 'folk super-group' Equation, with Rusby and Kathryn Roberts.

Lakeman's album *Kitty Jay*, nominated for the Mercury Music Prize in 2005, contained both original and traditional songs about the stories and legends of his birthplace and home, Dartmoor in south-west England. It was recorded for £300 in his kitchen. "I love folk song and I'm fascinated by the stories and the history," he says. "I don't regard myself in any respect as a traditional singer, but I am inspired by tradition and the area in which I grew up, and I play upon traditional stories."

In the mid 1990s, Lakeman discovered at first hand that folk music and the pop world can make uneasy bedfellows when Equation signed to Warner Brothers. The label tried to turn them into pop stars, and they ended up falling hopelessly between two stools: they were never quite accepted by the pop world and yet much of the folk music community felt betrayed. Rightly or wrongly, the group earned a reputation for arrogance – more of a sin in folk circles than adding electronic beats to a trad ballad – and the conflicting pressures killed the band.

Rusby was one of the first to quit, and says of her departure: "It was a big step to walk away from a major label deal but I knew I would be so unhappy in the pop world.

I just couldn't play that kind of music." Lakeman stayed until 2001 and then went solo himself. "To be honest, I never planned to be a solo artist," he says today. "I was always in the background in Equation and I thought I'd just play fiddle or guitar with other people and do a bit of work in the studio. So I didn't plan any of this. It just happened. I'm not on a crusade for folk music or anything and I can't really say why people like the songs, other than that I think they respond to stories. I've not purposefully tried to do anything different. It all feels natural to me, although I do enjoy a dramatic approach to songs."

While Lakeman has tended to flesh out his folk ballads with denser layers of sound that at times strays into folk-rock territory, The Devil's Interval, a young British band, have gone in an opposite but equally dramatic direction by stripping down their take on the traditional folk ballad to the basics of the unaccompanied human voice. They don't quite stick their fingers in their ears, and they do occasionally add discreet splashes of concertina and accordion, but essentially the trio of Jim Causley, Emily Portman, and Lauren McCormick sing unadorned vocal harmonies in the traditional style. Their effervescent approach makes them sound entirely new, and earned them the accolade of a cover feature in the British magazine *fRoots* before their first album had even been released.

Seth Lakeman, one of many young performers finding a new audience for traditional music.

The three met while doing a degree course in traditional music at Newcastle University, where they become entranced by listening to the source singers on Topic Records' vast *Voice Of The People* series. The set includes some of the earliest known recordings from almost a century ago. As several of the singers were in the sunset of their days even then, their voices represent the most direct and tangible link we have to the folk song of the pre-recording era, when a live performance was the only method by which a song could be disseminated. "We're drawn to those singers, not only because they sing great songs but because of the way they sing them," Lauren McCormick told *fRoots*. "They're not only bearers of a tradition, but creative musicians in their own right. We don't just listen out of a sense of duty. We listen to them for pleasure. They're great singers."

As a result of direct exposure to such source material, their folk club performances are blessed with a rare authenticity, moulded not by the histrionics of the rock'n'roll era but by the equally theatrical style of performers who never knew what a microphone was. And yet they are also doing entirely their own thing; the essence of traditional folk music has always been that there can be no 'correct' version of a song, for before the advent of the recording era, folk songs were subtly and often unknowingly altered by almost everyone who sang them. "There are lots of people who want to fix rules on to this music," Jim Causley says. "But we love it for the very opposite reason: that there's such room for freedom in interpretation. You take a lot of pop songs and sing them unaccompanied and they sound rubbish because they only use a few notes. Traditional songs were made to be sung unaccompanied and that's why the tunes are so great – they go all over the place and they can stand up on their own."

Whether they can sustain a career singing unaccompanied traditional song remains to be seen. "We love playing folk clubs and festivals," Lauren McCormick says. "But we're not naïve enough to think it will be easy to make a living out of performing. We all teach and have our hands in different projects."

In the hands of the great singers of the past, the presentation of a traditional folk song was always a dramatic art. In recent times nowhere can this be heard to more intensely theatrical effect than on Chris Wood's 2005 album *The Lark Ascending*. This is hardly surprising given that the singer and fiddler, who also recorded with Martin Carthy as part of the trio Wood, Wilson & Carthy, has worked with folk song at both the Royal National Theatre in London and the Royal Shakespeare Company in Stratford. "My jaw would drop every night at how these songs could become even more powerful if you set them up," Wood says of his experience in the theatre. "You could create exactly the right situation for a traditional song without being overtly folkie about it. Something would happen on stage and the only thing that could follow it was an incest ballad or something."

Seth Lakeman made a point earlier in this chapter about not being on a crusade for folk music. He no doubt had in mind that as soon as someone young, talented, and attractive appears on the scene singing folk songs rather than making pop music, they are liable to be seized upon by the elders of the folk establishment as the music's 'great white hope'. It's a path strewn with casualties for immediately the new young champion dares to step outside of the folk stockade, the cries of betrayal go up. It happened famously to Bob Dylan when he went electric at the Newport Folk Festival in 1965. Thirty years later, the much vaunted Equation suffered a similar backlash when Warner Brothers attempted to turn them into pop stars.

When 22-year-old Jim Moray burst on to the scene in 2003, with his extraordinary debut album *Sweet England*, the record was hailed by the London *Daily Telegraph* as "the biggest leap forward in folk for 30 years" and the most important English folk record since Fairport Convention's *Liege And Lief*. Suddenly he found himself cast as both hero and villain. To some diehards, his 21st-century fusion of traditional folk ballads with electronic beats, loops and synths, influenced in equal parts by Massive Attack and Martin Carthy, was anathema. To others, he was folk music's bold new crusader, ready to sally forth on his charger, convert Radio 1 to the folk cause with his updated take on the tradition and usher in a new (or in the current usage, 'nu') golden age.

Moray was flattered, but rightfully wary. "Folk music in England can be a very insular community," he says. "They're not always very open-minded and tend to think the music should be done the way it has always been done. But it would have been a lie for me to sing these songs acoustically in the vocal style of a 16th-century peasant, because I grew up listening to rock music and electronica and I can't pretend they didn't influence me. I don't think there is really anything unusual about what I do at a base level – traditional music has always been about taking the things you hear around you and making them into your own music. I try to be true to these songs and play them in a way that appeals to me as someone who listens to a lot of music."

By presenting such traditional ballads as 'Early One Morning' and 'Raggle Taggle Gypsies' (p136) in a contemporary style, Moray believes not only that he has captured the essence of the songs but prevented such well known material sounding hackneyed. "I discarded a lot of the folk wrapping to get at the stuff inside – the real core of the music," he says.

The reason he turned to traditional material rather than writing his own songs was very simple. "I'd been in a rock band as a teenager and it simply began to dawn on me that these were better songs than anything I could write because they're the ultimate collaborations," he explains. "I mean, you've had the best songwriters working on them for the past 500 years! Everybody who has ever sung a traditional ballad adds their own little bit, and it gets refined into a really amazing song."

Perhaps the boldest and most ambitious effort to update traditional folk song in recent times is the Imagined Village project, masterminded by Simon Emmerson. In the mid 1990s , he formed the Afro Celt Sound System, whose fusion of Irish roots music, West African rhythms and contemporary dance beats made them firm favourites on the global festival circuit. The band remains active, although for most of the past two years, Emmerson has been putting together the Imagined Village, which takes its title from Georgina Boyes's book of the same name. Boyes's book argues that the English folk revival of the last 50 years has been a direct and urgent response to a cultural crisis caused by the pressures of industrialisation and urbanisation.

Emmerson's brief was simple enough – to re-imagine traditional folk song for a post-industrial 21st century Britain via a series of collaborations between folk performers and artists working with such contemporary urban forms as drum'n'bass, trip-hop and rock, as well as imported styles that have become an integral part of our multicultural society, such as bhangra and reggae.

"Georgina's book pointed out that English folk music can never belong to any single group of people," Emmerson says. "Over the years it's been claimed by both right and left but it can't be appropriated or manipulated by anyone. We wanted to find an interface between the folk tradition and modern English roots music, which is a far broader concept that reflects the wider diversity in the community and is connected to the debate about multiculturalism and what English identity now means. Someone like Benjamin Zephaniah was a perfect fit because he's not only a UK rasta but he's a storyteller, and so a ballad like 'Tam Lin' was an ideal vehicle for him."

Other contributors to *The Imagined Village*, due for release on the Real World label in 2007, include Paul Weller, who has reworked the trad ballad 'John Barleycorn' with Martin Carthy; Damon Albarn, who

Jim Moray has won critical acclaim – and enraged purists – by presenting traditional songs in bold contemporary arrangements.

duets with Eliza Carthy; Transglobal Underground; Chris Wood, who teams up with the British-Asian singer Sheila Chandra; and Billy Bragg, who performs an updated version of 'Hard Times Of Old England' with The Young Coppers.

"The musicians were presented with unaccompanied versions of the songs so they weren't influenced in terms of their arrangements and accompaniment," Emmerson explains. "We wanted to move beyond folk-rock and to take the English folk song book and see how these great songs could interact and collide with contemporary idioms in as open and questioning a way as possible. What was fascinating was that people like Eliza Carthy were just as interested in opening up to bhangra and reggae forms as the musicians from those backgrounds were in exploring the English folk heritage. It really was a two-way street."

Some will love the results. Others may loathe them. But the project proves beyond any shadow of doubt that the opportunities for working with traditional song remain as thrilling and open-ended in 2007 as they were when the songs were first performed, centuries ago.

# Folk in America today

## BY DAVID SHEPPARD

I N MAY 2003, THE BRATTLEBORO FREE FOLK FESTIVAL took place, deep in rural Vermont. For two days a wildly eclectic community gathered in the small town: homespun troubadours, psychedelic noiseniks, savant balladeers, and unkempt improvisers. Part late-1960s hippy Arcadia, part anarcho-punk demi-monde, this alternative musical universe revolved around performers united only by their rejection of commercial pop and rock formulas and an associated, if implicit, political agenda. What was interesting was that this hodgepodge of outsider culture had chosen to gather beneath the penumbra of 'Free Folk'.

Among the observers was David Keenan, a writer for the British magazine *The Wire*. His account of the Free Folk Festival appeared in the August 2003 issue of the magazine under the heading *Welcome To The New Weird America*. Though superficially it appeared that it was the 'Free', not the 'Folk' element which was most pertinent, Keenan was quick to underline the connection between this genre-challenging musical miscellany and established notions of folk music: "Although the players' interpretation of what constitutes 'folk music' is unusually wide," he wrote, "they all relate to traditional folk forms in several significant ways. Primarily the music is an expression of a self-supporting community of like-minded individuals, all dedicated to finding their own voice and creating art as free from outside influence as possible."

Playing at Brattleboro that weekend were such colourfully monikered combos as Boston's Sunburned Hand Of The Man – a multiple-personnel, three-drummer troupe nominally led by John Moloney. Members of the band might already have been familiar to *Wire* readers, courtesy of their association with oft-mentioned, but little listened to experimental ensembles such as the Vibracathedral Orchestra and the No Neck Blues Band. Owing more to the improvisation of The Grateful Dead and the wanton dronescapes of Sonic Youth than to Donovan or The Incredible String Band, their spiralling ragas channelled 1960s psychedelia through pagan furies of percussion. Sunburned Hand Of The Man were the most uncompromising exemplars of the neo-folk idiom (and one of the first to attract another adjectival variant, 'freak folk'). With their religiously guarded independence, fluid personnel, anarchic spirit and disregard for orthodox notions of what 'a band' should be, they were, in effect, the neo-folk scene in microcosm.

Other key members of this mutable but irrefutable new tendency included Six Organs Of Admittance (essentially guitarist Ben Chasny, his finger-picked acoustic and frail, aching vocals), Scorces (the duo of guitarist Christina Carter and blood-drawing pedal-steel player Heather Leigh Murray), and Tower Recordings (the multi-faceted brainchild of Matt Valentine, Brattleboro resident and bespectacled lynchpin of the new folk underground). Under the Tower Recordings banner, Valentine released a tellingly titled debut album *Folk Scene* (a record that blends musique concrète montages with a very obvious debt to The Incredible String Band) as far back as 2001. The epitome of back-to-nature mellowness, Valentine lives in a wooden house set among the treetops just outside Brattleboro with his partner and muse Erika Elder. Together they also record and perform as MV & EE, adding an irreverent, splintered blues vocabulary to an eerie folk-rock blueprint.

Bringing together this miscellany of music under the *New Weird America* heading – now sometimes used as a label for the whole scene – was a direct response to a term coined by critic Greil Marcus in *Invisible Republic*. This ruminative book examines Bob Dylan and The Band and their self-imposed exile in Woodstock, upstate New York, at the end of the 1960s. Marcus discusses Dylan's attempt to divine a sense of place along the timeline of North American song, deliberately cutting against the progressive impulse of contemporary psychedelic experiment. Isolated in the Catskill Mountains, Dylan and friends immersed themselves in allegorical music, embracing traditional and old time styles and revelling in the arcane – everything from British Isles ballads to selections from Harry Smith's *Anthology of American Folk Music,* to Tin Pan Alley standards, hymns, and archaic country songs.

It was, according to Marcus, a purposeful reaching down into rich but forgotten cultural loam. It was also an investment in music whose superficial sobriety cloaked an uncanny mystique which, once unearthed, required no narcotic crutch or oil-wheel light-show to enthral and intrigue. Marcus saw this music as a reflection of a mythic American past, a time and a place before the homogenising grip of mass media and mobility; a period of idiosyncrasies and anomalies born of the collision of immigrant cultures with a vast and only partially mapped continent. This he dubbed *The Old Weird America.*

What Dave Keenan thought he had stumbled upon at Brattleboro was a 21st century update of this musical inheritance. None of the new, nominally 'folk' bands was attempting such a self-conscious unearthing of ancient music; and in their psychedelic flights, communal living, and anarchic politics they had as much in common with the hippy radicalism of 1960s northern California as the studied cultural revanchism of Dylan and the Band, holed up in their Woodstock lair. But they shared with the folk pioneers a delight in a backwoods sensibility, in music as an extension of communal society. The difference was a matter of musical vocabulary, with 21st century American folk as likely to embrace improvised composition based on ragas or drones as the hymnal progressions and tent-show hollers of Dylan's *The Basement Tapes.*

Will Oldham, who also performs as Bonnie 'Prince' Billy, brings a folk sensibility to the US alternative music scene.

When British Isles folk song was first imported into the Appalachian Mountains of the eastern USA, its essential character was inevitably changed by the needs of the transplanted populace. The pagan resonances of murder songs, Child ballads, and admonitory tales of doomed young lovers deep in the greenwood were too disquieting for struggling settlers carving society in a vast woodland landscape, dark, unknown and thick with wild animals. Instead they favoured work songs that hymned loggers, carpenters, and farmers. What were once cautionary tales quickly evolved into a participatory music, something to be played in reassuring family or community groups on well lit porches. To this day the communal music-making tradition lives on in the Appalachians, through fiddlers' conventions, house parties, and back porch jams.

The free folk movement sought, implicitly, to renew this tradition, at the same time re-injecting a certain mystery and incongruity: the old rural *weirdness* that no amount of cheerful Saturday night hoedowns had ever quite extinguished. With the Iraq War raging and America under severe global examination, the neo-folk movement can be seen as an attempt by disenfranchised youth to build a controllable cultural bulwark against a reactionary government – much as the original Woodstock generation sought to do in defiance of the Vietnam War.

Indeed, rather than being some antediluvian anomaly, the events of Brattleboro would prove symptomatic of a shift in underground music in post-9/11 America. Keenan's article identified a slow but significant change: a palpable ratcheting down of amplified rock in favour of diffuse, meditative, acoustic-based soundscaping and songcraft. Such 'unplugged' aesthetics had already been wowing the US independent scene for the best part of a decade, most obviously in the faux-Appalachian country-folk introspection of Will Oldham of Louisville, Kentucky, in his many guises: solo, as 'Palace', or as Bonnie 'Prince' Billy. Oldham's wearied croak, rudimentary guitar and lyrics of picaresque, Old Testament hue had been established in alternative circles since the early 1990s, and his considerable appeal to rock critics had helped make declamatory folk introspection (not to mention hillbilly dungarees, agricultural feed caps and luxuriant moustaches) fashionable. Suddenly the keening sound of the banjo was beginning to be heard on records that had nothing much to do with the bluegrass or mainstream country music with which the instrument was most readily associated.

Even as the epicentres of US independent rock shifted from the coasts toward Chicago, with the punk, grunge, hardcore scenes ceding to the catholic, genre-melding experimentation of post-rock, the seeds of renewed interest in folk were being sown. In 1996, members of post-rockers-in-chief Tortoise formed a splinter group, Pullman, to record *Turnstyles & Junkpiles*. An album of all-acoustic instrumentals that nodded more to the pastoral baroque of Nick Drake and the 'American primitivism' of Washington DC guitar maverick John Fahey than the dub and Krautrock influences of their main band, it was emblematic of a more widespread broadening of the alternative music

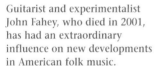

Guitarist and experimentalist John Fahey, who died in 2001, has had an extraordinary influence on new developments in American folk music.

church. Critically revered Dave Pajo – once a stalwart of influential Louisville post rockers Slint, as well as Tortoise - would soon supplant instrumental mood music with folk song, covering such traditional British ballads as 'The Unquiet Grave' (p86) and 'The Lass Of Roch Royal' on his 2001 album (as Papa M) *Whatever, Mortal*. It was proof of an undeniable shift.

John Fahey was the fulcrum around which the transformation of US underground music turned. Tortoise had named themselves after Fahey's own publishing company, Tortoise Music, while another revered Chicagoan experimenter, Jim O'Rourke, and his band Gastr del Sol, sought to update Fahey's audacious marriage of steel-string bluegrass guitar picking, musique concrète, spirituals, rural blues, and avant-garde classical music. O'Rourke would collaborate with Fahey several times before the latter's untimely death in 2001, and extrapolated his style on his 1998 instrumental opus *Bad Timing*. In 2000, O'Rourke moved to New York to join Sonic Youth (with neat circularity, that band's Thurston Moore would go on to release Sunburned Hand Of The Man's records on his own Ecstatic Peace imprint).

The sound and spirit of John Fahey (and other 1960s and 1970s solo guitar pioneers such as Sandy Bull, Leo Kottke and Robbie Basho) were important catalysts in the music of Boston's Cul-de-Sac, Portland's M. Ward, Brooklyn's Currituck Co and San Francisco's Vetiver. These were typical of a marginally less feral wave of new American folk artists whose finger-picking and intimate songwriting flowered at the same time as the Brattleboro Free Folk Festival. Meanwhile, Virginian guitarist Jack Rose, a sometime member of drone ensemble Pelt, has built a parallel career as a solo guitarist based almost exactly on the pattern set down by Fahey. In their wake came a succession of acts keen to present their own vision of folk music to American record buyers and downloaders. Among them were Philadelphia's sprawling acoustic-dirge specialists Espers and two further Brooklyn–based groups, Animal Collective and Akron/Family, who dripped liquid electronica over rural folk jams to universal critical applause.

More significantly still, from San Francisco came wild-haired, Venezuela-born Devendra Banhart, a colourful figure with an approach to songwriting that recalled the pixie strut of Marc Bolan as readily as any US troubadour stereotype. Banhart seemed to strike an immediate chord with those for whom Sunburned Hand Of The Man and their ilk were just a little astringent. Aside from his own increasingly successful albums, Banhart earned plaudits for curating *The Golden Apples Of The Sun* – a compilation CD released by Bastet (an imprint of the alternative/arts magazine *Arthur*) in the spring of 2004. It featured tracks from many of the artists mentioned here, as well as other rustic-hued, soon-to-be-notables such as CocoRosie, Iron and Wine, and Josephine Foster, and came to be regarded by many as the neo-folk movement's second defining moment.

Also on the compilation was a track by Joanna Newsom of Nevada City, California. Nowadays established as the poster girl of 21st century American folk, Newsom, a creative writing graduate of Mills College, wedded capricious, symbol-strewn lyrics, owing more to Emily Dickinson than Joni Mitchell, to a dextrously plucked orchestral harp. Though her untutored shriek of a voice was an acquired taste, she quickly beguiled herself to a wide audience after first touring with Will Oldham and then signing to revered Chicago independent imprint Drag City. Her debut album *The Milk-Eyed Mender* was a neo-folk benchmark, while her 2006 follow-up *Ys* – an ambitious five-track song cycle orchestrated by erstwhile Brian Wilson collaborator Van Dyke Parks

Joanna Newsom, whose acclaimed neo-folk albums have achieved the unlikely feat of making the harp fashionable.

As well as releasing his own albums, Devendra Banhart earned plaudits for putting together *The Golden Apples Of The Sun*, an influential compilation in the new American folk scene.

(and produced by Jim O'Rourke) – was a bold attempt to elevate the genre to new, esoteric, heights.

Since the genuine revolution of punk rock in the mid 1970s, rock journalism has kept an eye out for apparently autonomous 'scenes', keen to be in at the birth of this or that new direction. It has taken only a handful of acts operating in vaguely similar territory and living in the same provincial city for the media to imagine they've stumbled upon a zeitgeist-redefining enclave.

The reality is often a good deal more flimsy – the 'scene' sometimes non-existent – but what starts as a combination of journalistic conceit and vague serendipity can rapidly will itself into existence. Post-Millennial underground folk was something quite different – a genuine autonomous phenomenon, propagating itself in limited edition CDRs, short run vinyl singles, and self-promoted concerts. In this sense it was, and remains, a true folk movement. Even as the likes of Devendra Banhart and Joanna Newsom grace magazine covers, and television advertisers swathe their wares in folk songs old and new, it continues to move forward with its own unique and, yes, often weird, momentum.

# The music of English folk song

BY **RIKKY ROOKSBY**

THE MOST SIGNIFICANT SINGLE FACTOR RESPONSIBLE for giving folk tunes their musical character is the process by which they were created, revised, and passed from one generation to the next, mainly by ear. For this aural process to be possible, a folk melody needs certain musical traits. It must:

- be relatively short, both in bars and number of phrases;
- contain memorable rhythms and melodic touches;
- be formulaic, because formulas are easy to recall;
- be simple in structure;
- be performable by one singer without instrumentation.

A second characteristic arises because folk tunes as they have come down to us are the product of a community of singers, not an individual. The basis for any folk tune may have been composed by one person to get the process going, but these individuals are lost in time. As folk tunes pass down the generations, they are sung by many people. Starting as individual expression they become the product of collective expression. A folk song is not really a single entity, a single thing in the way that a song by The Beatles is a single thing, but a process sustained by individuals across time and place. However many times 'Ticket To Ride' is covered and arranged there is still the original recording issued on Parlophone in 1965. There is usually no such equivalent original for a folk song. With multiple variants of melody and lyric, a folk song is more akin to a musical space in which variants overlap and co-exist.

This process will tend to reject and smooth out features that would be regarded as eccentric when compared with the majority of tunes. Imagine a Sussex farm labourer who sang ballads. Having learned many local songs, he decides to invent one. His new tune has leaps of a major seventh, repeatedly raises the fourth of the scale by a semitone (half-step), and starts with a chromatic (ie, off-scale) approach to the key note using the third, second, and lowered second of the major scale. These features are unusual and tricky to sing, but not for the tune's composer, who likes them and therefore finds them easy to pitch. This melody reflects the taste of the individual who made it. However, the majority of singers who hear it, or learn it in later generations, don't like these oddities, which set the song apart from the other folk tunes they sing, and they find the intervals unfamiliar and awkward.

A communal conservatism comes into play. In time, other singers remove the altered notes, and smooth the seventh leaps by inserting a passing note or two. The individuality of the tune – felt by them as eccentric and challenging – is thus eroded. Of course, growing up surrounded by folk songs it is less likely (though not impossible) that our Sussex farmer would have developed a liking for odd intervals and chromatic notes. Nonetheless, this is the process identified by Cecil Sharp in *English Folk Songs* (1954): "The individual, then, invents; the community selects."

This communal process made folk song different from art song. Early in the 20th century, when introducing folk song to a middle-class audience, Sharp contrasted it with 'classical' art song, which he described as the creation of individuals, often after an education in the sophisticated techniques of classical music. An art song was composed in a relatively short space of time, primarily (though not exclusively – here Sharp exaggerated) expressed the individual's feelings, often used literary texts, and was given a final form in notation. The printed score fixed the melody, gave some directions as to tempo, phrasing and dynamics, and specified the harmony and accompaniment style. The score was the guarantee that the song would remain the same regardless of the nuances of an individual singer's performance. It would be sung in the parlour or the concert hall, not in a tavern or outdoors.

Later, recording technology would fix a song more definitively than a score. By contrast, a single unnotated folk melody existed in many forms, within the British Isles and outside it; there was no

Cecil Sharp

definitive version or performance of it. Ironically, during the 1960s–70s there were interpretations of traditional songs by singers and groups released on vinyl, then bought by hundreds of thousands of people, for whom these versions became definitive. For the record-buying public 'Scarborough Fair' (p236) meant Simon and Garfunkel, 'Matty Groves' meant Fairport Convention, and 'The Briery Bush' meant Led Zeppelin's 'Gallows Pole'. Singers sometimes took versions learned from records back into performance in the folk clubs. I used to perform a version of 'The Trees They Do Grow High' (p80) which I knew from an Alan Stivell album. This effect of technology made it difficult to see popular music as a modern equivalent to traditional folk music. The recorded performance, captured in the studio or in concert, meant popular music had more in common, in this respect at least, with art music.

## Lyric versus melody

In traditional folk songs, melody and rhythm are subordinate to the lyric. It is revealing that Cecil Sharp knew singers who couldn't remember the tune if they forgot the words, and singers who couldn't sing at all without words. The musical content of an unharmonised folk song is modest by comparison with that of art song or popular song. By contrast, a number of folk songs instead have long lyrics in relation to the length of their music. 'Matty Groves' runs to 28 stanzas; 'Lord Thomas and Fair Elron' has eight bars of melody to carry 18 stanzas. Folk tunes often have many more verses than popular songs, often as a result of the lyric telling a story. The longer the lyric the more likely there would be variations of verbal rhythm, which, in turn, require grace-notes or different rhythmic patterns in the tune – another example of the lyric dictating the music rather than the other way round.

Folk lyrics often have dramatic, fast-moving narratives. The melody is there to be a stage for the lyric. Listeners would be untroubled by the repetitious nature of a song based on a single musical verse because their attention was on the lyric's imagery, plot, emotion, and sometimes on decoding the erotic meaning of quibbling metaphors. The audience might also be focused on the meaning of small consecutive lyric changes in a refrain (as in 'The Trees They Do Grow High' p80), or following a different version of a familiar lyric.

Lyric formulas often dictate melodic formulas. Many folk melodies start on the last beat of a bar (the upbeat or 'anacrusis') because the first syllable of the words is likely to be unstressed, whereas the second syllable (which falls on the strong first beat of the next bar) will be stressed. This is the natural 'iambic' rhythm of English: an iambic rhythm consists of an unstressed syllable followed by a stressed syllable. In the line "The *ship* sailed out one bright summer morn", the word "ship" is the first beat of the first whole bar. The same applies to the ballad opening "As *I* walked out".

## The refrain

Folk songs often consist musically of only a verse (exceptionally, 'Spanish Ladies', p189, has a chorus section and a verse). The equivalent to a chorus in folk song is the refrain tagged onto the verse end, repeating the last line of the lyrics, as featured in 'Death And The Lady' (p70) and 'John Barleycorn' (p103). The refrain adds an extra phrase to the four in a standard 'strophic' verse (see below). Lyrically, the refrain may comment on or illustrate the preceding verse, and this meaning may vary. By contrast, the nonsense refrain – like the much-derided "fol-de-rol-diddle-o-day" type – has a musical purpose, a chance for listeners to join in, reinforcing the communality of the performance. The listeners do not have to know the lyric to do this; they quickly pick up the refrain. This also provides an opportunity for simple harmonisation, if anyone present has the ear and the bravado.

## Rhythm

The rhythms of folk tunes are not always straightforward, one reason why early collectors had difficulty putting the tunes in standard notation. When Vaughan Williams notated 'Bushes And Briars' in December 1903 he observed, "It is impossible to reproduce the free rhythms and subtle portamento effects of this beautiful tune in ordinary notation" (*Bushes and Briars: Folk Songs Collected By Ralph Vaughan Williams*, edited by Roy Palmer, 1999). The aural nature of folk song is responsible for various kinds of rhythmic irregularity.

First, if a tune was not written down, its performers never had to think about bars and bar-lines, or whether they were changing time signature or not. In some performances it is probably a safe assumption that there is no rhythmic system other than the phrase, and even within a phrase the words dictate pauses and gaps, not the counting of a metrical pulse. To seek to explain this variation by conceptualising it as an organic complexity, grasping for some undiscovered, underlying super-system, is to introduce mystification where none is needed.

This factor, coupled with the primacy of the lyric, accounts for the irregularity of pulse in many printed versions of folk melodies with fluctuating time signatures ( 'Lord Randal', p158, in some versions, is in 4/4, 3/4 and 2/4) or even unlikely asymmetrical signatures such as 5/4. To use such notations in the act of transcribing is not a crime against authenticity, but an attempt to represent the musical experience and bring a degree of order that allows accompaniment. Bars where an extra beat is added or taken away probably arose not for reasons of rhythm, but from the desire either to pause before delivering the next lyric line or to hurry on to it. The singers did not see any musical reason to trim such a pause or lengthen it to maintain regular bars.

The fact of solo performance is also relevant here. With no accompanying musicians, the folk singer is free to take liberties with the spaces between lyric lines. Having ended a phrase, he or she is under no obligation to count the exact beat(s) to fill the bar before the next phrase, even when counting beats in the first place. This would be difficult with a group of musicians, because everyone needs to know exactly how long gaps are between phrases.

## The strophic verse

The majority of folk songs consist of a single verse of music that is repeated, creating the 'strophic' song. This verse might be 8 or 16 bars, depending on how it was notated, and within it there will usually be four phrases, five if there is a repeated refrain. This contrasts on the one hand with the extremes of the 'through-composed' art song, which has no large-scale repeating sections, and the commercial song, which uses such structures as verse/chorus/middle 8, or the 32-bar A A B A pattern.

In many folk melodies there is a discernible pattern to the four phrases in terms of expressive function and pitch. If we label the four phrases A, B, C, D, it is often the case that:

- A makes an initial rising statement from the key note;
- B imitates A's shape but either starts or rises a little higher, introduces a rhythmic variation, and ends less securely;
- C rises higher still – often the highest note in the melody is found here – or reverses direction to A and B, curving decidedly lower;
- D recovers something of A's phrasing and creates a sense of completion, often falling to the key note on which the melody began.

It is as if a little drama is played out, with A as the start of an adventure, B as the determination to advance further, provoking C as a crisis of some kind, settled by the resolution of D. The effect of this purely musical action offsets whatever is the theme of the lyric; there is a subtle relation between the two, and the lyric may not provide the resolution that the music does. A good example of this sort of shape would be 'The Banks Of Sweet Primroses' (p110).

If there is an anacrusis the most popular note is the fifth of the scale, going up or down to the key note (tonic) on the first beat of the first bar; an alternative is a move from the fifth to the third.

The pitch range of an average folk song is between an octave and a tenth. In some versions 'Banks Of Green Willow' (p148) is an octave, 'Bruton Town' (p150) is a ninth, and 'Admiral Benbow' (p170) a tenth. The range could not be much wider otherwise the average voice would not be able to cope. Some are narrower: 'Keys Of Canterbury' (p140) is only a sixth. There is a fair amount of step-wise movement, with a few easy-to-pitch leaps, and simple rhythms.

In performance, tunes were subject to enormous and unconscious spontaneous variation, so much so that collectors had to tell their singers to sing over and over again to catch some of the variations. Long notes were apt to attract ornamentation, as was the attempt to adapt lyrics from one song to a different music.

## The unharmonised melody

If there is a single feature of traditional song that holds a lesson for contemporary popular songwriters, at a time when genres such as rap can often be defined by their indifference to melody, it is the phenomenon of folk's unharmonised melody.

Traditional folk song comprises a single unharmonised melodic line. It is a music focused on melody, even when such melodies suggest chords, and for earlier collectors, the addition of harmony to folk song was considered an artificial sweetener. But, from the 1920s onwards, most folk music has been harmonised in many styles, from the sophisticated modal arrangements of Vaughan Williams, or the modernist harmony of Britten, to the banjo and guitar chording of the 1960s folk revival, and the electric rock-influenced arrangements by Fairport Convention and Steeleye Span.

The unharmonised melody requires no more instrumentation than a voice. This alone makes it unusual, since most music is harmonised. To the modern ear, lack of harmony makes traditional song sound stark and bare. This is part of its appeal, especially if this bareness is perceived as 'pure', 'authentic', or 'natural'. In *An Introduction To English Folk Song* (1987) Maud Karpeles followed Sharp in affirming that yoking folk melody to keys and harmony, the "tonic-dominant form of accompaniment", was generally "unsuited to the structure of melody and has the effect of ironing out its distinctive qualities".

In *English Folk Songs*, written in 1919, Cecil Sharp observed that the fundamental difference between folk song and art song (and, we could add, most popular music), was the fact that folk melody was unharmonised, for folk music "being the product of those in whom the harmonic sense is dormant, is essentially a non-harmonic tune; whereas the later is demonstrably constructed upon a harmonic basis". He thought the harmonic sense of some tunes was at best elementary. He observed that some singers could not recognise their songs when they were played harmonised at a piano.

Sharp's ideas about folk music have been subjected to criticism and revision by later writers: many insist that the shape of many folk tunes implies a clear harmonic framework. For instance, many of the melodies use basic triads in arpeggio form. And there is plenty of evidence that singers of the 18th and 19th centuries would have experienced harmony, not least through church choirs and bands. But at the time these songs were collected and written down they were being sung in unharmonised versions.

In Sharp's day there were disagreements about the 'right' way to harmonise a folk song. Within the classical tradition there were some who felt that folk melodies had to fit into the scale and key system. For this to work the pitch of some notes was altered, because some folk melodies did not use the standard major or harmonic minor scale. Sharp's ideal was to use such chords as would preserve what he considered to be an expressive element that he considered the 'timelessness' of the melody. He drew up a set of guidelines, which included:

- not harmonising according to major and minor as commonly understood, to avoid losing the modal feel;
- harmonising using the diatonic chords of that mode – ie, the chords that naturally form on that scale;
- not raising leading notes (the seventh note in the scale) to a half-step (semitone) from the key-note if in the melody they are a whole step away. In other words, not turning flattened sevenths into major sevenths;
- not modulating to a key that contains the right accidentals. For instance, there are no accidentals in G mixolydian: its notes are G A B C D E F, the same as in C major. But Sharp would not approve of modulating to the key of C major. Similarly, A dorian contains the same notes as G major: A B C D E F# G. But Sharp felt the tune should not modulate into G major;
- never altering the melody to fit the harmony; the harmony must conform to the melody.

By contrast, Australian-born song collector and composer Percy Grainger (1882–1961) took a freer, more chromatic approach to harmonising folk melodies. This was partly influenced by his dislike of the dominant Germanic musical traditions in form and harmony of the late 19th century. Grainger was particularly active in British folk song in the years 1905–08.

## No modulation

One significant difference between folk song and art song (and to a lesser degree popular song) is that folk melodies generally do not change key or 'modulate'. Modulation has a significant effect on harmony, and is one of the glories of the tonal system developed in European music from around 1650. Trying to differentiate folk song from art song, Sharp insisted that "the genuine folk air never modulates, never wavers from its allegiance to one fixed tonal centre". Even so, harmony could make a folk tune *appear* to change key. This tonal centre might be a note, rather than a key, and the exception was that a folk tune might be based on two types of scale starting from the same note (see the discussion of modes, below). Since this involves changing one note's pitch, often this may have happened because a singer was more concerned to smooth out a phrase, rather than wanting to change mode.

Ralph Vaughan Williams and Percy Grainger, who collected and arranged folk song before becoming renowned composers.

## Pitch

We have already noted that musicologist collectors found it hard to notate the rhythms of folk melodies. A similar issue arose with pitch, which in turn had implications for harmonising. Sharp recorded that folk singers treated the pitch of the third note of the scale very freely – sometimes it was never sharp enough to be a major third and sometimes so flat as to be a minor third, and sometimes in the middle (ie, a quarter tone). In classical music the distinction between the major third and minor third is vital, since it is related to the expressive contrast between a major chord and a minor.

Sharp also claimed that the English country singer usually pitched the untempered natural seventh and not the minor seventh of the tempered scale.

It must also be said that some unaccompanied singers in recordings are largely indifferent to pitch. In some recorded performances, traditional singers start in one key and drift a semitone up within the first 20 seconds, or lose the sense of pitch half-way so that a song begun in E♭ ends a tone lower in D♭. This kind of 'pitch creep' occurs for three main reasons. First, the singer may begin a little low for his or her voice and adjust the pitch accordingly mid-performance. Second, moments of expression sharpen notes repeatedly by small degrees and then the singer finally snaps into the next key a semitone higher. Third, a note is mis-pitched half-way through, say as an A in E♭ – a sharpened fourth – and then re-interpreted harmonically as the fifth of D, the entire song then being pitched a tone lower.

## Folk melody and the modes

There are seven main modes (sometimes called the 'church' modes) or scales that date from ancient Greece and have always been present in Western music. One of them is the major scale. The other six modes are scales that use different patterns of intervals to the major. Each mode is a pattern of semitone (half-step) and tone (whole-step) intervals or gaps. It is this pattern that gives each its flavour. They can be played starting on any note as long as the distinctive progression of tone and semitone gaps is preserved.

Sharp noted, "English folk tunes are cast in the Dorian, Phrygian, Mixolydian, Aeolian, and Ionian (major) modes, and occasionally in the minor. Personally, I have never recovered an English folk tune in the minor mode, and very few have been recorded by other collectors. Minor folk airs are, no doubt, Aeolian airs that have been modernised by the addition of a leading note." He estimated that two-thirds of English folk-tunes were in the major mode, the remaining third divided evenly between Mixolydian, Dorian and Aeolian. He recalled how in the winter of 1906, "I sat one day from noon till four o'clock in the parlour of a primitive wayside inn on the peat moors of Somerset. The company numbered on the average some 12 or 14 men, and song followed song in quick succession, but not a single major or minor tune was sung throughout the whole of the four hours."

The Mixolydian is close to the pattern of a major scale but with the seventh note flattened by a semitone (in C: C D E F G A B♭). As popular music since the mid 1950s has flattened sevenths wherever there is the slightest blues influence, the Mixolydian mode is common today. The most common *minor* scale for folk singing is the 'natural minor' or Aeolian mode (in A minor: A B C D E F G). The Dorian mode can also be thought of as a minor mode (A Dorian: A B C D E F♯ G). The only difference between it and A Aeolian is that the sixth note is sharpened. Sharp's version of 'Rosebud In June' is in E Dorian in the chorus, with C♯ appearing instead of the C of E natural minor. The exceptionally rare Phrygian mode also has an affinity with the natural minor (A Phrygian: A B♭ C D E F G).

It should be noted that the usefulness and accuracy of applying these classic church modes to folk song has increasingly been questioned. Many musicologists feel the issue is more complex. Percy Grainger, for example, sometimes made as many as five recordings of a single song performed by the same singer. He found that the versions contained many variations of melody. Some of the tunes were purely modal and some were of mixed scales. This led him to argue that the tunes might be better understood as deriving from a scale whose third and seventh could be major or minor, and which might contain a sixth that was major or minor for decorative passing note purposes.

Be this as it may, at the start of the 20th century, art music considered modes archaic and outdated. Sharp knew most trained musicians believed that "a scale with a minor seventh is fundamentally false, and conflicts with natural law". This was because the all-important sense of closure in tonal music could seemingly only be generated by the rising leading note, one semitone away from the tonic, whereas the lowered seventh of the modes was a tone away. But when it came to pitching, Sharp added, "The flattened seventh possesses no terrors for the country singer. The leading note is much more likely to cause him difficulty." In the 1890s, as a student, Vaughan Williams often had his Royal College tutors complain about his use of a flattened seventh. But for him and others there was an exciting sense that modes offered new opportunities for musical expression. Many leading European composers of the early 20th century used them to generate a new form of extended tonality. Since the 1950s, harmonised modal scales have been a central part of rock, blues, and soul, to such an extent that many people no longer hear them as anything other than normal.

Ironically, the traditional tonal leading note and the cadence-driven sequences of extended tonal music may even seem more revolutionary to many listeners than the lowered sevenths we hear every day. But modal folk melody has made a permanent contribution to the harmonic vocabulary of music, in addition to its intrinsic historic, sociological, and aesthetic value as the music of the folk.

# Working with folk song

BY **MARTIN CARTHY**

CHOOSING SONGS TO PERFORM IS ALWAYS SUBJECTIVE, but I love narrative songs and tend to stick to those. I also want songs that will speak to people nowadays, and that have a bit of edge to them. It is not important that these songs are sometimes about characters and settings that are not of our own time. They can tell a story that applies just as strongly now as it ever did. I'm not one of those who think you should take all the horses out of a song and put motorbikes in instead. That is a school of thought – but I think it's profoundly silly. All it does is immediately date something that has hitherto been timeless.

Some of these songs are several hundred years old. What Cecil Sharp or whoever got, when the song was collected, was a four-and-a-half minute snapshot in that song's existence. We don't know what happened to it the next day or what it was like the day before. We know, for instance, that Sharp found the tunes were not fixed. He was absolutely potty about the modal character of the tunes, and he found that, with some singers, the mode would change depending on what day they were singing the song. I'm not saying that was a general rule, but with some singers things were pretty fluid.

And I get the impression that the words, with some singers, were the same: as long as they told the story, it didn't matter two hoots how they did it. So the language of the thing, in that sense, is not vital to its integrity. What's vital is that the story still speaks to people.

What I want is involvement. I want performers to be involved with these songs. Of course, I don't want them to be involved with them to the extent that they start copyrighting them, because they belong to everybody. It doesn't matter if it's a ten verse song and I've changed the equivalent of five verses; if I'm telling the same story, it remains a traditional song. It remains everybody's. I pass it on to the next person and they mess with it too. That's what tradition is, as far as I'm concerned.

I think if you are involved with the song, you are not going to lose its essence. You can go too far: I've done it myself. I've got a bee in my bonnet about a particular song and determined that it should go a particular way, and then determined to find something that the song wasn't telling me, and perhaps kicked it around too much to try to get that little notion in. I think that's probably a mistake.

If you've got what you think is the true essence of the song, you have to maintain a teeny bit of detachment, so you can take a step back and look at it and see if it works.

## Words and music

I love both words and music. But I won't sing words that I really don't like just because a song has got a great tune. I'll sit back and envy the tune and try to find a way of putting it to something else I find myself more comfortable with.

I'm not comfortable singing hare-hunting songs, for instance. I think hares are beautiful. Sharp collected a few absolutely sensational hare-hunting songs,

Martin Carthy in the early 1960s.

and they've got good words too. And a lot of those fox hunting songs from the Lake District have got fabulous words, but I'm not comfortable singing them.

And some of them have fabulous melodies. There's a particular hunting song that Sharp collected in Somerset, which he just calls 'Hare Hunting Song', which has got the most astonishing tune. I look at it, and every time I come across another set of words that has not got a tune, I see if I can shoe-horn those words into that tune. I've had no luck so far.

There are other songs I won't sing. Wife-beating songs, for instance. The one that comes to mind immediately is a marvellous tune that Harry Cox sings. He calls it 'The Man Of Burnham Town'. That's a wife-beating song. I recorded that with Dave Swarbrick back in 1967, I think, and when we were doing it in the studio I didn't have any problem with it because there wasn't an audience. Then I stood up and sang it in front of an audience, and you could feel this discomfort. Even in 1967! I was on the stage at the Manchester Sports Club singing with Dave and I swear to God there was a voice at my shoulder saying "Do you really want to sing this?" And I brought the song to an end and Dave and I never did it again. And Dave never asked. I was drawn to it because of the tune, and that was an object lesson as far as I was concerned.

But if I like the words of a song, but don't like the tune, I'd change that in a heartbeat. I suppose there are some people who think this stuff is Holy Writ and you shouldn't do that sort of thing, but I don't share that opinion. People were always very relaxed about this in the past. They got a set of words from a ballad-monger, and if they didn't remember the tune or they didn't like his tune they either bashed out a tune themselves or used a tune they already knew. I think it's time we all took responsibility for what we are doing.

For instance, I learned 'The Foggy Dew'. The version I learned had what you might call the standard tune, that Burl Ives sang, or Benjamin Britten and Peter Pears. And I don't like that tune, and I have sort of physical difficulty singing it: it completely eluded me. So I just found another Harry Cox song, took its tune and sort of fitted it to those words: it was more lyrical and seemed to carry the song absolutely beautifully. And as far as I was concerned it was a revelation. I feel that we are all free to do that.

## Reorganising songs

I will reorganise a song if I think it needs it. I think the most important thing to remember is that the people who were listening to these songs in the past had a background that we don't have. They knew the story and they knew what was happening. We have to be more clear when we are telling the story.

For me it's down to momentum. You must generate momentum. Sometimes a very long song needs trimming: but sometimes even a long song needs a verse added. Because there are always moments in a song where someone in the audience wants to look away and pick up their drink and sit back up and not have lost the thread. So you have repeated verses which allow you to relax for a second, and then the thread is picked up again and it starts to move on once more.

People are worried about repeats. They're sometimes a bit scared when they've got to sing them. But that's to misunderstand the way the thing works. I've heard people sing songs and I've heard them trim bits and I've thought they trimmed it unnecessarily. You don't need to do that. Let it relax. People can easily miss the point of a song: those repeats are there for a reason.

## Arrangement and harmony

We, my generation of instrumentalists, found a way of arranging traditional folk song. But that can't be the only way. So when people who are 20 years old come along and do things that sound outrageous to us, perhaps they aren't. Maybe it just works. Maybe they're doing what we all did when we were 20 and they're trying a few things out. And it's their right because it belongs to them too.

In my arrangements, I tend to avoid chords. In fact I think the ideal instrument for accompanying a lot of this stuff is the fiddle. You get all sorts of other things happening if you're playing the fiddle and you're not trying to play a clean line and eliminate everything else.

I never did learn the fiddle, but I did learn the guitar, and I have tried to make the guitar work like a fiddle. I like to approach it in that melodic way, rather than a harmonic way. Obviously a lot of this music has a harmonic structure: in fact the majority of it is not modal. But if you take that harmonic stuff and approach it from the melodic end, very interesting things can happen.

I think the problem with arranging stuff is that one tends to get too orchestral. One is approaching it from a harmonic point of view but it's much more interesting to approach it from the other end. You can't really call what happens accidental, because you are making choices all the time, but there are all sorts of interesting things that happen when you think like a fiddle.

In fact, I would suggest that young musicians, especially if they're guitar players, should listen to fiddle players. Not violinists so much, but fiddle players. Listen to those overtones and harmonics that start ringing in your ears and see if you can emulate those sounds. It's also useful to listen to a lot of American mountain banjo playing, because it has the same sort of feel. It's not harmonic, it's quite definitely melodic, but harmonic things are happening. You get all sorts of seconds and ninths generated, which, if you play a ninth on the guitar, don't sound right. But if it's all implied, and is just hanging on from the previous thing you just played, then you're beginning to get somewhere with it.

## Sing the song first

One of the things that people do is to try to tidy up the songs, to make the phrase lengths and verse lengths more regular. I wouldn't do that, because that is part of their character. In fact I would go so far as to try to emulate it sometimes. Stick in a long line, or clip another line short: that's the way people sing. People don't sing in a regular metre, 4/4 or 3/4, but they do sing in a pulse. You need to find a way of playing a song, accompanying a song, that means you're not playing in a strict metre but are implying a tempo and imparting a pulse to the thing.

The way to do this is to sing the song first, find out how you're going to sing it, and then try and play what you sing. It's great fun to do, and it's a step to the side from the way you might think it would be done. I love listening to the way people sing, people who are not thought of as musicians: there's so much to be learned from them. Harry Cox, for instance, was a wonderful musician. Walter Pardon was a wonderful musician. The musical thought that goes on with these traditional singers is wonderful, even when they are not instrumentalists.

You have to arrive at your own vocal style. All my favourite singers, if you were to play me records of them singing and records of them speaking, I could probably match the singing voice to the speaking voice. And that's something to be aimed at.

## Instrumentation

I think probably the best accompanying band I've ever heard are Shepheard, Spiers and Watson, from Scotland. It's an object lesson in how to do it. Nobody holds back; everybody plays and everybody sings, but there's a looseness there that takes your breath away. It's wonderful. They use a melodeon, a whistle and a fiddle.

I don't think any instrument can be excluded. I don't even see why you shouldn't accompany folk songs on piano. Eliza Carthy has played some of this stuff on piano, and you can do it, but you have to think hard. Any instrument can be made to work, but it depends on the imagination of the player. I would never have thought an autoharp could be made to do anything, but there's an autoharp player called Kilby Snow in America who is absolutely extraordinary.

You can't hurt this music. That's the most important thing. There's nothing you can do that is going to hurt it. You can go back and try again, and you can always refer back to the fabulous recordings made over the last 100 years or so. And if you do make a mess of it, someone else will come along and sing the same song, and it'll be a case of "Ah, there it is. It's all right."

# How to use the songbook

This songbook brings together a selection of songs collected in England at the turn of the 20th century. They are intended to be representative of the range of songs collected then, and still sung today, as well as being interesting and appealing in their own right. In addition the book includes transcriptions of the songs you can hear on the accompanying CD, collected more recently from singers in the same tradition. All the songs are intended for singing as much as for reading.

The songbook is unusual in that it is made up entirely of songs taken down from singers, rather than written for the page. Song collectors would travel the countryside, seeking out people with a reputation for singing, and would then write down what they heard. In some cases, the collector would write down both words and music. In others, two collectors would share the work. Sometimes, words and music would be collected at different times. Then the manuscripts would be sent to the Folk-Song Society in London for possible publication in its journal. Most of the book is based on those manuscripts.

Collection was not a straightforward process. The Folk-Song Society's *Hints To Collector Of Folk Music*, written by Kate Lee in 1898, explained how it should be done. It recommended that two people worked together, one to collect words, the other the tune. If the same collector had to do both, he should take down the words first, but not separately from the tune because that would confuse the singer. Nothing should be written down at all until the song had been sung once through. After taking down the words, with no alterations for the sake of grammatical correctness, the collector could turn to the tune, choosing to take down either rhythm or melody first but never both at the same time. Two or three repetitions were recommended for each half of the process, and finally one more repetition to check the transcript.

Anyone who has tried this knows how hard it can be, even for a skilled musician. The very early collectors did not use mechanical recording devices. Percy Grainger used the Edison Phonograph from 1906, but other collectors did not generally follow his lead. Furthermore, the singers did not always sing each phrase the same each time; and if the collector came back on a different day, the chances are the singer would be singing the song differently. So these tunes represent a snapshot of one performance, on one day, taken down quickly to the best of the collector's ability.

Cecil Sharp and his trusty bicycle, his usual companion on collecting trips.

PREVIOUS PAGE The influential folk-revival singer Ewan MacColl in full voice at The Enterprise pub in London in 1958.

In some cases, the collector painstakingly recorded all the tiny variations from verse to verse. We have mostly removed those for reasons of clarity, to create a single version of the tune. Sometimes, especially when words and music were collected separately, the words do not fit, and certainly not for every verse. We have sometimes had to adjust words or music very slightly to produce a version that fits the words of the first verse. But in every case, singers will need to work on these songs, to make them comfortable to sing. In the first place they will need to transpose them to fit their own preferred range; they will also have to make the words of each verse fit. Folk singing has always been a process of re-creation rather than merely one of exact reproduction. We have also altered punctuation, usually to make it clear who is speaking in a narrative song, and we have standardised spellings; but we have not altered grammar where, as so often, non-standard or dialect grammar is essential to the character of the song.

The early collectors were sometimes more interested in the music than in the words. The recommended collecting process, too, placed more emphasis on getting the music right. Sometimes they only collected one verse. On other occasions, they may have misunderstood the local pronunciation and dialect. In a few cases, they supplied sets of words that do not correspond to the words written under the notes in the music collected from the same singer.

All of this has consequences for those hoping to take inspiration from these songs or just to sing them for pleasure. Our aim has been to keep them as close to the original collected versions as possible. The result, in some cases, is that the songs don't entirely make sense. These singers learned them from other singers. In the process, they will have misheard or misunderstood them, and recast them into something that made sense to them. Folk singing is a creative process. If you want to sing some of these songs, and you want their stories to be coherent, you will, in some cases, need to add material from other sources. Where possible we have provided additional material for you to consider, particularly from the broadside ballads corresponding to these collected songs. One of the best sources for broadside material is the Bodleian Library's ballad website: http://www.bodley.ox.ac.uk/ballads/ballads.htm.

The second group of songs in the book were taken down from the recordings of singers that feature on the CD. By comparing the CD performances with the notation (created by Julian Elloway), you can see exactly how difficult it is to turn a complex and subtle performance into written music. Imagine how much more difficult it was for Cecil Sharp, George Gardiner, the Hammond brothers and all the other collectors in the days before reliable sound recording became available.

## How the song listings work

The songs are grouped according to their subject matter: love, death, the sea, etc. Each section has a general introduction that discusses the theme and the different ways the songs deal with it.

Traditional songs are known under many different titles. Here we have used generic titles that indicate the group of songs to which this example belongs;

it may have been collected under a different name, and that appears immediately afterwards in brackets. Where this has happened, we have clarified the situation in the section of the notes that refers to the circumstances of the song's collection.

In every case the song's title is followed by its 'Roud number'. This relates to The Roud Folk Song Index, a database created by Steve Roud, local studies librarian with the London Borough of Croydon. This is an index to songs collected from the oral tradition in the English language all over the world. Each song is given a Roud number, irrespective of the title under which it was collected. By using the number, all versions of the song can be tracked. The database can also be searched in many other ways, including by title, first line, singer's name, collector's name, type (sound, printed book, collector's manuscript, etc), geographical location, and so on. Roud also created The Roud Broadside Index, a database of songs in broadsides, chapbooks, songsters and other printed publications. Where songs also appear in Folk Song Index, they share a Roud number.

The Roud indexes, and several other indexes of individual collections, are available on the website of the Vaughan Williams Memorial Library at Cecil Sharp House in London, headquarters of the English Folk Dance and Song Society: http://library.efdss.org. It is important to note that the index itself does not contain the texts or music of the songs. For that you will need a library, with the Vaughan Williams Memorial Library being the principal source. Details of how to gain access to the library are available on the EFDSS website: http://www.efdss.org. In addition, songs in this songbook that appear in Francis Child's collection, *The English And Scottish Popular Ballads,* are given a 'Child number'.

Then comes a single-line melody for each song, taken from the manuscript found in the Vaughan Williams Memorial Library or, in the case of the songs on the CD, from the audio recording. These songs were generally collected in unaccompanied versions. Performers are, of course, at liberty to add their own harmonies and instrumentation. For those who are not comfortable with written music, MIDI versions of the songs are available at the accompanying website: www.folkhandbook.com. These can be listened to in a web browser or saved for use in a music program, where they can help with the process of transposition and arrangement.

Next come the texts that accompany the song in the library. These are often incomplete or obscure, and in those cases we have tried to supply additional words from other versions, including broadsides, to make it possible for you to create a performable version. Where a chorus is included, you will often have to make your own judgement about how often to use it.

The notes include some history of the song where this is known, its relationship with broadside printed versions, some comment on its meaning, and the story of its collection where this is known. Then follows a list of recordings. Some of these are unaccompanied, traditional versions recorded in the field, but we have also included more contemporary accounts to demonstrate the continuing life of the songs.

# Songs of death

Death takes many forms in English folk songs, from brutal murders, death in war, and the executions of criminals to supernatural encounters and lovers who pine away. This section brings together some songs that deal with death in a more general sense – songs that present death as an inescapable but natural process, not as an unpredictable and tragic occurrence.

The Dance of Death or *danse macabre* was a very common allegorical device, first found in the 14th century, usually depicting the figure of Death as a dancing skeleton or corpse leading all sorts and conditions of human beings to the grave. There is a famous series of woodcuts on the subject by the German artist Hans Holbein the Younger, published in 1538 in France. A preoccupation with death was an area of shared culture that spanned the religious rifts of the Reformation period, and the Dance of Death itself provides an example of continuity with the morality plays of medieval times. Broadside ballads treating the theme of death were common in the early modern period – from the 16th century on – and served, like depictions of the Dance of Death, as a *memento mori* – a reminder to human beings of the shortness and uncertainty of life and the certainty of death. "To keep the thought of death constantly in mind was the key to living virtuously in this life and preparing properly for the life to come," says Tessa Watt, in her *Cheap Print and Popular Piety, 1550–1640*, a study of popular religious literature in the English Reformation. Indeed, broadsides with titles such as 'A Warninge To Worldlings To Learne Them To Dye' were often illustrated with woodcuts of skeletal figures so as to serve as not just a recited or sung *memento mori* but a visual one too – and broadsides were often pasted on the walls of domestic dwellings, ale-houses, and the like.

The folk songs represented here can be considered to continue this earlier *memento mori* tradition, even though many of them cannot be shown to be actually any older than the 18th or 19th century. It would not do to exaggerate this, especially in the light of the many other kinds of folk songs from the same period represented in this anthology, but it does seem to be the case that a resigned and often lyrical acceptance of mortality was one aspect of the culture that is represented by English folk song.

It is often said that the two great themes of the English-language ballads are sex and death. This is too grand a generalisation as to be altogether meaningful, but it is nonetheless an epigrammatic way of saying that there is something universal about folk songs, something that speaks to the human condition; it must be presumed that this is one reason why they have retained their hold on the popular imagination for so long. Living in a hedonistic age in which death has become the last taboo, it is salutary to experience the resignation that pervades songs such as these.

## DEATH AND THE LADY ROUD 1031

As I walked forth one day, one day,
I met an old man by the way;
His head was bald, his beard was grey,
And his clothing made of the cold earth of clay
And his clothing made of the cold earth of clay.

"I say what man, what old man are you,
Or what country do you belong unto?"
"My name is Death, ha'n't you heard of me?
Both kings and princes bow down to me,
And you fair maid, must come along with me."

"I will give you gold, I will give you pearl,
I will give you costly rich robes to wear,
If you will spare me a little while,
A little long time my life for to amend,
A little long time my life for to amend."

"I'll have none of your gold, nor none of your pearl,
Neither your costly rich robes to wear."
"If you will spare me but a little while,
A little longer time my life to amend,
A little longer time my life to amend."

In six months after, this fair maid died.
"Let this be put on my tomb stone," she cried.
"Here lies a poor and distressed maid,
Just in her bloom as she was snatched away,
And her clothing was made of the cold earth clay."

This song, which relates an encounter between Death and a fair lady, is the prime example of the *danse macabre* tradition in English folk song. With the exception of a single record from Northern Ireland, all of the collected versions are from England.

None of the figures in Holbein's Dance of Death corresponds very closely to the fair lady of the folk song (there is, though, a figure of Death in the background of Dürer's *The Lady and the Gentleman*), but a broadside relating a dialogue between Death and a lady, with the title 'The Great Messenger of Mortality; Or, A Dialogue Between Death and the Lady' and commencing 'Fair lady, lay those costly robes aside', dates from the late 17th century. The Victorian musicologist William Chappell discovered a woodcut that appears to depict the encounter between Death and a lady dating from about 1572, and was inclined to assign the dialogue to the 16th century. The tune was printed in Henry Carey's *Musical Century* in 1738. Mary Lamb reused the first two lines of the song in a naïve dialogue between a mother and child in 1804.

Broadsides from the 18th and 19th centuries carry a wide range of imprints, including Kelsey (Boston), Bennett (Bristol), Turner (Coventry), Dash (Kettering), Aldermary Churchyard, Batchelar, Catnach, Dicey, Dicey and Marshall, Evans, Fortey, Jennings, Pitts, Stonecutter Street, Sympson (London), Marshall (Newcastle), Henson (Northampton), Walker (Otley), Williams (Portsea), Harkness (Preston), Butler (Worcester), Carrall[?] (York). This popularity with broadside printers would appear to have been matched among singers, but regrettably no sound recordings have survived. The song was, for example, in the repertoire of the Sussex singer Henry Burstow. This version most closely resembles a broadside called 'Death By The Way'. A very poor copy is held by the Bodleian Library, printer unknown and tentatively dated to 1760.

Other early broadsides carry similar dialogues between Death and an exciseman (dated to 1659), Death and a rich man ('The Midnight Messenger', printed by Pitts), or Death and a young gallant (printed 1633–34). A wall painting (only surviving in a later copy) depicting an encounter between Death and a brainless fop is said to have been executed in Salisbury Cathedral around 1460.

'There Was a Lady All Skin and Bone' (Roud 501), collected frequently in the USA, as well as in England and Scotland, is another take on the same theme, often used as a children's song and susceptible to dramatic performance, working up to the stage direction 'Here the lady screams' printed with the earliest text, around 1783. As a child, the poet Robert Southey, in tears, used to beg his family not to go on with the story.

This version was collected by Cecil Sharp from Mrs R. Sage at Chew Stoke, on January 11th, 1907. It is a concise account of a story that can run to 24 verses in the broadsides. Note that while the tune is generally in 5/4, it includes several bars of 6/4. In the typed-up version of Sharp's notes, the verses vary between four and five lines, but they can be made regular by repeating some of the last lines, as here. In *One Hundred Folksongs*, Sharp also amends the fourth verse so that Death answers the lady more directly:

"I'll have no gold, I'll have no pearl,
I want no costly rich robes to wear.
I cannot spare you a little while,
Nor give you time your life to amend,
Nor give you time your life to amend."

**Recordings** Shirley & Dolly Collins *Love, Death & The Lady*; John Fleagle *World's Bliss*; John Renbourn *A Maid In Bedlam*; Waterson:Carthy *A Dark Light*.

## THE DEATH OF QUEEN JANE CHILD 170; ROUD 77

Queen Jane was in labour,
For six days or more,
Till the women got tired,
And wished it all o'er.

"Good women, good women,
Good women if you be,
Will you send for King Henry?
King Henry I must see."

King Henry was a-sent for,
King Henry did come home,
For to meet with Queen Jane, "My love,
Your eyes look so dim."

"King Henry, King Henry,
King Henry if you be,
Will you have my right side cut open,
You will find my dear baby."

"Queen Jane, my love, Queen Jane, my love,
Such things were never known;
If you open your right side,
You will lose your dear baby."

"King Henry, King Henry,
King Henry if you be,
Will you build your love a castle,
And lie down so deep,
For to bury my body,
And to christen my dear baby."

King Henry went mourning,
And so did his men,
And so did his dear baby,
For Queen Jane did die-en.

And how deep was the mourning,
How wide was the bands,
How yellow was the flower, my boys,
She carried in her hands.

How she hold it, how she rumpled it,
How she hold it in her hand,
Saying, "The flower of old England
Shall never detain me long."

There was fiddling, there was dancing,
The day the babe was born.
To see that Queen Jane, my love,
Lying cold as a stone.

'The Death Of Queen Jane' is a threnody or lamentation for Jane Seymour, the third queen of Henry VIII. Having been married to the king in May 1536, shortly after the execution of her predecessor, Anne Boleyn, she gave birth to Henry's only male heir, the future Edward VI, in October 1537, but died 12 days later. There is some uncertainty as to whether the delivery was mismanaged, with one authority reporting that the prince "was not by natural passage delivered into the world, but that his mother's belly was opened for his birth, and that she died of the incision", while another states that the queen "died twelve days after the birth of this prince, having been well delivered, and without any incision, as others have maliciously reported". It seems most likely that she died of puerperal sepsis, also known as "childbed fever".

The ballad is first known from the 18th century, although there are records from the 16th century of broadsides with titles such as 'The Lamentation of Queene Jane', which may or may not refer to something similar. It has been collected in England, Scotland, Ireland, and the USA, and appeared on broadsides with imprints including Collard (Bristol), Morren (Edinburgh), Dicey and Marshall (London). Cecil Sharp collected versions both in Somerset and in the Appalachian Mountains.

Collected by Cecil Sharp from Mrs Sweet (aged 61) at Somerton, in Somerset, on August 2nd, 1906. In editing the song for book publication, Sharp removed the two extra lines at the start of verse six, and the whole of verse nine. The "flower" in verse eight became "the flamboys", meaning torches. The broadside versions use "torches".

**Recordings** Dave & Toni Arthur *The Lark In The Morning*; Joan Baez *Joan Baez 5*; Ian Bostridge *The English Songbook*; The Bothy Band *After Hours (Live In Paris)*; Martin Carthy & Dave Swarbrick *Straws In The Wind*; Douglas Kennedy *Field Trip – England: Collected by Jean Ritchie and George Pickow. Edited by Jean Ritchie;* Bascom Lamar Lunsford *Ballads, Banjo Tunes, And Sacred Songs Of Western North Carolina*; John Jacob Niles *American Folk Lore Vol. 3*; Joan Sprung *Pictures To My Mind*; Trian *Trian II*; Duncan Williamson *Travellers' Tales Vol. 2*.

Cecil Sharp's original notebook entry for Mrs Sweet's version of 'The Death Of Queen Jane'.

## GEORDIE CHILD 209; ROUD 90

Come bridle me my milk-white steed, Come bridle me my pony, That I might ride to fair London town, To plead for my Geordie.

Come bridle me my milk-white steed,
Come bridle me my pony,
That I might ride to fair London town,
To plead for the life of Geordie.
That I might ride to fair London town,
To plead for the life of Geordie.

And when she entered in the hall,
There were lords and ladies plenty,
Down on her bended knees she fall,
To plead for the life of Geordie.

Then Geordie look round the court,
And saw his dearest Polly,
He said, "My dear, you've come to late
For I'm condemned already."

Then the people looked down on him,
And said "I'm sorry for thee.
'Tis thine own confession hath hanged thee,
May the Lord have mercy upon thee."

Oh Geordie stole no cow nor calf,
Nor he never stoled any money.
But he sold sixteen of the King's white steeds,
And sold them in Bohenny.

Let Geordie hang in golden chains,
His crimes were never many,
Because he came from the royal blood,
And courted a virtuous lady.

I wish I was in yonder grove,
Where times I have been many,
With my broad sword and pistol too,
I'd fight for the life of Geordie.

This very popular ballad has been collected many times in England, Scotland, and North America.

Scottish writers have taken the subject of the song to be George Gordon, fourth Earl of Huntly, who incurred the Queen Regent's displeasure for failing to execute a commission against a Highland robber in 1554. Huntly was imprisoned in Edinburgh

Castle and his enemies urged that he be either banished or put to death. In fact, he escaped with a fine. Scottish versions of the ballad generally do have a happy ending, although their focus on Geordie's lady, her pleas for pardon for her husband, and her payment of his fine are probably more imaginative than historical.

However, a different strain is represented by the ballad as it is best known in England and North America. The story in a London broadside of the early 17th century, 'A Lamentable New Ditty, Made Upon The Death Of A Worthy Gentleman Named George Stoole', is told mostly by the eponymous gentleman himself, and ends with his execution:

I never stole no oxe nor cow,
Nor never murdered any,
But fifty horse I did receive,
Of a merchant's man of Gory.

For which I am condemned to dye,
Though guiltlesse I stand dying,
Deare gracious God, my soule receive!
For now my life is flying.

Later in the 17th century, broadsides appeared on 'The Life And Death Of George Of Oxford' who is a self-confessed highwayman. Here, although George of Oxford recounts his exploits (and endeavours in some degree to excuse them), attention is paid to 'Lady Gray', who pleads for his life. Nevertheless,

Georgy he went up the hill,
And after followed many.
Georgy was hanged in silken string,
The like was never any.

There are many later broadsides, and imprints include Walker (Bradford), Hook (Brighton), Collard, Smith (Bristol), Ward (Ledbury), Birt, Catnach, Disley, Fortey, Hodges, Jennings, Pitts, Such (London).

This last stanza is very like those that conclude so many of the English and American versions of the ballad collected from singers. These versions essentially tell of a lady's unsuccessful pleas to save the life of her husband or lover, who has been condemned for theft or some such misdemeanour that scarcely seems to warrant the death penalty. The relationship between the Scottish and the English–American strains of the story remains uncertain. Child (1882–98: IV, 126) acknowledged the influence of the broadsides on the Scottish ballads, but maintained that the latter "have a proper story, with a beginning, middle, and end".

Collected by Cecil Sharp from Mrs Emma Overd, at Langport, in Somerset, on August 17th, 1904. The last two lines of each verse are repeated as a chorus.

**Recordings** Joan Baez *The First 10 Years*; Martin Carthy *Crown Of Horn*; Shirley & Dolly Collins *Love, Death & The Lady*; The Green House Band *Mirage*; Maddy Prior & June Tabor *Silly Sisters*; Jasper Smith *Here's Luck To A Man*; Levi Smith *The Voice Of The People, Vol. 1*; *Trees On The Shore*.

## GEORGE COLLINS (GILES COLLINS) CHILD 85; ROUD 147

Giles Collins he said to his mother one day,
"Oh mother, come bind up my head,
For tomorrow morning before it is day,
I'm sure I shall be dead.

"Oh mother, Oh mother, if I should die,
As I am sure I shall,
Don't let me be buried in our churchyard,
But under Lady Alice's wall."

His mother she made him some water-gruel,
And stirred it up with a spoon.
Giles Collins he ate but one spoonful,
And died before it was noon.

Lady Alice was sitting in her turret so high,
A-mending of her night-coif.
She saw the prettiest corpse go by,
That ever she saw in her life.

"What bear ye there ye six tall men?
What bear ye there on your shrine?"|
"We bear the body of Giles Collins,
Who was a true lover of thine."

"Down with him, down with him upon the grass,
The grass that grows so green,
For tomorrow morning before it is day,
My body shall lie by him."

Her mother she made him some plum gruel,
With spices all of the best,
Lady Alice she ate but one spoonful,
And the doctor he ate all the rest.

Giles Collins was laid in the lower chancel,
Lady Alice was laid in the higher,
There grew from her breast a lily-white rose,
And from Giles Collins a briar.

The grew and they grew to the very church top,
Until they could grow no higher.
They twisted and twined in a true lover's knot,
Which made all the parish admire.

Widely collected in England and the USA, 'George Collins', 'Giles Collins', or 'Johnny Collins' is often little more than a lament for dead lovers, which Child entitled 'Lady Alice', and which has readily lent itself to parodies such as the marvellous piece included in the *Universal Songster* (1825–26).

A number of versions, however, begin much more mysteriously, with a maid washing her "white marble stone", who foresees the death of George Collins. In England, such versions are only known from Hampshire, having been first collected by George B. Gardiner, and later by Bob Copper from Enos White of Axford. Subsequently Bob Copper sang it himself.

Some scholars have endeavoured to connect this 'marble stone' form with the Scottish ballad 'Clerk Colvill' (Child 42) which tells of a fateful encounter with a mermaid or water-sprite, in turn connected with either the banshee of Celtic folklore or an elf woman of Scandinavian ballads. This scholarship is probably overly imaginative but still highly suggestive. A marble stone in English folklore tends to signify the grave, as in this rhyme from 'The Old Witch', a fairy tale collected in London in the late 19th century by Alice Gomme, a friend of Cecil Sharp:

> Apple tree, apple tree hide me,
> In case the old witch will find me.
> If she do she'll break my bones,
> And bury me under the marble stones.

Foretelling George Collins's death gives the song an air of frightening determinism, allied with a memorable tune.

This version, called 'Giles Collins', was collected by Cecil Sharp from Sister Emma, an Anglican nun, at a convent in Clewer, Berkshire, on February 27th, 1909. Sharp noted that Sister Emma, who was born in 1837, had learned her songs from her mother, who learned them from her grandmother, who had been born before 1753.

**Recordings** Shirley Collins *The Sweet Primeroses*; Bob Copper *When The May Is All In Bloom*; Jacquey Gabriel *Up In The North And Down In The South*; Roy Harvey & North Carolina Ramblers *Man Of Constant Sorrow And Other Timeless Mountain Ballads*; Nathan Hicks *Nothing Seems Better to Me*; Enos White *The Folk Songs Of Britain, Vol. 5.*

## ROSIN THE BEAU ROUD 1192

Oh when I am dead and laid out on the counter,
The ladies they'll all want to know,
Just lift up the lid of the coffin,
And in it's old Rosum the Beau.
And in it's old Rosum the Beau,
And in it's old Rosum the Beau,
Just lift up the lid of the coffin,
And in it's old Rosum the Beau.

Go and get me twelve young and healthy young fellows,
And stand them all round in a row,
And let them drink out of half gallon bottle,
To the health of old Rosum the Beau.

Alfred Williams, the poet and railway worker, collected 'Rosin The Beau' from an old thatcher and his wife for his *Folk Songs Of The Upper Thames*. He noted that he had never heard it anywhere else. In fact, it has been collected a few times in England (by Cecil Sharp among others), Scotland, and Ireland, and rather more often in America. It also appeared under 19th-century broadside imprints such as Walker (Durham), Sanderson (Edinburgh), Goode, Hodges, Paul, Such (London), and in American songsters.

Williams also observed, "Rosin the Beau was evidently a popular and well-known figure, probably the keeper of a noted hostelry", suggesting that he thought of it as a drinking song. Indeed, it could just as easily have found its way into the Drink section of this book. The final stanza of Williams's version, though, gives it a more philosophical turn than many of the drinking songs, and faces death with characteristic resignation and equanimity.

An adaptation beginning "I'm a Yankee boy seeking my fortune", printed by Harkness (Preston) and others, keeps little more than the name of Rosin the Beau, and no doubt the tune, but drops both the themes of drinking and mortality altogether.

Collected by Cecil Sharp from Louie Hooper at Hambridge, in Somerset, on January 6th, 1904. In the typescript, though not in the music manuscript, the hero is referred to as "Rosum the Beau". Sharp notated the tune in 6/8 throughout, even though the first bar is in 9/8. For clarity, we have started in 9/8 and changed to 6/8.

This is obviously an extremely truncated version. Alfred Williams's account, collected from William and Patty Warren, at South Marston in Wiltshire, is much fuller:

I've travelled this wide world over,
And now to another I'll go,
For I know that good quarters are waiting,
To welcome old Rosin the Beau.
To welcome old Rosin the Beau,
To welcome old Rosin the Beau,
For I know that good quarters are waiting,
To welcome old Rosin the Beau.

When I'm dead and laid out on the counter,
A voice you will hear from below,
Crying out "Whisky and water,
To drink to old Rosin the Beau."
To drink, etc.

And when I am dead, I reckon,
The ladies will want to, I know,
Just lift off the lid of the coffin,
And look at old Rosin the Beau.
And look, etc.

Then get a full dozen stout fellows,
And stand them all round in a row,
And drink out of half-gallon bottles,
To the name of old Rosin the Beau.
To the name, etc.

Then get half a dozen young fellows,
And let them all staggering go,
And dig a great hole in the meadow,
And in it toss Rosin the Beau.
And in it toss, etc.

Then get you a couple of tombstones,
Put one at my head and my toe,
And do not fail to scratch on it,
The name of old Rosin the Beau,
The name, etc.

I feel that great tyrant approaching,
That cruel, implacable foe,
That spares neither age nor condition,
Not even old Rosin the Beau.
Not even, etc.

**Recordings** The Clancy Brothers & Tommy Makem *Greatest Hits*, as 'Rosin the Bow'; Bob Dylan recorded this song with The Band during the *Basement Tapes* sessions, using the title 'Ol' Roison The Beau'; Walter Pardon *Put a Bit of Powder On It, Father*.

# THE TREES THEY DO GROW HIGH
## (THE TREES THEY GROW SO HIGH) ROUD 31

The trees they grow high, and the leaves they grow green,
The days are gone and past, my love, which you and I have seen.
Saying, once I had a true love, but now I've got ne'er a one,
So fare you well, my bonny lad, for ever.

"Oh father, dear father, you've done me much harm,
You've married me to a young man that were so very young."
"Oh daughter, dear daughter, if you'll only lie alone,
A lady you shall be while he's a-growing.

"I'll send him to some college for one year or two,
That in a short time he might do for you.
I'll buy him some white ribbon to tie all round his bonny waist,
To let the ladies know that he's married."

She had not been away from her own true love six months,
She went up to his college, she looked over the wall,
Where four and twenty young men were playing at the ball,
She enquired for her own true love, but they would not let him go alone,
Because he was too young and a-growing.

At the age of fourteen, he were a married man,
At the age of sixteen, he was father of a son,
At the age of eighteen, Oh, his grave was growing green,
And that put an end to his growing.

I'll make him a shroud of the holland so fine,
And all the while I'm making it the tears were in my eyes,
Saying, once I had a true love, but now I've got ne'er a one,
So fare you well, my bonny lad, for ever.

'The Trees They Do Grow High' or 'Still Growing' appears to have been an exceptionally popular song with traditional singers. It has been collected right across England and there are records from Scotland, Ireland, Australia, Canada, and the USA. It appeared on 19th-century broadsides from Disley, Fortey, Such (all London), and Walker (Newcastle).

Various commentators have repeated the claim that the ballad is founded on a true incident. In 1631 Sir Robert Innes obtained the guardianship of the young Lord Craigton, and soon afterwards married him to his eldest daughter, Elizabeth Innes. The young husband died in 1634. There is, however, no substantial evidence of a direct connection. Marriages involving minors, arranged in the interests of family alliances, were common in the early modern period and beyond, especially but perhaps not exclusively among the social elite. The song, though, cannot be traced back before the early 19th century. Some of the earliest records are Scottish, however, and the earliest broadsides are probably the Newcastle rather than the London printings, so a Scottish connection is not implausible.

Scholars have also maintained that 'The Trees They Do Grow High' is one of the ballads that Child 'overlooked' or 'omitted', but such speculations are largely fruitless. More to the point is the elegiac quality of the song, which can be presumed to have contributed to its lasting currency regardless of any possible historical connections. Robert Burns rewrote the words of 'Still Growing' as 'Lady Mary Ann'.

Collected by Clive Carey from Stephen Spooner, at Midhurst Union workhouse in Sussex, on September 11th and 13th, 1912. The notation of the tune is exactly as it appears in the library's handwritten copy, made by Frank Purslow from Carey's notebook, including the irregular bars five and six, which have nine and ten quavers (eighth-notes) respectively, rather than the usual eight. Purslow includes several adjustments of the tune to accommodate the words of the different verses. We have omitted these for clarity. The words are also reproduced here as they appear in the original typescript, but in our notation they have been adjusted slightly to fit. The fourth verse has an extra line: Purslow suggests that the second line should be sung twice to accommodate it.

**Recordings** Joan Baez *Volume 2*; Martin Carthy *Martin Carthy*; Bob Copper *When The May Is All In Bloom*; Mary Ann Haynes *Here's Luck To A Man*; Lizzie Higgins *The Voice Of The People, Vol. 17*; Fred Jordan *A Shropshire Lad*; Walter Pardon *A World Without Horses*; Pentangle *Sweet Child*; Scafell Pike *The Month Of Maying*; Duncan Williamson *Travellers' Tales, Vol. 2*.

## THE UNFORTUNATE RAKE
**(THE UNFORTUNATE LAD)** ROUD 2

1. One day as I strolled down the Ro-yal Al-bi-on, Dark was the morn_ ing,
2. He called for a can-dle to light him to bed, Like-wise an old flan-nel to

cold was the day, Then who should I spy__ but one of my ship-mates,
wrap round his head, His poor head was ach-ing, his poor heart was break-ing,

Draped in a blan-ket far cold-er than clay.
For he was a young sailor cut down in his prime. We'll

beat the drums loud-ly and play the pipes mer-ri-ly

Play the dead march as we carr-y him along, Take him to a church-yard and

fire three vol-leys o-ver him, For he's a good sai-lor cut down in his prime.

One day as I strolled down the Royal Albion,
Dark was the morning, cold was the day,
Then who should I spy but one of my shipmates,
Draped in a blanket, far colder than clay.

He called for a candle to light him to bed,
Likewise an old flannel to wrap round his head,
His poor head was aching, his poor heart was breaking,
For he was a young sailor cut down in his prime.

Chorus:
We'll beat the drums loudly and play the pipes merrily,
Play the dead march as we carry him along,
Take him to the churchyard and fire three volleys over him,
For he's a young sailor cut down in his prime.

His poor aged father, his good old mother,
Oft times had told him about his past life,
Along with the flash girls his money he squandered,
Along with those flash girls he took his delight.

But now he is dead and laid in his coffin,
Six jolly sailor lads march on each side,
And each of them carries a bunch of white roses,
That no-one might smell him as we pass 'em by.

At the corner of the street there's two girls standing,
Each to the other does whisper and say,
"Here come a young fellow whose money we squandered,
Here comes a young sailor cut down in his prime."

On top of his tombstone these words they are written,
"All you young fellows take a warning from me,
And never go courting those girls of the city,
For those girls of the city were the ruin of me."

'The Unfortunate Rake', just as widely known by titles such as 'The Young Man Cut Down in his Prime', and the source of American standards such as 'St James' Infirmary', or 'The Streets of Laredo', is one of the finest examples of the adaptability of traditional song.

The song's origins are unknown. The earliest record is a stanza dated to *c*1790 in P.W. Joyce's *Old Irish Folk Music And Songs*, which appears to describe a military funeral, so the dead character may well have been a soldier at this stage. In the mid 19th century, broadsides titled 'The Unfortunate Lad' or 'The Buck's Elegy' describe a funeral in Covent Garden, or elsewhere, and they are usually quite explicit that the cause of death is a sexually transmitted disease. Printers include Stewart (Carlisle), Such (London), Ross (Newcastle), and there are several sheets without imprints; Such's text begins, "As I was a walking down by the Lock Hospital", "lock hospital" being a generic term for institutions for the treatment of venereal diseases. Texts describe treatments including sweating, induced by wrapping the patient in flannel, and the administration of mercury pills, which was probably just as dangerous as the disease itself.

In the broadsides the victim is no longer a soldier, more a man about town, but the traditional song, collected from very many singers throughout England, Scotland, Ireland, and North America, often tells of "The Trooper Cut Down in his Prime", "A Sailor Cut Down in his Prime", and so forth. The disease may be explicit or simply suggested by the smell of the corpse, or warnings against the flash girls of the town. And in some instances the victim herself is such a girl, in songs with titles such as 'The Bad Girl's Lament', or even 'The Whore's Lament'.

When the song appears in North America it has often become 'The Dying Cowboy' or 'The Streets of Laredo', and the cause of his demise is not disease but a life of gambling and drinking, ending in a bar-room brawl. In black American blues and jazz tradition, as 'St James' Infirmary', the focus is on the funeral procession itself, with little surrounding narrative. That version of the song has been recorded and sung by everyone from Louis Armstrong, Cab Calloway, and Bobby Bland to Janis Joplin, The Doors, Dr John, Joe Cocker, and The Stray Cats. Other American variations tell of 'The Wild Lumberjack' or of a copper miner dying of silicosis. Then there are versions that

seem closer to parody, such as 'The Lineman's Hymn', in which an electricity lineman meets his death by falling from an electricity pole. Like his American compatriots, he still requests a military-style funeral, which seems to draw on the song's ancestry.

Collected by Henry Hammond from William Curtis, at Lyme Regis, in Dorset, in March 1906. His version of the song is recorded as 'The Unfortunate Lad'. Note that two verses are sung before the chorus.

**Recordings** Louis Armstrong *The Complete Hot Five And Hot Seven Recordings*, as 'St James Infirmary'; Crooked Jades *The Unfortunate Rake, Vol. 2*; Johnny Doughty *The Voice Of The People, Vol. 12*; Texas Gladden *Ballad Legacy*, as 'One Morning In May'; Bob Hart *A Broadside*; Harry Holman *Just Another Saturday Night*; Mr. Howe *Songs And Stories From East Coast Fishermen, Voice Of Suffolk, No. 6*; Fred Jordan *A Shropshire Lad*; Moses 'Clear Rock' Platt *Deep River Of Song: Black Texicans*, as 'St James Hospital'; Harry Upton *The Voice Of The People, Vol. 2*; The White Stripes *The White Stripes*, as 'St James Infirmary'; Fred Whiting *Songs Sung In Suffolk*.

Cecil Sharp's field notes of two versions of 'The Unfortunate Rake' collected in Somerset in 1908. They are 'Royal Harbour' (opposite), from Esau Porter of Enmore, and 'Bath Hospital', from Alfred Emery of Othery.

# THE UNQUIET GRAVE (COLD BLOWS THE WIND)
(CHILD 78; ROUD 51)

Cold blows the wind tonight, true love,
Cold blows the drops of rain.
I never had but one true love,
And in the greenwood she lays slain.

I'll do as much for any true love,
As any young man may.
I'll sit and weep upon her grave,
For a twelvemonth and a day.

And when this twelvemonth and one day was up,
Her ghost began to speak:
"What makes you sit upon my grave
And will not let me sleep?"

"One kiss, one kiss from your clay-cold lips,
One kiss is all I crave,
One kiss, one kiss from your clay-cold lips,
And return back to your grave."

"If you should kiss my clay-cold lips
Your days will not be long,
For my lips are cold as any clay,
My breath smells (very?) strong."

"Bring me a note from a dungeon deep,
And water from a stone,
And milk, white from a maiden's breast,
When maid she never had known.

'The Unquiet Grave' is one of the sub-group of ballads in the Child corpus which see the return of a ghost, or *revenant*, from beyond the grave. These ballad revenants are living corpses, who conduct themselves in a remarkably human manner and communicate with the living on equal terms (the revenant babes of 'The Cruel Mother' provide another example).

'The Unquiet Grave' is one of the most widespread of such ballads, especially in England. Its brief, rather lyrical story gives form to the general notion that excessive grieving for the dead will disturb their rest; or, to put it another way, it offers an objective correlative to a psychological inability to come to terms with the fact of death.

The ballad has been most widely collected from singers in England, with occasional records from North America and Scotland. The ballad was printed on broadsides of the early 19th century under the titles 'Cold Blows the Wind' or 'The Weeping Lover'. These are unusual in that of five known imprints, four are of Birmingham printers – Heppel, Jackson, Pratt, and Wright – the other being Williams of Portsea. This is the earliest date that can be ascribed to the song, although Bronson (II, 234) makes a tenuous connection with a carol preserved in a manuscript of around 1500, beginning "There blows a cold wynd todaye, todaye".

Some of the broadside texts, and some of the versions collected from singers (including this one), incorporate a stanza or two in which tasks are set, in the manner of riddling ballads like 'Scarborough Fair' and this may give an edge to the encounter between the living and the dead. Note also that the genders of the two characters, living and dead, are interchangeable in different versions of the song.

Collected by Clive Carey from Mr and Mrs Stemp, at Trotton, Sussex, in January 1912. A note on Frank Purslow's handwritten manuscript, copied from Carey's notebook, suggests the song is sung "Also to Auld Lang Syne(!)" There is also a note of an exchange between Sharp and Carey: "This I think has come through children at school (C.S)? Yes, it has! (C.C.)." On the typescript of the lyrics, Dorothy Marshall, who collected with Carey, has typed "The last line is corrupt, I suppose." A reasonable guess, used by Sharp in his printed version of the song, would be to replace "maid" with "man" or "young man". The "note from a dungeon deep" is often a "nut", but it does appear in this form in some of the broadside versions.

**Recordings** May Bradley *Garners Gay*, as 'Cold Blows The Wind'; The Ian Campbell Folk Group *Across The Hills*; Shirley Collins *False True Lovers*; The Dubliners *36 Irish Favourites*; George Dunn *Chainmaker*, as 'Cold Blows The Wind'; Gryphon *Gryphon*; Papa M *Whatever, Mortal*; Jean Ritchie *Ballads From Her Appalachian Family Tradition*; Kate Rusby *Sleepless*.

# WHAT IS THE LIFE OF A MAN?
## (THE FALL OF THE LEAF) (ROUD 848)

As I was a-walk-ing one morn-ing at ease, View-ing the leaves as they fell from the trees, They was all in full mo-tion ap-pear-ing to me, But now they are with-ered, and fal-len from the tree. What is the life of a man, an-y more than the leaves? The man has his sea-son and why should he grieve? Al-though in this world he may prove fine and gay, But like the leaves he shall with-er and soon fade a-way.

As I was a-walking, one morning at ease,
A-viewing the leaves as they fell from the trees,
They was all in full motion appearing to me,
But now they are withered, and fallen from the tree.

Chorus:
What is the life of a man, any more than the leaves?
The man has his season, and why should he grieve?
Although in this world he may prove fine and gay,
But like the leaves he shall wither and soon fade away.

If you'd seen those leaves but a short time ago,
How beautiful and green they did all seem to grow,
But the frost came upon them and withers them all,
And as the rain beat upon them, why down they did fall.

(Chorus)

If you look in our churchyard all names you will see,
Has fallen like leaves from the trees.
Old age and affliction upon them did fall,
And like the leaves they did wither and down they did fall.

(Chorus)

Like 'Death And The Lady', 'The Life Of A Man' is a vernacular English *memento mori*. Here the iconography of death is pastoral, the inevitability of decay and death figured not by a corpse or skeleton and reminders of the grave but through the cycle of the seasons.

'The Life Of A Man' has been collected almost exclusively from singers in England, and southern England at that. Prominent among them are the Copper family from Sussex. However, under the title 'Fall Of The Leaf', or 'Fall Of Leaves', the song appeared on broadsides with a variety of northern imprints, including Swindells (Manchester), Pearson (Manchester), Harkness (Preston), Walker (Newcastle), Ross (Newcastle), Dalton (York), Stewart (Carlisle), Sanderson (Edinburgh).

There is something very similar in versions of 'The Moon Shines Bright' (Roud 702):

The life of a man it is but a span;
It's like the morning flower.
We're here today, tomorrow we're gone,
We're dead all in one hour.

That song, too, is mostly known from singers in the southern half of England, but it was also printed by southern broadside printers.

'The Life Of A Man' in its present form probably dates from around the beginning of the 19th century, which is the period of the earliest known broadsides. The idea, though, was not a new one. It appears in Homer, when Glaucus says: "Men in their generations are like the leaves of the trees. The wind blows and one year's leaves are scattered on the ground; but the trees burst into bud and put on fresh ones when the spring comes round. In the same way one generation flourishes and another nears its end" (*Iliad*, VI).

This broadside of 'The Fall Of The Leaf' was printed by Harkness in Preston in the middle of the 19th century.

It would have been familiar, too, from the Bible: 'We all fade like a leaf, and our iniquities, like the wind, take us away' (Isaiah 64:6). In the *Roxburghe Ballads* (I, 142–47) there is a black-letter broadside of the 17th century running to some 34 stanzas, lacking its title but headed with the following quatrain:

A comparison of the life of man,
Concerning how fickle his estate doth stand,
Flourishing like a tree, or vine, or dainty flower,
Or like a ship, or raine, that's turn'd each houre.

Collected by Cecil Sharp from William Spearing at Isle Brewers, Somerset, on January 6th, 1904. It is recorded as 'The Fall Of The Leaf'. A note on the music manuscript remarks, "Not, of course, a genuine folk air." Bars seven and sixteen are irregular, having an extra quaver (eighth-note); this is how Sharp took them down.

**Recordings** Jumbo Brightwell *Songs From The Eel's Foot*; Harry Holman *Just Another Saturday Night*; George Townshend *Come Hand To Me The Glass*.

# Songs of drinking

Songs concerning the pleasures of drink have long been popular and are, in fact, found among the folk songs of most, if not all, European nations. Such songs celebrate not just drink for its own sake, but the conviviality associated with it. The English ale house or public house was one of the recognised sites for the singing of folk songs. The pub was, though, essentially a male environment, and a male viewpoint comes through strongly at times in some of these songs.

A chapter in Flora Thompson's fictionalised memoir of life in late-19th-century Oxfordshire, *Lark Rise To Candleford*, is set in the Wagon and Horses pub and makes mention of the various kinds of songs that were sung there, from popular hits of the day and music hall songs through to classical English ballads. Though somewhat romanticised, her account testifies to the importance of rural village pub singing in England.

## ALL FOR ME GROG (THE NOBBY HAT) ROUD 475

Where is my hat, oh my nobby, nobby hat,
The hat which I wear in cold weather?
For the brim is wore out and the crown is kickin' about,
And the linin's gone to look for better weather.
Then he shouted out hurrah for his grog and tobacco,
For I spent all my tin with the women a-drinking o' gin,
And across the briny ocean I must wander.

Oh where is my coat, my nobby, nobby coat,
The coat which I wear in cold weather?
The collar is wore out and the fronts are kickin' about,
And the sleeves are gone to look for better weather.
Then he shouted, etc.

Where is my waistcoat, my nobby, nobby waistcoat,
The waistcoat which I wear in cold weather?
The fronts are wore out and the back is kickin' about,
And the collar's gone to look for better weather.
Then he shouted, etc.

Oh where is my breeches, my nobby, nobby breeches,
The breeches which I wear in cold weather?
For the waist is wore out and the fronts kickin' about,
And the arse is gone to look for better weather.
Then he shouted, etc.

Where is my shirt, my nobby, nobby shirt,
The shirt which I wear in cold weather?
For the collar is wore out and the sleeves are kickin' about,
And the tail is gone to look for better weather.
Then he shouted, etc.

Oh where is my stockings, my nobby pair of stockings,
The stockings which I wear in good weather?
For the toe is wore out, and the heel is kickin' about,
And the legs is gone to look for better weather.
Then he shouted, etc.

Oh where is my boots, my nobby pair of boots,
The boots which I wear in cold weather?
The uppers are wore out, and the bottoms are kickin' about,
And the lace is gone to look for better weather.
Then he shouted, etc.

Though not printed on broadsides, this seems to have been a popular song in England. Cecil Sharp collected a version (from a female singer, Louie Hooper), as did George B. Gardiner, Alfred Williams, and several later collectors.

Williams observed at the head of his manuscript: "An old song, though not a particularly inspiriting one. Nevertheless, in spite of the poet's poverty, he could be optimistic, though I fear such optimism was rather feigned than real." John Baldwin, who collected the song in much the same area in 1969, told a rather different story:

"The man who used to sing it (in the pub, of course) apparently removed each article of clothing as he sang about it, until such a stage was reached, when he was left with only his pants, that the landlady would shout 'You can stop singin' that song ... You're not takin' anythin' else off in here ...!'" (FMJ, 1.5 (1969), 341).

Most of the collected versions are from England, but the song has also been found occasionally in Scotland and Canada, as well as in Australia, where it turns up in Banjo Patterson's *Old Bush Songs*.

This version, recorded as 'The Nobby Hat', was collected by George Gardiner from Charles Chivers, at Basingstoke, in Hampshire, in August 1906.

**Recordings** The Dubliners *Wild Rover*; George 'Tom' Newman *The Voice Of The People, Vol. 13*; Walter Pardon *Put A Bit of Powder On It, Father*; The Watersons *Early Days*.

## THE BARLEY MOW ROUD 944 As sung by Harry Chambers.

CD TRACK 1

1. Here's good luck to the pint pot, here's luck to the Bar - ley Mow,

Here's good luck to the pint pot,— here's luck to the Bar - ley Mow, To the

pint pot, gill pot, half a gill, lil - li - get, ben, ben- mow, and here's

luck, here's luck to the Bar - ley Mow._____

Here's good luck to the pint pot, here's luck to the Barley Mow,
Here's good luck to the pint pot, here's luck to the Barley Mow,
To the pint pot, gill pot, half-a-gill, lilliget, ben, benmow,
And here's luck, here's luck to the Barley Mow.

Here's good luck to the quart pot, here's luck to the Barley Mow,
Here's good luck to the pint pot, here's luck to the Barley Mow,
To the quart pot, pint pot, gill pot, half-a-gill, lilliget, ben, benmow,
And here's luck, here's luck to the Barley Mow.

(Then adding a new element each time)

Here's good luck to the gallon pot...

Here's good luck to the barrel...

Here's good luck to the barmaid...

Here's good luck to the landlady...

Here's good luck to the landlord...

(Ending)
Here's good luck to the company, here's luck to the Barley Mow,
Here's good luck to the company, here's luck to the Barley Mow,
To the company, landlord, landlady, barmaid, barrel, gallon pot, quart pot, pint pot,
    gill pot, half-a-gill, lilliget, ben, benmow,
And here's luck, here's luck to the Barley Mow.

Another popular drinking song, which has occasionally been collected in Canada and Australia, 'The Barley Mow' was popular throughout rural England and was often used to finish a singing session in the pub. Mike Yates notes that singers pride themselves on being able to get through it without making a mistake.

Alfred Williams observed: "'The Barley-Mow Song' was in general use at harvest-homes as long as they were observed under the old order of things in the country. I am unable to fix its age, or even to suggest it, though doubtless the piece has existed for several centuries" (*Folk-Songs of the Upper Thames*, p289). The earliest datable printing is in *Ancient Poems, Ballads and Songs of the Peasantry* (1846 and later editions), and there are a few broadsides, albeit without imprints, which probably belong to the 19th century. Dixon and Bell likewise associated the song with harvest-homes: "This song is sung at country meetings in Devon and Cornwall, particularly on completing the carrying of the barley, when the rick, or mow of barley, is finished", adding, "The effect of the 'Barley-Mow Song' cannot be given in words; it should be heard, to be appreciated properly, – particularly with the West-country dialect" (p159). The tune is included in William Chappell's *Popular Music of the Olden Time* (1858–59). It is also mentioned in Thomas Hardy's *The Return Of The Native*, published in 1878.

Fred Whiting from Suffolk (born 1905) sang a rather different song, to essentially the same tune, which has more narrative content, telling about the harvesting of the barley. At the end of the recording, he commented: "Now if you were in Debenham Cherry Tree 60 years ago, about nine o'clock on a Saturday night, you'd hear 'Barley Mow'. Now if you were down there and sung it I don't suppose anyone would know it." Dixon and Bell also give a Suffolk text of 'The Barley Mow' that differs from the usual cumulative song, though it is not the same as the one Fred Whiting sang.

Chambers' "lilliget, ben, benmow" are substitutes for a variety of liquid measures found in other versions of the song, notably "nipperkin and brown bowl".

**Recordings** Harry Chambers *Songs Sung In Suffolk*; George Fradley *It Was On A Market Day, Vol. 1*; Hair Of The Dog *Release The Hounds*; Revel Players *The Wild Mountain Thyme*; George Spicer *The Voice Of The People, Vol. 13*; Fred Whiting *Songs Sung In Suffolk*.

Harry Chambers

# DRINK OLD ENGLAND DRY ROUD 882
As sung by Will Noble and John Cocking.

CD TRACK 2

Now come, my brave boys, As I've told you be - fore, Come

drink, my brave boys, And we'll bold - ly call for more. For the

French have in - vi - ted us, And say that they will try, will try, They

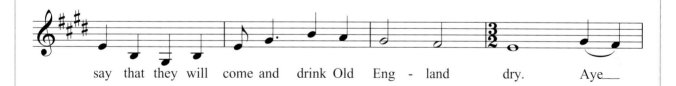

say that they will come and drink Old Eng - land dry. Aye___

dry, aye___ dry, me boys, aye dry,_____ They

say that they will come and drink Old Eng - land dry.

Now come my brave boys as I've told you before,
Come drink my brave boys and we'll boldly call for more,
For the French have invited us and say that they will try, will try,
They say that they will come and drink Old England dry.
Aye dry, aye dry me boys, aye dry,
They say that they will come and drink Old England dry.

Supposing we should meet with the Germans by the way,
Ten thousand to one we will show them British play.
With our swords and our cutlasses, we'll fight until we die, we die
Before that they shall come and drink Old England dry.
Aye dry, etc.

Then up spake bold Churchill of fame and renown,
He swears he'll be true to his country and his crown,
For the cannons they will rattle and the bullets they will fly, will fly,
Before that they shall come and drink Old England dry.
Aye dry, etc.

Then it's come my brave boys, as I told you before,
Come drink my brave boys till you cannot drink no more,
For those Germans they may boast and shout but their brags are all my eye, my eye,
They say that they will come and drink Old England dry,
Aye dry, etc.

Will Noble and John Cocking

Although 'Drink Old England Dry' could just as easily be listed under songs about war or soldiers' songs, it is particularly associated with the Haxey Hood Game and is sung in the pubs in the Lincolnshire village of Haxey, on Old Christmas Day, January 6th. The Haxey Hood Game, which has been described as a version of "rugby-cum-rollerball", is played across the muddy fields between Haxey and Westwoodside with a leather ball known as the 'hood', the name deriving from the apocryphal story of the game's origin. It is said that in the 14th century, Lady de Mowbray, wife of a local landowner, was riding by on January 6th when her hood blew off. Thirteen men tried to bring it back, and she was so delighted by their efforts that she gave each man a grant of land on the basis that the scene would be re-enacted each year, which it is, with 13 men playing key roles. No historical evidence has been found for any of this, the game not being recorded before 1815.

The song has been occasionally collected elsewhere in England, but there seems to be just a single record of a broadside printing, by Pratt of Birmingham. From the mention of the French in the first stanza, the song is assumed to date from the time of Napoleon's threatened invasion, but in various versions it has been updated with references to the Crimean War, Lord Roberts, Winston Churchill, the Germans, and the Russians.

**Recordings** Will Noble and John Cocking: *Yon Green Banks*; Haxey Singers *The Folk Songs Of Britain, Vol. 8*.

# FATHOM THE BOWL ROUD 880

Come all you bold heroes, give an ear to my song, Singing in the praise of good bran - dy and rum. There's a
clear, cry - stal foun - tain ov - er Eng - land doth flow,— Give to
me the punch lad - le, I'll fa - thom the bowl.

Come all you bold heroes, give an ear to my song,
Singing in the praise of good brandy and rum.
There's a clear crystal fountain over England doth flow,
Give to me the punch ladle, I'll fathom the bowl.
I'll fathom the punch with a full-flowing bowl,
Give to me the punch ladle, I'll fathom the bowl.

From France we get brandy, from Jamaica comes rum,
Sweet oranges and lemons from Portugal come.
Good beer and good cider over England doth flow,
Give to me the punch ladle, I'll fathom the bowl.
I'll fathom the punch, etc.

My wife, she comes in as I sit at my ease,
She scolds and she grumbles, does nothing to please,
She may scold and she may grumble till she's black as a coal,
Give to me the punch ladle, I'll fathom the bowl.
I'll fathom the punch, etc.

My father, he lies in the depths of the sea,
With a stone round his neck, what matters for he?
There's a clear crystal fountain, over him it doth flow,
Give to me the punch ladle, I'll fathom the bowl.
I'll fathom the punch, etc.

Another very well-known drinking song, 'Fathom The Bowl' has apparently been collected only in southern England. Broadside imprints such as Boyes (Brighton), Marshall (Bristol), Sharman (Cambridge), Catnach, Fortey, Hodges, Pitt, Such (London), Peirce (Southborough) would seem to confirm that impression. The broadsides are titled 'The Punch Ladle' or 'Give Me the Punch Ladle'. Fortey's printing pairs the song with 'John Barleycorn Is a Hero Bold' (Roud 2141), which seems appropriate enough, but Pitts has it alongside 'The Stage of Life', a religious meditation upon mortality, so not too much can be read into such juxtapositions.

Collected by Clive Carey from Richard West, at Stedham in Sussex, in August 1911. No separate chorus is provided, so presumably it was sung by repeating the last two lines of the tune.

**Recordings** John C. Reilly *Rogue's Gallery: Pirate Ballads, Sea Songs, & Chanteys*; The Watersons *Early Days.*

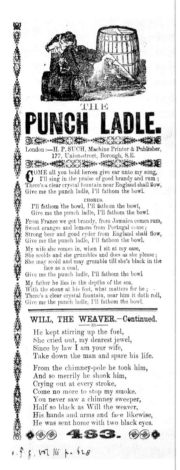

A broadside version of the song, printed by Such in London towards the end of the 19th century.

## GOOD ALE (HOME BREWED ALE) (ROUD 203)

In come the landlord, he look so big,
With his high crowned hat and his powdered wig.
With his high crowned hat and his high heeled boots,
And it's you and I have to pay for that.
Home brewed ale,
Thou art my darling,
Thou art my comfort,
Night and morning.

In come the landlady, she look so fine,
With her big-sleeved gown and her fine lace cap.
With her big-sleeved gown and her fine lace cap,
For it's you and I have to pay for that.
Home brewed ale, etc.

In come the son, as I suppose,
With his billy-cocked hat and his turned-up nose.
With his billy-cocked hat and his high-heeled shoes,
For it's you and I have to pay for that.
Home brewed ale, etc.

In come the daughter, she looks so gay,
Not many do exceed the flowers of May.
Not many do exceed the flowers of May,
For her hair she plaits and scents with musk.
Home brewed ale, etc.

In come the tapster, he looks so pale,
He will either draw it new or stale.
And if there is no small beer in the tap,
Then the landlord say then go the droppings.
Home brewed ale, etc.

So now my friends we are all a-met,
We are not going to part just yet,
We are going to chit and to chat,
Drink and we'll smoke and we'll have
Home brewed ale, etc.

'Good Ale' or 'O Good Ale, Thou Art My Darling' is another song associated with the Copper family, but has also been collected elsewhere in England and in Scotland. In fact, the earliest record actually seems to be in the *Scots Musical Museum* (1803) in a text 'corrected' by Robert Burns.

The song was also printed in the *London Melodist* (*c*1831), and broadsides bear the imprints of Mason (Belper), Such (London), Swindells (Manchester), and there is another unascribed sheet printed in York. It appeared, too, in an American songster, and there is a single record of a version, possibly something of an adaptation, collected in America.

Collected, as 'Home Brewed Ale', by Cecil Sharp from Elizabeth Coles (aged 76) at Nether Stowey, Somerset, on August 10th, 1906.

**Recordings** The Copper Family *Come Write Me Down: Early Recordings*; Lou Killen *Sea Shanteys*.

The original notebook entry made by Cecil Sharp when he took down the song from Elizabeth Coles.

## JOHN BARLEYCORN (ROUD 164) As sung by Tom Smith.

CD TRACK 3

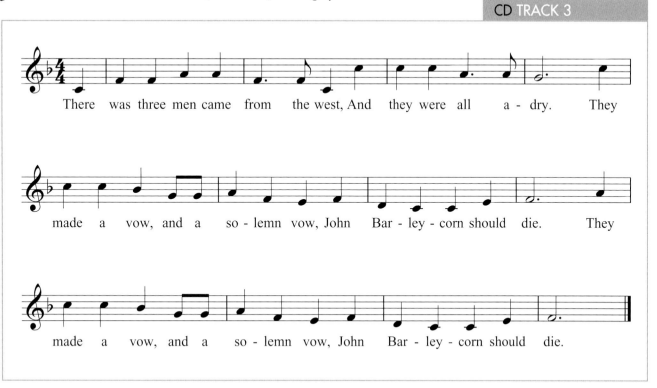

There was three men came from the west, And they were all a-dry. They made a vow, and a solemn vow, John Barley-corn should die. They made a vow, and a solemn vow, John Barley-corn should die.

There was three men came from the west,
And they were all a-dry.
They made a vow, and a solemn vow,
John Barleycorn should die.
They made a vow, and a solemn vow,
John Barleycorn should die.

They ploughed him in the ground so deep,
Put clods all over his head.
They made a vow, and a solemn vow,
John Barleycorn was dead.
They made a vow, and a solemn vow,
John Barleycorn was dead.

Now he lay sleeping 'neath the ground,
When the rains from heav'n did fall.
Then he sprang up so very high,
He did amaze them all.
Then he sprang up so very high,
He did amaze them all.

About Michaelmas time or a little before,
He grew very yellow, and then,
John Barleycorn he grew a long beard
And soon became a man.
John Barleycorn he grew a long beard,
And soon became a man.

They hired men with scythes so sharp,
They cut him right down to the knee.
And after they'd served him so, my boys,
They called it barbary.
And after they'd served him so, my boys,
They called it barbary.

They hired men with pitchforks stout,
They pierced him through the heart.
And after they'd served him so, my boys,
They tied him to a cart.
And after they'd served him so, my boys,
They tied him to a cart.

They wheeled him up and down the land,
They took him to the barn.
They made a vow, and a solemn vow,
They'd done poor John no harm.
They made a vow, and a solemn vow,
They'd done poor John no harm.

They hired men with stiff staff cram,
They thrashed him skin from bones.
And after they'd served him so, my boys,
They ground him between two stones.
And after they'd served him so, my boys,
They ground him between two stones.

They put him in the tub so round,
They scald him almost blind.
And after they'd served him so, my boys,
They gave him to the swine.
And after they'd served him so, my boys,
They gave him to the swine.

Put brandy in a glass, my boys,
Put cider in a can,
Put barley broth in an old brown pot,
He'll become the brightest man.
Put barley broth in an old brown pot,
He'll become the brightest man.

Tom Smith

Probably the best-known of songs in praise of beer, 'John Barleycorn' is among the oldest and the most complicated. Peter Wood ('John Barleycorn: The Evolution of a Folk-song Family', *Folk Music Journal*, 8.4 (2004), 438–55) has traced at least seven different interlinked song families on the theme. There is even a rewriting of the song by Robert Burns.

To cut a long story short, the earliest traces are in a song or poem, 'Allan-a-Maut', in a Scottish manuscript of the 16th century. But something more readily recognisable as 'John Barleycorn' emerges in 'A Pleasant New ballad. To Sing Evening and Morn, of the Bloody Murder of Sir John Barleycorn', printed in London by Henry Gosson and recorded in the Stationers' Register on 14 December 1624. 'The Little Barley-Corne', a witty broadside describing the effect of beer on its drinkers was entered in the Register in November 1632, but does not appear to have survived among singers.

A further song, 'Hey, John Barleycorn' or 'John Barleycorn Is A Hero Bold' (Roud 2141), which is sung to a different tune from 'John Barleycorn', appears to date from the mid 19th century and concentrates on the theme of Barleycorn as beer (rather than beginning with its growth in the fields). Although printed on broadsides – mostly in London, though there is a sheet from Harkness (Preston) – this song does not seem to have been especially popular, although it was in the repertoire of Walter Pardon and a few other English singers.

'John Barleycorn' itself has been collected throughout the English-speaking world, and appeared on early and mid 19th-century broadsides, with imprints including Jackson, Russell, Whiting (Birmingham), Collard (Bristol), Willey (Cheltenham), Evans, Such (London), Kiernan (Manchester), Marshall (Newcastle), Plant (Nottingham). Early folklorists saw in the song a representation of the death and resurrection of the old corn god, but there is no need to imagine pagan beliefs to follow the song's metaphor for the cycle of the seasons and the process of brewing ale or beer, which has no doubt outlasted many deities.

'John Barleycorn, My Jo' (Roud 6051) is a unique Scottish piece, said to have been "composed by the late George Burton, shoemaker, at one time working at Auchnagatt, who ... composed his poetry when drunk and swore at it when sober".

**Recordings** Bob Blake *Down In The Fields*; Martin Carthy *Sweet Wivelsfield*; Fairport Convention *Tipplers Tales*; Austin Flanagan *The Voice Of The People, Vol. 14*; Bob Hart *A Broadside*; Fred Jordan *A Shropshire Lad*; John Renbourn *A Maid In Bedlam*; Tom Smith *Songs Sung In Suffolk*; Steeleye Span *Below The Salt*; Traffic *John Barleycorn Must Die*; Duncan Williamson *Travellers' Tales, vol. 2*; The Young Tradition *Galleries*.

## WHEN JONES'S ALE WAS NEW
### (WHEN JOAN'S ALE WAS NEW) ROUD 139

The next come in was a tai - lor, With his bod - kin shears and thim - ble, No man could be more nim - ble, To join the jo - vial crew. He sat and called for ale and chalk, Till this poor tai - lor he was broke, When Joan's ale was new, my boys, When Joan's ale was new.

There was three jolly tradesmen,
And they all fell a-drinking,
They all sat down all to be merry,
'Twas over a bottle or two a good sherry
To help them over the hills so merry,
When Joan's ale was new, my boys,
When Joan's ale was new.

The first came in was a hatter,
And he asked what was the matter,
To join the jovial crew.
He hold his hat all on the ground,
Saying every man shall spend a crown,
They sat and drinked his health all round,
When Joan's ale was new, etc.

The next come in was a tailor,
With his bodkin shears and thimble,
No man could be no nimbler,
To join the jovial crew.
He sat and called for ale and chalk,
Till this poor tailor he was broke,
And he was obliged to put on his coat,
When Joan's ale was new, etc.

The next came in was a dyer,
No man could be no slyer,
To join the jovial crew.
He told the landlord to his face
That the chimney corner was his place,
There he would sit and wash his face,
When Joan's ale was new, etc.

The next came in was a mason,
He swore he'd drink out of the basin,
To join the jovial crew.
He threw his hammer against the wall,
Praying that all the churches and chapels might fall,
Then would be work for masons all.
When Joan's ale was new, etc.

The next came in was a soldier,
No man could be no bolder,
To join the jovial crew.
He swore he'd fight for English ground,
Before the nation should be run down,
He sat and drinked his health all round,
When Joan's ale was new, etc.

The next came in was a ragman,
With his rag-bag on his shoulder,
No man could be no bolder,
To join the jovial crew.
He sat and called for glasses and glasses,
Till they were all as drunk as jackasses,
And burn the rag-bag all to ashes,
When Joan's ale was new, etc.

A 19th-century broadside of
'Joan's Ale Was New', printer and
date unknown.

This old song, which appeared in Thomas D'Urfey's *Pills to Purge Melancholy* (1719–20), has often been collected in England and also occasionally in Scotland and the USA. There is a Stationers' Register entry for 'Jones ale is newe' from as early as 1594, although the song is first known from later printings, including London broadsides of the mid to late 17th century. It was also included in Thomas D'Urfey's six-volume collection of songs, *Pills To Purge Melancholy* (1719–20). Broadside imprints from the 19th century include Russell (Birmingham), Willey (Cheltenham), Poet's Box (Glasgow), Fordyce (Hull), Birt, Catnach, Fortey, Jennings (London), Fordyce (Newcastle), Harkness (Preston), Baird (Cork), and a sheet ascribed to Dublin.

The text in Robert Bell's *Ancient Poems, Ballads and Songs of the Peasantry of England* (pp197–99) includes the name 'Nolly', prompting the editor to suggest that the song was a lampoon on Oliver Cromwell and his wife, who was nicknamed 'Joan' by the Royalists. The Protector's low-life acquaintances are depicted paying him a congratulatory visit on his change of fortune. If so, this must have been a later adaptation of a pre-existing song. No doubt part of its appeal has always lain in the possibility of varying the cast of characters to amuse or satirise whatever company happens to be present. D'Urfey's text has a Welshman and a Dutchman in addition to the usual tradesmen.

This version ('When Joan's Ale Was New') was collected by Cecil Sharp from Edward Harrison (aged 65) at Langport, in Somerset, on April 6th, 1906. It is not entirely coherent. In the first verse you may wish to replace "They all sat down to be merry", which seems to have been mis-remembered, with the repeated "To join the jovial crew" refrain. Elsewhere you will notice that not all the verses have the same number of lines (a characteristic also found in broadside versions of the song). This seems to have presented certain problems to Sharp when he wrote out the tune. He chose to base his notation on the third verse, which has three lines (rather than the usual two) before the "To join the jovial crew" refrain. But then he omitted to notate a line in the second half of each verse, just before "When Joan's ale was new". A handwritten note on the typescript suggests repeating bars eleven and twelve to fill the gap. This is a case where singers will need to exercise their ingenuity to produce a convincing version.

**Recordings** Bob & Ron Copper *Twankydillo*; George Fradley *It Was On A Market Day, Vol. 1*; Fred Jordan *The Voice Of The People, Vol. 17*.

# Songs of love

Predictably, love in all its forms is one of the great themes of English folk song. Songs about lovers can be found in virtually all of the other sections in this book – not least among the bawdy songs and murder ballads.

Here are included songs about faithful and unfaithful lovers, ranging from lyric songs to narrative ballads. Several songs concern the reunion of lovers who have long been parted, which are sometimes generically designated the 'broken token' songs, since the returned true-love is often only recognized by some kind of token. The custom of lovers breaking an item such as a cheap ring or a coin between them as a token of fidelity was apparently widespread in England in earlier times.

The course of true love, though, does not always run smooth. Just as frequently, lovers in folk songs find themselves thwarted by their social and economic circumstances. 'Family opposition to lovers' is one of the standard themes of English-language balladry, represented by songs including 'Died for Love' and 'The Butcher Boy', and also found motivating murder ballads such as 'Bruton Town' and 'The Constant Farmer's Son'.

In 'The Daemon Lover' or 'The House Carpenter', divided loyalties bring about tragic and sometimes supernatural consequences. The supernatural as such is not so strong a theme in English folk song (although there are elements of supernatural retribution in some of the murder ballads, such as 'The Cruel Ship's Carpenter'), but a more benign manifestation also occurs in 'The Grey Cock'; and 'The Unquiet Grave' (included under Songs of Death) could also be classed as a song about love.

## THE BANKS OF SWEET PRIMROSES (ROUD 586)
As sung by Vic Legg

CD TRACK 4

As I strolled out___ on a bright spring morn-ing, For to roam the val-leys and to take fresh air, All on the banks of the___ sweet prim-ro - ses, And who should I spy but a mai - den fair?

Vic Legg

As I strolled out on the bright spring morning,
For to roam the valleys and to take fresh air,
All on the banks of the sweet primroses,
And who should I spy but a maiden fair?

With three long steps and I was beside her,
But not knowing me she passed me by,
It was all in a long of a bright spring morning,
She appeared to me like a lovely bride.

I said, "Fair maiden, where are you a-going?
And what is the reason for all your ails?
I will make you as happy as any young lady,
If you your kindness on me prevail."

She said, "Stand off, stand off, you are false and deceitful,
You are a false and a wicked young man.
It is them like you that caused me to wander,
And to bring me comfort is all in vain.

"So I'll go down to some lonely valley,
Where no man nor mortal there can be found,
And the pretty little songbirds keep changing their voices,
And I can sleep safely on the ground."

So come all you young men who've a mind to go courting,
And pay attention to what I have to say.
For there's many a dark and a gloomy morning
Turns out to be a sunshine day.

Truly one of the classic English folk songs, 'The Banks of Sweet Primroses' appears in all the major collections and both tune and text remain remarkably stable. The Hammond brothers noted that the primroses "were so numerous we did not stop to gather any"! With the occasional record from Canada or Scotland, the song seems to have been confined to England and Wales, though its popularity there cannot easily be overstated.

It is also well represented on broadsides, which again tell the short, familiar story widely collected from singers. Imprints (which all seem to be from England) include Jackson, Pratt, Russell (Birmingham), Stewart (Carlisle), Keys (Devonport), Smith (Leicester), Birt, Catnach, Disley, Fortey, Hillatt and Martin, Morgan, Paul, Such, Taylor (London), Pearson, Swindells (Manchester), Ross, Walker (Newcastle), Henson (Northampton), Ordoyno, Plant (Nottingham), Harkness (Preston), Sefton (Worcester), and Dalton (York).

**Recordings** Blue Murder *No One Stands Alone*; Martin Carthy & Dave Swarbrick *But Two Came By*; The Copper Family *Coppersongs 2*; Bob Hart *A Broadside*; Fred Jordan *A Shropshire Lad*; Martin Simpson *The Bramble Briar*; June Tabor *At The Wood's Heart*; Phil Tanner *The Gower Nightingale*.

## BARBARA ALLEN (CHILD 84; ROUD 54) As sung by Vic Legg.

**CD TRACK 5**

It being the springtime of the year,
The flowers were freshly blooming;
A young man from my own country,
Fell in love with Barbara Allen.

This young man took sick and went to bed,
And called for Barbara Allen,
And when she came 'twas what she said,
"Young man, I think you're dying."

"I am not dying," this young man did cry,
"One kiss from you would cure me."
"One kiss from me you'll never see,
Though I thought your heart was breaking.

"Do you remember last Sunday night,
Above in the ballroom dancing?
You danced all night with the village pride,
And you slighted Barbara Allen."

"I do remember last Sunday night,
Above in the ballroom dancing.
I danced all night with the village pride,
But I still love Barbara Allen."

He rang a bell for the serving maid
But she was slow in coming.
"There's a watch and chain in the window there,
Give them to Barbara Allen."

She had not been gone too very far,
When she heard the church bells tolling,
And each toll that those church bells made
Was cruel Barbara Allen.

She had not been gone but a mile or two
When she saw his funeral coming.
"Lay down, lay down his corpse," she cried
"So that I may gaze upon him."

They laid his corpse down on the road,
And there she fell lamenting.
"Oh why, oh why?" A young man cried,
"Can this be Barbara Allen?"

She ran till she came to her father's gate,
And there she stopped lamenting.
"Oh father, father, dig my grave,
And dig it deep and narrow.
A young man died for me today,
I'll die for him tomorrow."

They both were buried in St Mary's churchyard,
But she was buried higher,
And from her grave a red rose grew,
And from his grave a briar.

They grew till they reached the old church wall
Till they could grow no higher,
And there they formed a true lovers' knot,
The red rose and the briar.

The Roud index lists more than a thousand entries for 'Barbara Allen', surely the most popular of all the ballads of the English-speaking world.

The ballad first appears on black-letter broadsides of the 17th century; and Samuel Pepys has a diary entry for January 2, 1666, recording, "In perfect pleasure I was to hear her [Mrs Knipp, an actress] sing, and especially her little Scotch song of Barbary Allen", suggesting that the song might have originated on the stage. Oliver Goldsmith wrote of his pleasure in the ballad in an essay on 1765, and in the same year it was printed in Thomas Percy's *Reliques Of Ancient English Poetry*. Broadsides continued to be printed in the 18th and 19th centuries, with English and Scottish imprints too numerous to list, as well as American printings.

The story remains relatively stable, with variations in the setting – 'Scarlet Town', 'Reading Town', and so forth – and in the name of Barbara's lover. The twining branches motif often appears at the end of the ballad. The main point of variation, however, concerns the motivation of the story, the lover's culpability and/or the justice of Barbara's accusations, with American versions often at least hinting at some complexity in this regard.

**Recordings** Garrett & Norah Arwood *Far In The Mountains*; Joan Baez *Volume 2*; Andy Cash *From Puck To Appleby*; Debbie/Pennie Davis *The Birds Upon The Tree And Other Traditional Songs And Tunes*; Doris Day *The Best Of The Big Bands*; Bob Dylan *Live At The Gaslight 1962*; Patsy Flynn *The Hardy Sons Of Dan*; Texas Gladden *Ballad Legacy*; Bob Hart *A Broadside*; Joe Heaney *The Road From Connemara*; Fred Jordan *Classic Ballads Of Britain And Ireland, Vol. 1*; Sarah Makem *The Voice Of The People, Vol. 17*; Jessie Murray *Classic Ballads Of Britain And Ireland, Vol. 1*; Jean Ritchie *Ballads From Her Appalachian Family Tradition*; Phoebe Smith *The Yellow Handkerchief*; Wiggy Smith *Band Of Gold*; Phil Tanner *The Gower Nightingale*; Charlie Wills *Classic Ballads Of Britain And Ireland, Vol. 1*; Jim Wilson *Just Another Saturday Night*.

# A BLACKSMITH COURTED ME (ROUD 816)

For the blacksmith courted me, nine months and better
When first he won my heart, he wrote me a letter,
With the hammer in his hand, Oh he do strike so mighty and clever,
And if I was with my love I would live for ever.

Good news has gone abroad, bad news is carried,
Good news has come at last, my first lover's married,
For I wish him well to do though he is not much here for to hear me,
For to think I love that young man when he proved deceitful.

"It's bring your witness now, then never I shall deny you."
(Missing line)
"Witness I've got none, only the Almighty,
And he will punish you for a-slighting of me."

For he looked in the glass, his poor head was aching,
And he looked all in the glass, his poor heart was breaking,
Oh his face looks pale and wan, Oh indeed his poor body trembles,
For to think he did love that young girl and he proved deceitful.

'Twas down in yonder's meadows they were gathering up roses,
'Twas down in yonder meadows were his cheeks like roses,
For I'm afraid this scorching sun will scorch and spoil all your beauty,
For I never shall die for love, now young girls believe me.

Collected exclusively in England, 'A Blacksmith Courted Me' is usually sung to the same tune as 'Our Captain Called All Hands', which Vaughan Williams borrowed for his setting of John Bunyan's 'To Be a Pilgrim'. Sometimes the faithless lover is a shoemaker.
  Ewan MacColl and Peggy Seeger (*Travellers' Songs from England and Scotland*, pp198–99) identified lines in common with early broadsides:

She:  Did you not promise me when you lay by me
That you would marry me, can you deny me?
He:  If I did promise thee, 'twas but to try thee.
Call up your witnesses, else I defie thee.

This particular dialogue was reprinted in Durfey's *Pills to Purge Melancholy* (1719). The lines, however, are commonplace and do not mean that 'The Blacksmith' is that old. In fact, the only broadside imprint that has been identified is that of Such (London) from the 19th century.

This version was collected by George Gardiner from James Ray at Passfield, in Hampshire, on April 14th, 1909. It bears very little resemblance to the famous 'To Be A Pilgrim' tune, but it is notable because it is the only manuscript version in the library at Cecil Sharp house that includes lyrics. Vaughan Williams originally recorded only the tune, from Mrs Powell in Weobley, Herefordshire, in 1909. In editing the song for the 1959 *Penguin Book Of English Folk Songs*, he had to supply words. He seems to have based them on the Such broadside:

A blacksmith courted me, for nine months or better,
And when he won my heart, he wrote to me a letter.
With his hammer in his hand, he looks so mighty clever,
Was I with my love, I could live for ever.

It's not what you promised when by me you did lie,
You promised to marry me and never me deny.
If I promised to marry you it was only to try you,
So bring your witness in and I never will deny you.

Witness I have none but the Almighty,
And he'll surely punish you for slighting of me.
Looking in the glass makes my poor heart tremble,
To think I loved a man who proved so deceitful.

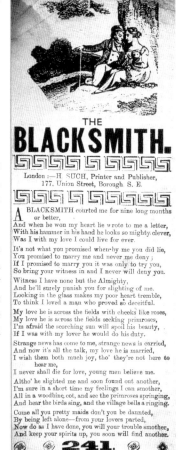

The only known broadside of 'The Blacksmith', printed by Such in London at some point between 1863 and 1885.

My love he is across the fields with cheeks like roses,
My love he is across the fields, seeking primroses.
I'm afraid the scorching sun will spoil his beauty,
If I was with my lover, he would do his duty.

Strange news has come, strange news is carried,
And now it's all the talk, my love he is married.
I wish them both much joy, though they're not here to hear me,
I never shall die for love, young men believe me.

Although he slighted me, and soon found out another,
I'm sure in a short time my feelings I can smother,
All in a woodbine cot, and see the primroses springing,
And hear the birds sing and the village bells a-ringing,

Come all you pretty maids, don't you be daunted,
By being left alone – from your lovers parted.
Now do as I have done, you will your trouble smother,
And keep your spirits up, you will soon find another.

**Recordings** Harry Brazil *The Voice Of The People, Vol. 11*; Shirley Collins *Sweet Primeroses*; Martin Simpson *Kind Letters*; Phoebe Smith *Songs Of The Travelling People*.

Peggy Seeger, writing with Ewan MacColl, suggested 18th century origins for the song.

# THE BOLD FISHERMAN (ROUD 291)

As I went out one May morning,
Down by the riverside,
There I beheld a bold fisherman,
Come rowing down the tide,
Come rowing down the tide,
There I beheld a bold fisherman,
Come rowing down the tide.

Good morning to you bold fisherman,
How came you fishing here?
I came fishing for your sweet sake,
All on this river clear.

He tied his boat unto a stand,
And to this lady went,
For to take hold of her lily-white hand,
It was his full intent.

Then he unbraced his morning gown,
And gently laid it down,
When she beheld three chains of gold,
Went twinkling three times round.

Then she fell on her bended knees,
And mercy did she call,
Calling you a bold fisherman,
I'm sure you are some lord.

I'll take you to my father's house,
And married we will be.
For you shall have a bold fisherman,
To row you on the sea.

'The Bold Fisherman' has proved particularly popular with English singers, with just a few other records from Scotland and North America. The songs was printed a number of times in the 19th century, but the only imprint outside of London that has come to light is that of Jackson (Birmingham); London imprints include Catnach, Disley, Fortey, Hodges, and Such.

Lucy Broadwood argued at some length (*JFSS* 5 (1915), 132–35; 7 (1923), 36–40) that the song is a secularised religious allegory, with several of its elements, such as the river, the sea, the royal fisher, the robes, and the mystical union of bride and groom, having their origins in ancient Gnostic symbolism. Although some scholars have tended to accept her arguments, more recent opinion has been decidedly sceptical, not least because the song is not known before the early 19th century. Renwick (*English Folk Poetry*, pp21–53) argues that the main narrative theme of 'The Bold Fisherman', is that of the unrecognised returned lover. Certainly the lord is in disguise, and it may be that the lady already knows him. Renwick points out that the song's language and imagery, are in fact very typical of English folk songs concerning love relationships.

This version was collected by Cecil Sharp from Edmund Jupp (aged 73) at Newbuildings, Southwater, Sussex, on April 23rd, 1908. The last two lines of each verse are reused to create a chorus, as happens with the first verse.

**Recordings** The Copper Family *Coppersongs: A Living Tradition*; Harry Cox *The Bonny Labouring* Boy; Tim Hart and Maddy Prior *Folk Songs Of Olde England Vol. 2*; Walter Pardon *A World Without Horses*; The Young Tradition *The Young Tradition*.

# THE BONNY LABOURING BOY (ROUD 1162)

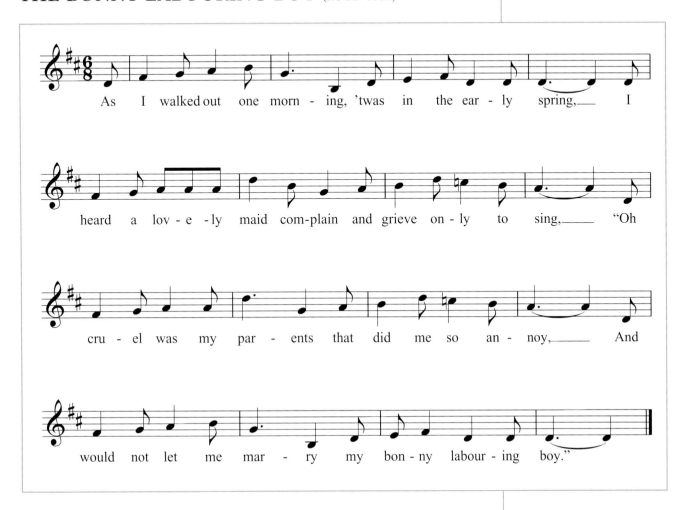

As I walked out one morning, 'twas early in spring,
I heard a lovely maid complain and grieve only to sing,
"Oh cruel was my parents that did me so annoy,
And would not let me marry my bonny labouring boy.

"His cheeks are like the roses, his eyes as black as sloes,
He's manly neat and handsome wherever that he goes,
But ...
In spite of my parents' malice, with my labouring boy I'll go.

"I courted him for twelve long months, but little did I know,
That my cruel parents would prove my overthrow.
They watched us close one evening, whilst in a shady grove,
Pledging our vows together in some constant bands of love.

"My father stepped up to me and seized me by the hand,
He swore he'd send young Johnny unto some foreign land.
He locked me up in my bedroom my comforts to annoy,
And kept me to weep and mourn for my bonny labouring boy.

"My mother came next morning and unto me did say,
'Your father he's intending to appoint your wedding day.'
I nobly made my answer, 'With him I'll never comply,
But single will I remain for my bonny labouring boy.'

"Says your daughter to the mother, 'Your talk is all in vain.
Lords, dukes and earls, their riches I disdain,
I'd rather lead a humble life my time for to employ,
Increasing nature's prospects with my bonny labouring boy.'"

Fill up your glasses to the brim, let the toast go merrily round,
Here's a health to every labouring boy that ploughs and hoes the land.
When his work is over, his home he will enjoy,
And happy is the girl that gets a bonny labouring boy.

'The Bonny Labouring Boy' provides a classic example of the 'family opposition to lovers' theme that is so common in English folk song, and has been widely collected in England, Ireland, and North America. Broadside imprints include Forth (Hull), Disley, Fortey, Hodges, Pitts, Ryle, Such (London), several sheets from Dublin printers, and also Lindsay (Glasgow), even though the song does not appear to have been collected from singers in Scotland.

Collected by George Gardiner from Mrs Davy in Hampshire. The song is in the Mixolydian mode. There's a missing line in the third verse. The version printed by Disley in London has this:

His cheeks are like the roses, his eyes as black as sloes,
He's mild in his behaviour wherever that he goes.
He's manly, neat and handsome, his skin as white as snow,
And in spite of my parents' malice with my labouring boy I'll go.

**Recordings** Paddy Beades *The Voice Of The People, Vol. 5*; Bob Blake *The Birds Upon The Tree And Other Traditional Songs And Tunes*; Shirley Collins *Sweet England*; Harry Cox *The Bonny Labouring* Boy; Tony Harvey *Songs Sung In Suffolk*; Jeff Wesley *Down In The Fields*.

## CLAUDY BANKS (ROUD 266)

It was one summer's morning all in the month of May, Down by some flower-y gardens I care-less-ly did stray. I ov-er heard a dam-sel in sor-row to com-plain, All for her ab-sent lo-ver that ploughed the rag-ing main.

It was of one summer's morning all in the month of May,
Down by some flowery gardens I carelessly did stray.
I overheard a damsel in sorrow to complain,
All for her absent lover that ploughed the raging main.

I stepped up to her, which put her in surprise,
I own she did not know me, I being in disguise,
I says, "My charming creature, my joy and heart's delight,
How far are you going to travel, this dark and stormy night?"

"Now the way, kind sir, to the Claudy Banks if you do please to show,
So pity a maid in all despair for there I has to go.
In search of a faithful young man and Johnny is his name,
It is on the banks of Claudy I'm told he does remain.

"If Johnny was here this night he would keep me from all harm,
He is in the field of battle all in his uniform,
He's in the field of battle, all foes he will destroy,
Like a royal king of honour, all in the wars of joy.

"Now it's six weeks or better since my true love left this shore,
And he's cruising the wide ocean where foaming billows roar,
He's cruising the wide ocean, for honour and for gain."
"I'm told the ship was wrecked all on the coast of Spain."

Oh when she heard those dreadful news, she fell in to despair,
In wringing of her hands and a-tearing of her hair,
"But since he's gone and left me, no man on earth I'll take,
Down in some lonesome valley, I'll wander for his sake."

His heart was filled (with) joy till he could no longer stand,
He fell into her arms, saying, "Betsy, I'm the man.
I am that very young man that you have thought was slain,
And since we have met on Claudy Banks we never will part again."

Like 'The Dark-Eyed Sailor' and other broken-token songs, 'Claudy Banks' is yet another take on the unrecognised lover's return. Collected in England, Scotland, Ireland, North America, and Australia, 'Claudy Banks' has remained very popular among singers, with the Copper family being closely associated with the song.

The earliest dated printing is an Edinburgh chapbook of 1818, and there are numerous broadside imprints to attest to its popularity, including Bloomer, Jackson, Pratt (Birmingham), Hook (Brighton), Marshall (Bristol), Stewart (Carlisle), Clift (Cirencester), Walker (Durham), Sanderson (Edinburgh), Lindsay, McIntosh (Glasgow), Batchelar, Birt, Catnach, Disley, Edwards, Fortey, Hill, Hodges, Pitts, Such (London), Pearson, Swindells (Manchester), Ross, Walker (Newcastle), Williams (Portsea), Harkness (Preston), Dalton (York), as well as several Irish and American printers.

Collected by George Gardiner from William Hill in Hampshire. We have omitted the word "of" in the opening phrase to make the words fit. Note that the narration, which has been in the first person throughout, abruptly changes to third person in the final verse. Some singers will want to amend that.

**Recordings** The Copper Family *Come Write Me Down: Early Recordings*; Fairport Convention *Five Seasons*; Joe Heaney *The Road From Connemara*; Fred Jordan *A Shropshire Lad*; Waterson:Carthy *Common Tongue*; Frederick White *A Century Of Song*.

# COME WRITE ME DOWN (ROUD 381)

Come_ write me down, ye po - wers a - bove, The first I fan-cied was a young man's love. It is a je - wel all in my eyes, And where my_ joy and com - fort_ lies.

Come write me down, ye powers above,
The first I fancied was a young man's love,
It is a jewel all in my eyes,
Where my joy and comfort lies.

"I will give you gold, I will give you pearl,
If you can fancy me, my girl.
Here's costly robes that you shall wear,
If you can fancy me, my dear."

"It's costly robes shall never entice,
For I don't mean to follow a young man's voice."
Then he turned round to go away,
She called him back and bid him to stay.

"Oh stay, Oh stay, young man," said she,
"For I can't fancy none but thee."
"Go along, go along, proud and scornful dame,
If you propose I can do just the same.

"I make no doubt that I can find
Some handsome young girl to please my mind."
"Now, love, do as we've done before,
And nothing but death shall part us any more."

Richard Adams

One of the great English love anthems, associated especially with the Copper family, but collected from a number of other singers in England, Scotland, and North America. 'Come Write Me Down' also appeared on broadsides under a variety of titles such as 'Second Thoughts Are Best', 'The Lamenting Lovers', 'The Powers Above', or 'The True Lovers'. Imprints include Wilson (Bideford), Pratt, Whiting (Birmingham), Bennett (Brighton), Sharman (Cambridge), Mate (Dover), Armstrong (Liverpool), Birt, Catnach, Evans, Pitts (London), Fordyce (Newcastle), Pierce (Southborough), and Robertson (Wigton).

Collected by Cecil Sharp from Richard Adams, at East Harptree, in Somerset, on August 25th, 1906. The sequence of events is clearer in the broadsides. This is the Wilson of Bideford version, called 'Second Thoughts Are Best':

Come write me down, ye powers above,
That first created man to love,
I have a diamond in my eye,
Where all my joy and comfort lie.

"I'll give you gold, I'll give you pearl,
If you can fancy me my girl,
Rich costly robes too you shall wear,
If you can fancy me my dear.'

"It's not your gold shall me entice,
To leave my pleasure to be a wife.
I never do intend at all,
To be at any young man's call."

"Oh go your way, you scornful dame,
If you are shy I'll be the same,
For I don't fear that I can find
Another fair maid to my mind."

"Oh stay young man, be not in haste,
You seem afraid your time to waste.
Let reason rule your roving mind,
And unto you I will prove kind."

My sorrow and trouble now are past,
My joy and comfort's come at last,
But the girl that always said me nay,
Now proves my comfort night and day.

**Recordings** Peter Bellamy *Wake The Vaulted Echoes*; The Copper Family *Come Write Me Down: Early Recordings*; Arthur Family *Voices: English Traditional Song.*

# THE DÆMON LOVER (CHILD 243; ROUD 14)
## (WELL MET, WELL MET MY OWN TRUE LOVE)

Well met, well met, my own true love,
Long time have I been absent from thee.
I am lately come from the salt sea,
And 'tis all for the sake, my love, of thee.

I have three ships all on the salt sea,
And (by) one of them has brought me safe to land.
I've four and twenty mariners on board;
You shall have music at your command.

The ship, my love, that you shall sail in,.
It shall be of the fine beaten gold.
I've four and twenty mariners on board;
It is a beauty for to behold.

'The Daemon Lover', also known as 'The House Carpenter', first appears as "A Warning for married women, being an example of Mrs Jane Reynolds (a West-Country Woman), born near Plymouth, who having plighted her troth to a Seaman, was afterwards married to a Carpenter, and at last carried away by a Spirit", entered in the Stationers' Register in 1657 and printed on broadsides of the 17th and early 18th century. The early broadsides tell the familiar ballad story at some considerable length: a young man is press-ganged into the navy, dies abroad, and leaves his betrothed to marry the carpenter. Later he returns as a spirit and tempts her away. Printed texts from the 18th century are closer to the ballad as later collected from singers. The story has not been linked to any known actual occurrence.

Joan Baez is one of many American singers to sing this song as 'The House Carpenter'.

Later Scottish versions retain the supernatural element, when once on board ship the wife spies her lover's cloven foot, before he causes the ship to sink and they are both drowned. One or two versions have been collected from England and Scotland, but on the whole the ballad does not seem to have survived well in Britain – unlike in America where it has remained very popular with singers. Likewise, the only later broadside printings are American.

Rarely in America, though, does the demonic nature of the returned lover become evident. Instead, there is a tendency towards sentimentality, as the wife starts to weep for the husband and babies she has left behind. In contrast, in the early broadside texts it is apparent that she belongs rightly with her first lover, who later returns to claim her, rather than with the carpenter, whom she has married in the meantime, and their children.

Rather like those of 'The Gypsy Laddie', the sexual politics of 'The House Carpenter' can be read in a number of ways, with American versions tending to emphasise the centrality of the family unit. It is perhaps not coincidence that the earliest texts should belong to a period in England when there was much public and literary debate over the status of marriage and the family. 'Warning' broadsides were a common genre in the 17th century, employed to make various ideological and/or theological points.

This version, recorded in the original notebook as 'James Harris, The Daemon Lover', was collected by Henry Hammond from Mrs Marina Russell at Upwey, Somerset, in January 1907. It is an extremely truncated account of the story, including only a small part of the lover's tempting of the carpenter's wife. Singers will want to seek out a longer and more elaborate version, either from Child or the broadsides. This version, known as 'The Distressed Ship Carpenter' was published by John Ashton in his *Real Sailor-Songs* collection of 1891:

Well met, well met, my own true love,
Long time have I been seeking thee,
I am lately come from the salt salt sea,
And all for the sake, love, of thee.

I might have had a King's daughter,
And fain she would have married me,
But I've forsaken all her crowns of gold,
And all for the sake, love, of thee.

If you might have had a king's daughter,
I think you much to blame,
I would not for five hundred pounds,
That my husband should hear the same.

For my husband is a carpenter,
And a young ship carpenter is he,
And by him I have a little son,
Or else, love, I'd go along with thee.

But, if I should leave my husband dear,
Likewise my little son also,
What have you to maintain me withal,
If I along with you should go?

I have seven ships upon the seas,
And one of them brought to land,
And seventeen mariners to wait on thee,
For to be, love, at your command.

A pair of slippers thou shalt have,
They shall be made of beaten gold,
Nay, and be lin'd with velvet soft,
For to keep thy feet from cold.

A gilded boat then thou shalt have,
Thy oars shall be gilded also,
And mariners to row thee along,
For to keep thee from thy overthrow.

They had not been long upon the sea,
Before that she began to weep;
What weep you for my gold? he said,
Or do you weep for my fee?

Or do you weep for some other young man,
That you love much better than me?
No, I do weep for my little son,
That should have come along with me.

She had not been upon the seas,
Passing days three or four,
But the mariner and she were drown'd,
And never heard of more.

When tidings to old England came,
The ship's carpenter's wife was drown'd,
He wrung his hands, and tore his hair,
And grievously fell in a swoon.

Oh! cursed be those mariners,
For they do lead a wicked life,
They ruin'd me a ship carpenter,
By deluding away my wife.

**Recordings** Clarence Ashley *Anthology Of American Folk Music*, as 'The House Carpenter'; Joan Baez *In Concert*, as 'The House Carpenter'; Bob Dylan *The Bootleg Series Volumes 1-3*, as 'The House Carpenter'; Almeda Riddle *Southern Journey, Vol 6*, as 'The House Carpenter'; Jean Ritchie *Ballads From Her Appalachian Family Tradition*, as 'The House Carpenter'.

# THE DARK-EYED SAILOR
## (FAIR PHOEBE AND HER SAILOR) (ROUD 265)

It's of a comely young lady fair,
Who was walking out for to take the air.
She met a sailor upon her way,
So I paid attention, so I paid attention,
To hear what they did say.

Said William, "Lady, why roam alone?
The night is coming, the day near gone."
She said, while tears from her eyes did fall,
"It's my dark-eyed sailor, it's my dark-eyed sailor,
That proved my downfall.

"It's two long years since he left the land,
I took the gold ring from off my hand.
We broke the token – here's a part with me,
And the other rolling, and the other rolling,
At the bottom of the sea."

Said William, "Drive him from off your mind,
Some other sailor as good you'll find.
Love turns aside and soon cold does grow,
Like a winter's morning, like a winter's morning,
When the lands are covered in snow."

These words did Phoebe's fond heart inflame,
She said, "On me you shall play no game."
She drew a dagger and then did cry,
"For my dark-eyed sailor, for my dark-eyed sailor,
A maid I'll live and die."

"His coal-black eyes and his curly hair,
And pleasing tongue did my heart ensnare.
Genteel he was, not a rake like you,
To advise a maiden, to advise a maiden,
To slight a jacket blue."

"But still," said Phoebe, "I'll ne'er disdain
A tarry sailor, but treat the same.
So drink his health – here's a piece of coin –
But the dark-eyed sailor, but the dark-eyed sailor,
Still claims this heart of mine."

Then half the ring did young William show,
She seemed distracted midst joy and woe.
"Oh, welcome, William, I've land and gold,
For my dark-eyed sailor, for my dark-eyed sailor,
So manly and bold."

Then in a cottage, down by the sea,
They joined in wedlock and well agree.
All maids be true when your love's away,
For a cloudy morning, for a cloudy morning,
Brings forth a sunshiny day.

'The Dark-Eyed Sailor' is a classic example of the 'broken token' class of love songs. With its theme of lovers parted for so long that they do not immediately recognise one another, it can be related to the 'return song' pattern of the *Odyssey* and of romances such as King Horn, from which the ballad 'Hind Horn' (Child 17; Roud 28) was adapted. For this reason it belongs here rather than with the songs about sailors.

The song has remained very stable over the large number of times it has been collected in England, Wales, Scotland, Ireland, and North America, and A.L. Lloyd believed that all the collected versions derive ultimately from a broadside printed by James Catnach, who published in London between 1813 and 1838. But there is no certainty that this definitely was the first printing. Lloyd thought the tune older, and suggested that the song shows a sophistication that might derive from the stage.

Broadside imprints certainly attest to the song's great popularity, and include Russell, Whiting, Wright (Birmingham), Phillips (Brighton), Stewart (Carlisle), Willey (Cheltenham), Ford (Chesterfield), Clift (Cirencester), Walker (Durham), Sanderson (Edinburgh), Lindsay, M'Intosh (Glasgow), Osbaldeston (Gloucester), Woolcock (Helston), Child (Hereford), Fordyce, Forth (Hull), Williams (Kington), Barr (Leeds), Edwards, Hinton (Leominster), Birt, Catnach, Disley, Fortey, Hill, Hillatt and Martin, Hodges, Paul, Pitts, Sharp, Such, Taylor (London), Bebbington, Jacques, Pearson, Wheeler (Manchester), Fordyce, Ross, Walker (Newcastle), Henson (Northampton), Plant (Nottingham), Forth (Pocklington), Williams (Portsea), Harkness (Preston), Jones (Sheffield), Houghton (Worcester), Dalton (York), and it was also printed in America.

Another example of the genre is the song variously known as 'The Broken Token', 'The Young and Single Sailor', or 'A Fair Maid Walking All in her Garden' (Roud 264). This song (which Lloyd thought gave rise to 'The Dark-Eyed Sailor'), has been collected in even greater numbers and was printed in the *Vocal Library* (1822) as well as on a wide selection of broadsides.

This version, called 'Fair Phoebe And Her Sailor' was collected by Clive Carey from Richard Hopkins, at Chithurst in Sussex, in February 1911.

**Recordings** Mary Cash *From Puck To Appleby*, as 'The Broken Token'; Daisy Chapman *Ythanside*; Jack Clark *Good Order!*; Bob Hart *A Broadside*; Fred Jordan *A Shropshire Lad*; Christy Moore *Prosperous*; Sarah Anne O'Neill *The Voice Of The People, Vol. 10*; Walter Pardon *A World Without Horses*; Charlotte Renals *Catch Me If You Can*; Kate Rusby And Kathryn Roberts *Kate Rusby And Kathryn Roberts*; Steeleye Span *Hark! The Village Wait*; June Tabor And The Oyster Band *Freedom And Rain*; Phil Tanner *The Gower Nightingale*.

# THE DROWNED LOVER (ROUD 185)

As I was a-walking down in Stokes Bay,
I met a drownded sailor on the beach as he lay,
And as I drawed nigh him put me to a stand
When I knowed it was my true love by the mark on his
	hand.

As he was a-sailing from his own native shore,
Where the stormy winds and the raging seas they'll begin
	for to roar,
You never behold his own love any more.

Down on her bended knees she fall,
Most bitterly did cry,
And the wringing of her hands and the tearing of her hair.
I'm contented to lie by your side,
And in a few moments this lover she died.

Come all you pretty maidens that have got lovers on the
	main,
Don't ever expect them to turn back again,
For the stormy winds and the raging seas begin for to roar,
And you never beheld your own love any more.

In Robin churchyard this couple do lay.
Come all you pretty fair maids that pass by this way,
Mark what the tomb did say.
Cruel, cruel weather throwed my love on shore,
And I never shall see him any more.

'The Drowned Lover', 'Scarborough Town', 'Robin Hood's Bay', or 'Stow Brow' is an archetypal lament, which has been widely collected in England and Scotland, and also in North America. Frank Kidson stated that this was a Yorkshire song, and certainly the places mentioned – Scarborough, Robin Hood's Bay, and Stow Brow, a tract of land to the south of Robin Hood's Bay – seem to give it a localised setting between Scarborough and Whitby. Extensive efforts, however, have failed to identify any local events that fit the story.

On the other hand, it has been claimed that the song derives from a 17th-century broadside concerning the finding of the Earl of Sandwich's drowned body after the Battle of Sole Bay (1672), and John Howson notes that Harold Smy, who piloted sailing barges on the Suffolk coast, claimed it as a local song.

Most of the broadside imprints that can be confidently identified with the song are northern, including Stewart (Carlisle), Forth (Hull), Ross (Newcastle), Harkness (Preston), Dalton (York), and yet Pitts (London) and Williams (Portsea) also issued sheets naming Robin Hood's Bay in the title.

The drowned lover motif occurs in other songs too, such as 'Down by the Sea Shore' (Roud 466), which is in the repertoire of the Copper family; and 'Susan Strayed the Briny Beach' (Roud 1896), collected in Ireland and Canada.

This version was collected by Cecil Sharp from James Bale, at Bridgwater, Somerset, on August 16th, 1905. The words are particularly chaotic. The version Sharp published in *One Hundred English Folksongs* (1916), using this tune, has the same words in the first verse but develops quite differently. In his notes, Sharp claims that "The words are almost exactly as they were sung to me." He notes that the tune is in the Dorian mode.

As I was a walking down in Stokes Bay,
I met a drowned sailor on the beach as he lay;
And as I drew nigh him, it put me to a stand,
When I knew it was my own true love, by the mark on his hand.

As he was a sailing from his own dear shore,
Where the waves and the billows so loudly do roar,
I said to my true love, "I shall see you no more,
So farewell, my dearest, you're the lad I adore."

She put her arms around him, saying "Oh my dear!"
She wept and she kissed him, ten thousand times o'er.
"Oh I am contented to lie by thy side."
And in a few moments, this lover she died.

And all in the churchyard these two were laid,
And a stone for remembrance was laid on her grave.
"My joys are all ended, my pleasures are fled,
This grave that I lie in is my new married bed."

James Bale

**Recordings** Harry Cox *The Bonny Labouring* Boy; Texas Gladden *Ballad Legacy*, as 'Down By The Sea Shore'; Gordon Hall *Good Things Enough*; Sam Larner *Now Is The Time For Fishing*; Harold Smy *When The Wind Blows*; Ron Spicer *When The May Is All In Bloom*; Frank Verrill *The Voice Of The People, Vol. 12*.

## GREEN BUSHES (ROUD 1040)

"I will buy you fine beavers and fine silver gowns, I will buy you fine petticoats with the flounce to the ground, If you will prove constant and loyal to me, I'll forsake my own true love and get married to thee."

"I will buy you fine beavers and fine silken gowns,
I will buy you fine petticoats with the flounce to the ground,
If you will prove royal and constant to me,
I'll forsake my own true love and get married to thee."

"I wants none of your petticoats and fine silken gowns,
I never was so poor as to marry for clothes,
But if you will prove royal and constant to me,
I'll forsake my own true love and get married to thee.

"Come let us be going, kind sir, if you please,
Come let us be going from yonder green woods,
For my true love is coming down yonder I see,
Down by the green bushes where he thinks to meet me."

And when he came there and found she was gone,
He stood like some lambkin that was for ever undone,
Saying "She's gone with some other and has forsaken me,
So adieu to green bushes for ever," cried he.

"Now I'll be like some schoolboy, spend all my life in play,
I never will be foolish to throw myself away,
For she's gone with some other and has forsaken me,
So adieu to green bushes for ever," cried he.

This song, which casts affairs of the heart in a cynical, even bitter, light has been widely collected in Scotland, Ireland, Canada, the USA, Australia, and especially in England. Mike Yates has noted the similarity of situation with medieval *pastourelles*, the typical subject of which is a meeting between a knight and a shepherdess, followed by a kind of debate, after which she may or may not succumb to the knight – though the extreme ease of the young woman's capitulation in 'Green Bushes' and the change of viewpoint in the final stanzas suggest a particular take on that tradition.

The song was featured in J.B. Buckstone's stage play *Green Bushes*, a Victorian tear-jerker staged in 1845, and the text printed in *Davidson's Universal Melodist* (1847) is described as "Sung by Mrs Fitzwilliam in the popular drama". It was also in the repertoire of the Irish tenor John McCormack. Later, George Butterworth, who had collected the song in Sussex, made use of it in his orchestral idyll *The Banks of Green Willow* (1913).

Comment on the age of the song has been rather inconclusive, with claims of Irish descent, Baring-Gould's statement that the words are "substantially old", and the possible influence of 'A Dialogue In Imitation of Mr H. Purcell – Between A Town Spark And A Country Lass', in Carey's *Musical Century* (1740). Baring-Gould and Cecil Sharp both favoured a Scottish origin in the mid 18th century. But other than Frank Kidson's precise statement that it was sung in Stockport about 1838, and printings on early-19th-century broadsides, there is little firm evidence for a much earlier date.

'Green Bushes' ('The False Lover' is another title used) was widely printed on broadsides, with imprints including Wright (Birmingham), Baller (Bristol), Stewart (Carlisle), Keys (Devonport), Stone (Exeter), Forth (Hull), Lindsay (Glasgow), Ward (Ledbury), McCall (Liverpool), Catnach, Disley, Fortey, Hodges, Pitts, Such (London), Kiernan (Manchester), Fordyce, Ross, Walker (Newcastle), Walker (Otley), King (Oxford), Williams (Portsea), Harkness (Preston), Burridge (Truro), Dalton (York), as well as Irish and American imprints and several appearances in songsters. None of these, however, serve to place the song any earlier than the early 19th century.

Louie Hooper (top) and Lucy White, who were half-sisters, had a huge repertoire of songs.

Collected by Cecil Sharp from Louie Hooper and Lucy White, at Hambridge, Somerset, in September 1903. This is one of those cases in which the words in the music manuscript do not match those in the typescript of the lyrics. The music has "silver gowns" rather than "silken gowns", and "constant and loyal", as opposed to "royal and constant". In the version Sharp published in *One Hundred English Folksongs*, he omitted the last stanza and supplied two introductory verses:

As I was a-walking one morning in spring,
For to hear the birds whistle and the nightingales sing,
I saw a young damsel so sweetly sang she,
"Down by the green bushes he thinks to meet me."

I stepped up to her and thus I did say,
"Why wait you, my fair one, so long by the way?"
"My true love, my true love," so sweetly sang she,
"Down by the green bushes he thinks to meet me."

**Recordings** Joseph Leaning *Unto Brigg Fair*; Geoff Ling *The Voice Of The People, Vol. 1*; Walter Pardon *Put a Bit of Powder On It, Father*; Cyril Poacher *Plenty Of Thyme*; Phoebe Smith *The Yellow Handkerchief*.

## THE GREY COCK (CHILD 248; ROUD 179)
## (THE LOVER'S GHOST or THE TIME IS COME)

The time is come I must be going,
The burning tempest I have to cross,
All over the mountains I've rode with pleasure,
This very night I'll be with my lass.
All over the mountains I've rode with pleasure,
This very night I'll be with my lass.

I came unto my true love's window,
I knelt down gently upon a stone,
'Twas through a pane that I whispered slowly,
Saying, "My dear girl, are you alone?"
'Twas through a pane that I whispered slowly,
Saying, "My dear girl, are you alone?"

She rose her head from her soft down pillow,
Snowy was her milk-white breast,
Crying "Who is there outside my window,
That have deprived me of my night's rest?"
Crying "Who is there outside my window,
That have deprived me of my night's rest?"

"It's your true love, do not discover,
I pray, love, rise and let me in.
I am fatigued after my long journey,
Besides I'm wet unto the skin.
I am fatigued after my long journey,
Besides I'm wet unto the skin."

My love she rose with greatest pleasure,
Opening the door for to let me in,
We kissed, shook hands, embraced each other,
Till that long night were at an end.
We kissed, shook hands, embraced each other,
Till that long night were at an end.

When that long night were gone and over,
The cocks they did begin to crow,
We kissed, shook hands, in sorrow parted,
I took my leave and away did go.
We kissed, shook hands, in sorrow parted,
I took my leave and away did go.

My love has skin as the snow in winter,
Her cheeks is red as the rose in June,
Her black sparkling eye like a blazing star,
In a winter's night, and it freezes too.
Her black sparkling eye like a blazing star,
In a winter's night, and it freezes too.

'The Grey Cock' belongs to the tradition of 'night-visiting' songs, in which a man visits his lover at night for obvious reasons and leaves in the morning. It also draws on the *aubade* or 'dawn song', which expresses the regret of parting lovers at daybreak. Examples are said to be found in almost all the world's literatures, with the earliest European examples dating from end of the 12th century. Among the most celebrated in English are the exchange between Romeo and Juliet at the end of their wedding night, and that beginning "Myn hertes lif, my trist, and my plesaunce, / That I was born, allas, what me is wo, / That day of us moot make disseveraunce!" when Criseyde hears the cock crow in Book III of Chaucer's *Troilus and Criseyde*.

In some versions of 'The Grey Cock' – though not this one – it becomes apparent that the lover is in fact a ghost. Hugh Shields ('The Grey Cock') argues that the supernatural element has in fact been borrowed from a different song – an Anglo-Irish broadside song called 'Willy-O' which is a reworking of 'Sweet William's Ghost' (Child 77; Roud 50). On this basis the supernatural ballad might be distinguishable from the more usual run of night-visiting songs with titles such as 'Saw You My Father?', 'Here's A Health To All True Lovers', and so forth.

The various songs together have been collected quite frequently in England, Scotland, Wales, Ireland, and North America. 'Saw You My Father?' was in print in the 18th century; and a few broadsides are known, mostly without imprints, though at least one hails from Dublin. A version was collected from Cecilia Costello in Birmingham in 1951 (she was of Irish descent), called 'The Grey Ghost'. It has vivid imagery – 'The burning Thames I have to cross', 'O Mary dear, the clay has changed me' – and a number of 'impossibles' or *adynata* (to use the rhetorical terminology) in the last stanza. These have made it especially influential with revival singers.

Collected by George Gardiner from William Stockley (56), at Locksheath, in Hampshire, in September 1907. He called the song 'The Lover's Ghost' or 'The Time Is Come'. The tune was annotated by J.F. Guyer.

**Recordings** Bill Cassidy *From Puck To Appleby*; Norah Cleary *The Voice Of The People, Vol. 3*; Cecilia Costello *Classic Ballads Of Britain And Ireland, Vol. 2*; Fred Jordan *In Course Of Time …*; Kathy And Carol *Kathy And Carol*; Ewan MacColl *The Manchester Angel*; Vergie Wallin *Far In The Mountains*; Waterson:Carthy *Waterson:Carthy*; Roisin White *The First Of My Rambles*.

## THE GYPSY LADDIE (THE DRAGGLETAIL GYPSIES)
(CHILD 200; ROUD 1)

There was three gypsies a-come to my door,
One sang high and the other sang low,
The one sang high and the other sang low,
And the other sang bonny bonny biscay O.

This lady come down in a silken gownd,
Put on her Spanish livery O,
Says she, "This night I'll resign,
To follow the draggletail gypsies O."

'Twas late at night when her lord came home,
Inquiring for his lady O,
The servants replied on every side,
She's gone with the draggletail gypsies O.

Come saddle me my milk-white steed,
Come bridle me my pony too,
That I might ride and seek for my bride,
She's gone with the draggletail gypsies O.

The he rode high and he rode low,
He rode through woods and copses too,
He rode till he came to the woodside,
And there he found his lady O.

What makes you leave your house and land,
What makes you leave your money too?
What makes you leave your new-wedded lord
To follow the draggletail gypsies O?

What care I for house and land?
What care I for money O?
What care I for my new wedded lord?
I'll follow the draggletail gypsies O.

Last night you could lay on a good feather bed,
And into the arms of your Johnny too.
And now you must ride on the wide open land,
Along with the draggletail gypsies O.

'The Gypsy Laddie', also known as 'The Raggle-Taggle Gypsies', is first known on an English broadside tentatively dated to 1720, and was then printed in Scotland in the 1740 edition of Allan Ramsay's *Tea-Table Miscellany*, although Child was determined that the ballad was Scottish in origin. The song has remained popular throughout the English-speaking world (second only to 'Barbara Allen' in the Roud index). There is the expected range of 19th-century broadsides, with imprints including Forth (Bridlington), Stewart, Whinham (Carlisle), Willey (Cheltenham), Ford (Chesterfield), Walker (Durham), Stephenson (Gateshead), Fordyce (Hull), Catnach, Hodges, Jennings, Pitts, Such (London), Swindells, Wheeler (Manchester), Fordyce, Ross (Newcastle), Harkness (Preston), Dalton, Kendrew (York), as well as Irish and American printers.

Perhaps the main source of variation is a tendency in American versions to condemn the wife for leaving her husband and children to elope with the gypsies, or 'Black Jack Davey'. In some versions she is abandoned by the Gypsy lover and ends up destitute. On the other hand, the ballad has, unsurprisingly, proved popular with Gypsy and traveller singers, who do not give this interpretation to the story.

This version, 'The Draggletail Gypsies', was collected by Cecil Sharp from Mrs Emma Overd at Langport, Somerset, on August 4th, 1904.

**Recordings** Harry Cox *The Bonny Labouring* Boy; Cilla Fisher & Artie Tresize *Cilla And Artie*; Texas Gladden *Ballad Legacy*; Woody Guthrie *Anglo-American Ballads, Vol. 1*, as 'Gypsy Davy'; Eunice Yeatts MacAlexander *A Century Of* Song; John Jacob Niles *Folk Balladeer*; Walter Pardon *The Voice Of The People, Vol. 6*; Jean Ritchie *Ballads From Her Appalachian Family Tradition*; Jeannie Robertson *The Voice Of The People, Vol. 17*.

Emma Overd

## HEAR THE NIGHTINGALE SING (THE GRENADIER)
(ROUD 140)

Oh as I was a-walking one morning in May,
I saw a young couple together did stray,
The one was a fair maid, a beauty I declare,
And the other was a soldier, a bold grenadier.

"Come sit yourself down by some crystal stream,
For to see the pretty flowers grow,
Hear the nightingale sing."

The soldier took the fair maid so slender round the middle,
And out of his knapsack he drew a fiddle,
And he played such a tuney, boys, which made the groves ring.
"Hark, hark," said the fair maid, "How the nightingales sing."

"Oh soldier," said the fair maid, "Will you marry me?"
"Oh no," said the soldier, "That never could be.
For I've got a wife 't home in my own countree,
And she's as nice a woman as ever you see.

"Now I am bound to the Injies and there to remain
For the space of three long years crossing the ocean again,
But if ever I do return it shall be in the Spring,
For to see the pretty flowers grow, hear the nightingales sing."

Despite the fiddle metaphor, 'Hear the Nightingale Sing', also known as 'The Grenadier And The Lady' or 'The Soldier and the Lady', manages to be a sensual, rather than bawdy, song of seduction, which has been popular with singers in England and North America (though apparently not in Scotland or Ireland).

'The Nightingale's Song; or The Soldier's Rare Musick, and Maid's Recreation' was printed in black-letter by W. Onley (London, 1689–1709), on a sheet topped with a woodcut of a rather large nightingale (or at least a generic bird – it looks more like a pigeon). The only later broadsides that are known, however, seem to be under the provincial imprints of Willey (Cheltenham), Forth (Hull).

('The Nightingale', beginning "My love he was a rich farmer's son", is a different song, in which a young woman's true-love is press-ganged on board a ship called the *Nightingale* and his ghost reappears when the ship is lost.)

This version was collected, as 'The Grenadier', by Cecil Sharp from Alfred Emery at Othery, in Somerset, on April 4th, 1908. It is in the Mixolydian mode. The second verse is shown exactly as collected but it is clearly truncated. You might fill the gap with this verse from the Onley broadside:

A dainty clear river, was running them by,?
A bank of sweet violets, and primroses nigh:
Then said the young gallant, "Sit down by this spring,
We'll here take our pleasure till the nightingale sing.'

**Recordings** Raymond & Frederick Cantwell *Songs Of Seduction*; George Dunn *Chainmaker*; Neil Morris *Ozark Frontier*; Charlie Pitman *Old Uncle Tom Cobleigh And All*; Doug & Jack Wallin *Family Songs And Stories From The North Carolina Mountains*.

Alfred Emery

## THE KEYS OF CANTERBURY (ROUD 573)
## (MADAM I WILL GIVE TO THEE)

"Ma - dam I will give you a fine sil - ver pin, To pin up your hair ___ and your fine mus - e - line.

Ma - dam will you walk, ma - dam will you talk, Ma - dam will you go a - ny - where ___ with me?"

"Madam, I will give you a fine silver pin,
To pin up your hair and your fine mus-e-line.
Madam will you walk, madam will you talk,
Madam, will you go anywhere with me?

"Madam, I'll give you a petticoat of blue,
To wear in the morning and to dabble in the dew.
Madam will you walk, etc.

"Madam I'll give some boots of cork,
The one made in London, and the other made in York.
Madam, will you walk, etc.

"Will you accept a kiss of Canterbury,
When all the bells in England shall ring to make us merry?
Madam, will you walk, etc."

"Yes, I'll accept the kiss of Canterbury
When all the bells of England shall ring to make us merry.
And I'll walk, and I'll talk,
And I'll go anywhere with you"

"When you could, you would not.
Now you will, you shall not.
So fare you well, gay lady."

Widely collected in England, Scotland, Ireland, and North America, 'The Keys of Canterbury' is not known before the 19th century. The Hammond brothers collected a version that was interspersed with dancing, and Steve Gardham (*An East Riding Songster*, p59) records that other versions were performed at concerts where the performers would dress up for the parts. It has been argued therefore that the basic form of the song derives from the Elizabethan stage jig.

A Scottish text is titled 'The Deil's Courtship': when the man offers the woman he is courting a purse of gold, she agrees to go away with him, but before they have gone a mile she spies his cloven hoof, rather in the manner of 'The Demon Lover' (and in a reversal of the 'Riddles Wisely Expounded' scenario). This is most unusual, but the song does seem amenable to a wide range of interpretation from the comic reversal that comes at the end of Johnny Doughty's version to the slightly flowery sentiment of the 'If Thou Wilt Walk with Me' text collected by Alfred Williams.

'The Keys of Canterbury' sometimes shows some confusion with 'No, John, No' (Roud 146).

This version was collected by George Gardiner from Mr Harrington in Hampshire as 'Madam I Will Give To Thee'. The last three lines are a kind of coda, but Gardiner has not recorded a separate tune for it. We have split the second beat in bar four in two to accommodate the word "mus-e-line". The "kiss of Canterbury" is a corruption of the more usual "keys of Canterbury".

**Recordings** Johnny Doughty *The Voice Of The People, Vol. 12*; Oscar Brand & Jean Ritchie *O Love Is Teasin'*.

## PLEASANT AND DELIGHTFUL (ROUD 660)
As sung by Tommy Morrissey and Charlie Pitman.

Oh pleasant and delightful on a bright summer's morn,
O'er the hills and the meadows were covered in corn,
And the blackbirds and thrushes sang from every greenwood tree,
And the larks they sang melodious at the dawning of the day.
And the larks they sang melodious,
And the larks they sang melodious,?
And the larks they sang melodious at the dawning of the day.

Said the sailor to his true love as they walked one day,?
Said the sailor to his true love, "I am bound far away,?
I am bound for the Indies where the loud cannons roar,
I must go and leave my Nancy, she's the girl I adore.
I must go and leave my Nancy,
I must go and leave my Nancy,
I must go and leave my Nancy, she's the girl I adore."

Then the ring from her finger she instantly drew,
Saying, "Take this dear William and my heart goes too."
And as he embraced her, tears from her eyes fell,
Saying, "May I go along with you?" "Nay Nancy, farewell."
Saying, "May I go along with you?"
Saying, "May I go along with you?"
Saying, "May I go along with you?" "Nay Nancy, farewell."

"Fare thee well dearest Nancy, I can no longer stay,
For the topsail is hoisted and the anchor's aweigh.
Our good ship lies awaiting for the next flowing tide,
And if ever I return again, I'll make you my bride.
And if ever I return again,
And if ever I return again,
And if ever I return again, I'll make you my bride."

Charlie Pitman and
Tommy Morrissey

'Pleasant and Delightful' has been mostly collected in England, with a few records from Scotland and Canada. It seems to have been first printed, by Jennings, London, as 'The Sailor And His True Love' around 1809–15. Other versions tell of a soldier and his true-love. A poignant 'broken token' song of enforced separation, with a highly memorable tune, 'Pleasant and Delightful' has been particularly frequently collected in East Anglia.

**Recordings** Velvet Brightwell *Good Order!*; Shirley & Dolly Collins *Anthems In Eden*; Cliff Haslam & John Millar *Colonial And Revolutionary War Sea Songs And Chanteys*; Lou & Sally Killen *Bright Shining Morning*; Tommy Morrissey and Charlie Pitman *Uncle Tom Cobley And All*.

## SEVENTEEN COME SUNDAY (ROUD 277)
### (SIXTEEN COME SUNDAY) As sung by Jean Orchard.

CD TRACK 7

"Where are you go-ing to Hen-ry my son? Where are you go-ing to my pret-ty one?" "In the mea-dow, In the mea-dow, In the mea-dow while I'm sick to my heart, and I want to lay down and I want to lay down."

"Where are you going, my fair pretty maid?
Where are you going, my honey?"
She answered me, yes quite cheerfully,
"On an errand for my mammy."
With my rue dum a day, for the diddle-ay,
Right for the lor a li do.

"May I come too, my fair pretty maid?
May I come too, my honey?"
She answered me, yes quite cheerfully,
"You may for me and welcome."
With my rue dum a day, for the diddle-ay,
Right for the lor a li do.

Now she was tall, and her clothes were smart,
And her hair hanged down in ringlets,
Her eyes were blue, and her shoes were black,
And her buckles shone like silver.
With my rue dum a day, for the diddle-ay,
Right for the lor a li do.

Jean Orchard

"How old are you, my fair pretty maid?
How old are you, my honey?"
She answered me, yes quite cheerfully,
"I'll be sixteen come next Sunday."
With my rue dum a day, for the diddle ay,
Right for the lor a li do.

"What is your father, my fair pretty maid?
What may he be, my honey?"
She answered me, yes quite cheerfully,
"My father he's a farmer."
With my rue dum a day, for the diddle ay,
Right for the lor a li do.

"Will you marry me, my fair pretty maid?
Will you marry me, my honey?"
She answered me, yes quite cheerfully,
"I'll have to ask my mammy."
With my roo dum a day, for the diddle ay,
Right for the lor a li do.

"Now if I go down, to your mammy's house,
When the moon is shining clearly,
Will you come down, and let me in,
For your mammy she won't hear me."
With my rue dum a day, for the diddle ay,
Right for the lor a li do.

And he goes down, to her mammy's house,
When the moon was shining clearly,
And she goes down, and she lets him in,
And he laid in her arms till morning.
With my rue dum a day, for the diddle ay,
Right for the lor a li do.

This song is generally known as 'Seventeen Come Sunday', but Joan Orchard, a Gypsy from Devon, learned this version ('Sixteen Come Sunday') from her grandmother, Dehlia Cracker. Collected right across England, Scotland, Ireland, North America, and Australia, there is perhaps not a lot to say about the song other than that it is one of the truly popular folk songs about love – or at any rate, seduction. Broadside imprints include Watts (Birmingham), Sanderson (Edinburgh), Booksellers (Falkirk), Disley, Fortey, Hodges, Jennings, Paul, Pitts, Ryle, Such (London), Bebbington, Pearson (Manchester), Harkness (Preston), Dalton (York).

**Recordings** Mary Delaney *From Puck To* Appleby; Seamus Ennis *Traditional Songs Of Ireland*; Fairport Convention *Cropredy Box*; Bob Hart *A Broadside*; Joe Heaney *The Voice Of The People, Vol. 1*; Fred Jordan *A Shropshire Lad*; Walter Pardon *Put a Bit of Powder On It, Father*; Charlotte Renals *Catch Me If You Can*; Steeleye Span *Storm Force Ten*.

# Songs of murder

It is scarcely surprising to find that murder should be one of the perennial themes of English folk song, given how common it is in popular literature of all kinds, certainly since the 16th century. In Elizabethan times, murder stories were staged in plays such as *Arden of Faversham* and broadside ballads circulated relating the same events. The *Newgate Calendar* was a generic label given to various 18th- and 19th-century collections describing the careers of notorious criminals. They proved highly popular for their presentation of sensational and salacious detail within a framework of moral disapproval, very much in the manner of today's tabloid newspapers. The social commentator Henry Mayhew recorded in *London Labour and the London Poor* (1861–62) the comment of a street vendor: "There's nothing beats a stunning good murder, after all." Mayhew also noted that the broadside of 'The Murder of Maria Marten' supposedly sold more than a million and a half copies.

Murder ballads, like all the other kinds of murder literature, were often formulaic, relating time and again a similar sequence: the youth, upbringing, and past deeds of the criminal; the events leading up to the crime itself; pursuit, capture, confession, and trial; execution. Anne B. Cohen (*Poor Pearl, Poor Girl!*) has shown how exactly the same formulaic pattern can be identified both in 'murdered-sweetheart ballads' (which, as the term indicates, relate the murder of lovers) and in popular newspaper accounts of the same events. Some of these ballads were cast in the form of the criminal's supposed account of his own life, delivered as he faced the gallows – the so-called 'goodnight ballads' or 'sorrowful lamentations' – although it is most improbable that they were in fact composed by the condemned men and women.

Many of the broadsides were crude, ephemeral pieces, but some at least seem to have formed the basis of songs that became popular with singers. Usually the versions collected from singers have become much more concise, episodic, and dramatic than the often laboured accounts printed in broadsides, although in the case of ballads such as 'The Cruel Ship's Carpenter' and 'The Wexford Girl', later broadside texts seem to be much closer to those circulating among singers. Thus when murder ballads have survived as folk songs, they have often moved away from the tabloid news story and towards something more archetypal.

Folk songs about murder quite often invoke a supernatural element, suggesting that "murder will out", as the proverb has it. Equally, though, they are quite capable of dwelling on the cold-blooded cruelty of such acts. They reflect a real world in which people earnestly desire justice and order to prevail, and at the same time give a glimpse into the chaos that follows when, inevitably, such ideals break down.

# BANKS OF GREEN WILLOW (CHILD 24; ROUD 172)

Go home and get your father's gold,
And some of your mother's money,
And you shall go and board with me,
For to be my dear honey, for to be my dear honey.

He had not sailed many miles,
Not many miles nor scarcely,
Before he was troubled,
With her and her baby, with her and her baby.

He tied a napkin round her head,
And he tied it to the baby,
And then he throwed them overboard,
Both her and her baby, both her and her baby.

See how my love she will try to swim,
She how my love she will taver,
She how my love she will try to swim,
To the banks of green willow, to the banks of green willow.

I will have my coffin made for my love,
And I'll edge it all with yellow,
Then she shall be buried,
On the banks of green willow, on the banks of green willow.

'Banks Of Green Willow', also known as 'Bonnie Annie', is usually a rather cryptic song, which might equally be classed as a murder ballad or with songs concerning love in its various aspects. The story appears to concern a young woman who robs her parents and runs away to sea with her lover; then, during a storm, she gives birth to a baby. The sailors, taking the storm to be a sign that there is a wrongdoer on board, throw her overboard. The song can, though, make it appear that it is the lover who is responsible for the woman's death, as in this version. The motif of the wrongdoer on board ship, echoing the biblical story of Jonah (see the Book of Jonah 1) is the same as occurs in the murder ballad 'Captain Glen' (Roud 478).

Nevertheless, in spite of this apparent obscurity, 'Banks Of Green Willow' has proved especially popular with singers in England, and there are a handful of further records from Scotland, Ireland, and North America. Ralph Vaughan Williams used a phonograph to make a recording of the song in 1909, probably sung by David Clements of Basingstoke, Hampshire. His friend George Butterworth, who collected 300 songs, used it as the basis of an orchestral piece in 1913. He was killed in World War I.

This version was collected by Cecil Sharp from Louie Hooper at Hambridge, Somerset, on December 28th, 1903. He notes on the music manuscript that she originally sang "some of your father's gold", then omitted the "some", then, when reminded, put it back in. "It should clearly be omitted," he concluded. The word "taver" in the fourth verse is defined by the *Oxford English Dictionary* as "to strike out at random with the arms and legs". This is an economical account of the story, omitting the role of the sailors or sea captain. Sharp collected nine versions in Somerset alone. A version collected from William Spearing at Isle Brewers on April 6th, 1904 provides a different slant on the plot, with the girl appearing to sacrifice her life and that of her baby for the sake of the sailors:

It's of a sea captain O,
Lived by the seaside O,
He courted a pretty girl,
Till he got her by child O.

She went for to sail
[Line omitted]
Then had not sailed many miles O,
Before she was delivered of a beautiful baby.

"Oh take me back again,
Here's fifty pounds I will to thee,
To row me safe back again,
Both me and my baby."

"Oh I cannot turn the ship O,
For to turn it would lose too many lives O."
"It's better to lose my life,
Than so many O."

"Oh fetch me a napkin O
And bind my head so easy,
And overboard throw me,
Both me and my baby."

Oh they fetched him a napkin,
And bound her head so easy,
And overboard he threw his love,
Both she and her baby."

"Oh see how my love's a rollin'
Oh see how my love's a tumblin'
Oh fetch to me the lifeboat,
And bring my love back safe again,
Both she and her baby."

"Oh make my love a coffin,
Of the gold that shines yellow,
And she shall be buried,
On the banks of green willow."

**Recordings** Frankie Armstrong *And The Music Plays So Grand*; Martin Carthy *Sheerwater*; David Clements *A Century Of Song*; Cynthia Gooding *Queen Of Hearts: Early English Folk Songs*, as 'Bonnie Annie'; Nic Jones *Nic Jones*; Ewan MacColl & Peggy Seeger *Popular Scottish Songs*, as 'Bonnie Annie'; Tony Rose *On Banks Of Green Willow*.

## BRUTON TOWN (ROUD 18)

In Bruton Town there lives a farmer,
Who had two sons and one daughter dear,
By day and by night they was courting,
To fill their parents' heart with fear.

She told her secrets to no other,
But unto her brother she told them to.
"I think our servant courts our sister,
I think they has a great mind to wed.
I'll put an end to all their courtship.
I'll send him silent to his grave."

A day of hunting was prepared,
Thorny woods and valley where briars grow.
And they did this young man a-murder,
And into the brake his fair body thrown.

"Welcome home, my dear young brothers,
Pray tell to me, where's that servant man?"
"We've a-left him behind where we've been a-hunting,
We've a-left him behind where no man can find."

She went to bed, crying and lamenting,
Lamenting for her heart's delight.
She slept, she dreamed, she saw him lay by her,
Covered all over in a gore of bled.

Then she rose early the very next morning,
Unto the yonder brook she went.
There she found her own dear jew-y-el,
Covered all over in a gore of blood.

She took her handkerchief out of her pocket,
For to wipe his eyes for he could not see.
"And since my brothers have been so cruel
To take your tender life away,
One grave shall hold us both together,
And along, along with you to death I'll stay."

Under various titles, such as 'Bruton Town', 'The Bramble Briar', and 'The Brake of Briars', this is a classic song of the kind sometimes labelled "family opposition to lovers", and at the same time a classic murder ballad. The story has a long pedigree and can be traced through the *Decameron* (*c*1358) of Boccaccio (Day 4, Book 5), several versions by the German poet and dramatist Hans Sachs (1494–1576), and Keats's *Isabella; or, The Pot of Basil* (1820).

The ending of the song varies a good deal – the brothers flee in a ship and are drowned; the sister poisons both herself and her two brothers; the brothers are arrested, imprisoned, and hanged – and the supernatural dimension, comprising the dead lover's appearance in a dream, may be more or less apparent. Collected in both England and the USA, there is just a single (unconfirmed) report of a broadside printing in America. The element of class difference is obvious in this version, motivating the brothers' hostility towards their sisters' chosen partner, and giving this murder ballad something of the edge of a protest piece.

This version was collected by Cecil Sharp from Mrs Overd, at Langport, in Somerset, on August 4th, 1904. Note that the second and final verses have six lines, compared with the usual four. There are other inconsistencies. In verse four of the typescript, "brook" has been changed to "brake", meaning a thicket, though it turns back into a brook in verse six. "Bled", in verse five, is in the original typescript but is probably a mis-hearing or mis-typing of "blood".

When he came to produce a printed version of the song, for *Folk Songs From Somerset*, Sharp noted that both versions of the song he had collected were "very corrupt". He edited them into something more coherent and consistent. Verse two here becomes two verses:

One told his secret to none other,
But unto his brother this he said:
"I think our servant courts our sister,
I think they have a mind to wed.

"If he our servant courts our sister,
That maid from such a shame I'll save.
I'll put an end to all their courtship,
And send him silent to his grave.

To make the sixth verse regular, he adapted the two last verses from a version he collected from George Whitcombe at Meare in Somerset, 18 months later:

She took her kerchief from her pocket,
And wiped his eyes though he was blind.
"Because he was my own true lover
My own true lover and friend of mine.

And since my brothers have been so cruel,
To take your tender sweet life away,
One grave shall hold us both together,
And along with you in death I'll stay."

**Recordings** Blowzabella *A Richer Dust*; Alex Campbell *Yours Aye, Alex*; Davy Graham *Large As Life And Twice As Natural*; Tim Hart & Maddy Prior *Folk Songs Of Olde England Vol.1*; Carolyne Hughes *Blackdog & Sheepcrook*; Pentangle *Sweet Child*.

# THE CONSTANT FARMER'S SON (ROUD 675)

There was a wealth-y nob-le-man in Lon-don Town did dwell, He had but one daugh-ter, a far-mer loved her well. She was ad-mired by lads and squires but all their hopes were vain,— For there was one, 'twas a far-mer's son, young Ma-ry's heart could gain.

There was a wealthy nobleman in London Town did dwell,
He had but one daughter, a farmer loved her well.
She was admired by lads and squires but all their hopes was vain,
For there was one, 'twas a farmer's son, young Mary's heart could gain.

Long time young William courted her, fixed the wedding day,
Her parents they consented, but her brothers they did say,
"There was a lord who pledged his word and him she shall not shun,
We will betray and then we'll slay the constant farmer's son."

As she lay on her pillow, she had a dreadful dream,
She dreamt she saw his body, down by a crystal stream.
Then she arose, put on her clothes, to seek her love's return.
When dead and cold she did behold her constant farmer's son.

Hunger it came creeping on, poor girl she shrieked with woe,
To try to find his murderers she straightaway home did go,
Saying "Parents dear, you soon shall hear, a dreadful deed is done,
In yonder vale lies dead and pale my constant farmer's son."

Up stepped the eldest brother, "Indeed it is not me."
Then up stepped the other and swore more bitterly.
Young Mary said, "Don't turn so red, nor try the laws to shun,
For you done the deed and you shall bleed, for my constant farmer's son."

'The Constant Farmer's Son' tells essentially the same story as 'Bruton Town'. It appeared on numerous 19th-century broadsides, with imprints including Russell (Birmingham), Stewart (Carlisle), Lindsay (Glasgow), Elliott (Hereford), Fordyce (Hull and Newcastle), Catnach, Fortey, Hodges, Pitts, Ryle, Sharp, Taylor (London), Fordyce, Ross, Walker (Newcastle), King (Oxford), Harkness (Preston), Dalton (York), Birmingham (Dublin). Collected versions come from England, Scotland, Ireland, and North America. Class is again central to the plot of this song, with the brothers determined that their sister should have an advantageous marriage.

Collected by George Gardiner from Mrs Barnes, in Hampshire.

**Recordings** Josie Connors *From Puck To Appleby*; James McDermott *The Hardy Sons Of Dan*.

A 19th-century broadside of 'The Constant Farmer's Son', printer unknown.

# THE CRUEL SHIP'S CARPENTER (ROUD 15)

In fair Worcester city in Worcestershire,
A handsome young damsel she lived there,
A handsome young man courted her to be his dear,
And he was by trade a ship-carpenter.

Now the king wanted seamen to go on to the sea,
Which caused this young damsel to sigh and to say,
"Oh William, dear William, don't you go to sea,
Remember the vow that you made to me."

It was early one morning before it was day,
He went to his Polly these words he did say,
"Oh Polly, Oh Polly, you must go with me,
Before we are married our friends for to see."

He led her through groves and valleys so deep,
Which caused this young damsel to sigh and to weep,
Saying, "William, dear William, you've led me astray,
On purpose my innocent life to betray."

"It's true, it's true," these words he did say,
"For all this night long I've been digging your grave,
Your grave has been open, the spade standing by."
It caused this young damsel to sigh and to cry.

It was early one morning before it was day,
Our captain came up, these words he did say,
"There's murder on board, which has lately been done,
For our ship she's in mourning and can't sail along."

Up stepped one, "Indeed it's not me."
Up stepped another, the same he did say.
Up stepped young William, he stamped and he swore,
"Indeed it's not me, sir, I vow and declare."

As he was a-turning from the captain with speed,
He saw his dear Polly, it made his heart bleed.
She stripped and she tore him, she tore him in three,
For murdering her innocent baby and she.

'The Cruel Ship's Carpenter' has been very widely collected in England, Scotland, Ireland, and North America, and printed on numerous broadsides and in chapbooks from the 18th century onwards, under titles such as 'The Gosport Tragedy; or, The Perjured Ship-Carpenter' and 'Polly's Love; or, The Cruel Ship Carpenter'. 19th-century imprints include Pratt (Birmingham), Bennett and Boyes (Brighton), Marshall (Bristol), Willey (Cheltenham), Turner (Coventry), Besley, Healey (Exeter), Forth (Hull), Beaumont (Leeds), Kiernan/Duckett (Liverpool), Batchelar, Catnach, Davenport, Disley, Evans, Fortey, Hodges, Jennings, Pitts, Such (London), Bebbington, Pearson, Swindells, Wrigley (Manchester), Walker (Newcastle), Harkness (Preston), Pierce (Southborough). The ballad was also printed in American songsters.

Versions collected from singers are similar to the 'Polly's Love' broadsides and are much pared-down in comparison with the earlier, 18th-century broadsides, suggesting the possibility of a conscious rewriting of the story. However, the central elements, including the supernatural apparition, remain. David C. Fowler in a closely argued article ('The Gosport Tragedy: The Story of a Ballad') has identified the ship named in the early broadsides as HMS *Bedford*, whose carpenter, John Billson, died on September 25th, 1726, and has reconstructed a possible scenario which means that the ballad may well be based on fact and therefore date from 1727.

In any case, the shipboard discovery of murder is a well-established motif, which is also encountered in 'Brown Robyn's Confession (Child 57; Roud 3882) and 'Captain Glen', or 'The New York Trader' (Roud 478). More generally, the fear aroused by the presence of a wrongdoer on board ship is to be found in the Book of Jonah.

This version was collected by George Gardiner from Mrs Barnes in Hampshire, England. It is very close to the common 19th-century broadside version sometimes known as 'Polly's Love', but it omits three verses that are crucial for the plot. Here are three taken from a broadside printed by Harkness in Preston some time between 1840 and 1866. They come after verse five above.

"O William, O William, O pardon my life,
I never will covet to be your wife.
I will travel the country to set you quite free,
O pardon, O pardon my baby and me."

"No pardon I'll give thee, there's no time to stand,"
So with that he had a knife in his hand,
He stabb'd her heart till the blood it did flow,
Then into the grave her fair body did throw.

He covered her up so safe and secure,
Thinking no one could find her he was sure;
Then he went on board to sail the world round,
Before that the murder could ever be found.

**Recordings** Harry Cox *The Voice Of The People, Vol. 17*; George Dunn *Chainmaker*; Sam Larner *Now Is The Time For Fishing*; A.L. Lloyd *Leviathan!*, as 'The Cruel Ship's Captain'; Wiggy Smith *Band Of Gold*; Dave Van Ronk *Inside*, as 'The Cruel Ship's Captain'; Mike Waterson *Mike Waterson*.

# LAMKIN (LANKIN) (CHILD 93; ROUD 6)

Said my Lord to my Lady as he mounted his horse, "Beware of Long Lankin that lives in the moss." Said my Lord to my Lady as he rode away, "Beware of Long Lankin that lives in the hay."

Said my Lord to my Lady as he mounted his horse,
"Beware of Long Lankin that lives in the moss."

Said my Lord to my Lady as he rode away,
"Beware of Long Lankin that lives in the hay.

"Let the doors be all bolted and the windows all pinned,
And leave not a hole for a mouse to creep in."

So he kissed his fair lady, and he rode away,
And he was in fair London before the break of day.

The doors were all bolted and the windows all pinned,
Except one little window where Long Lankin crept in.

"Where is the Lord of this house?" said Long Lankin.
"He's asleep in his cradle," said the false nurse to him.

"We'll prick him, we'll prick him all over with a pin,
And that'll make my Lady to come down to him."

So he pricked him, he pricked him all over with a pin,
And the nurse held a basin for the blood to flow in.

"Oh nurse how you slumber, Oh nurse how you sleep.
You leave my little son Johnson to cry and to weep.

"Oh nurse how you slumber, Oh nurse how you snore,
You leave my little son Johnson to cry and to roar."

"I've tried him with apples, I've tried him with pears.
Come down my fair lady and rock him in your chairs.

"I've tried him with milk, I've tried him with pap,
Come down my fair lady and nurse him in your lap."

"How can I come down, 'tis so late in the night,
There's no fire burning nor candle to give light."

Her maiden looked out from the turret so high,
And she saw her master from London riding by.

"You have three silver mantles as bright as the sun,
Come down my fair lady all by the light of one."

"Oh master, Oh master, don't lay the blame on me.
'Twas the false nurse and Lankin that killed your fair Lady."

My Lady came down the stairs thinking no harm.
Long Lankin stood ready for to catch her in his arms.

Long Lankin was hung on a gibbet so high
And the false nurse was burnt in a fire close by.

Collected widely in England, Scotland, Ireland, and North America, various attempts have been made to link 'Lamkin' with actual places – Balwearie Castle in Scotland, for example – but none of these have been very convincing. The ballad can, however, be traced back to the 18th century, in both England and Scotland; and a single broadside printing, with the imprint of Pitts (London), is known from the early 19th century.

Although in some of the Scottish versions the atrocity seems motivated clearly enough, in that Lamkin (or Lankin) is a mason who has not been paid for his work, in many versions there is no such explicit explanation. Anne Gilchrist argued that two distinct strands of the story arose at an early date, perhaps in the Scottish Border region, as a result of the loss of the beginning of the tale which explained the motive for the crime; they also acquired different tunes, one Scottish and one English in character (JEFDSS, 1.1 (1932), 1–32).

The problem of motivation has continued to trouble scholars. Some suggestions have revolved around the name Lamkin, which has been understood as an ironic taunt aimed at the builder's apparent meekness, or else as derived from an Irish term meaning an outcast leper. Lord Wearie himself has been identified with the fairy folk or the Devil. While 'Lamkin' does not have European analogues as such, the blood shed in the ballad has also been related to a blood-sacrifice required so that a building should stand firm, as in the Hungarian ballad of 'Clement Mason'. Finally, Lamkin himself has been identified with the Devil. Child referred to "the bloody mason" as "the terror of countless nurseries" – that much is not in dispute.

This version was collected by Cecil Sharp from an Anglican nun, Sister Emma (71), at Clewer, in Berkshire, England, on February 27th, 1909. She called it 'Lankin'. Sharp used a different version, collected in Cambridgeshire, in his own song books, but this melody and words were used by Ralph Vaughan Williams and A.L. Lloyd in the 1959 *Penguin Book Of English Folk Songs*.

**Recordings** Ben Butcher *The Voice Of The People, Vol. 3*; Martin Carthy & Dave Swarbrick *But Two Came By*; George Fosbury *Classic Ballads Of Britain And Ireland, Vol.1*; George Fradley *It Was On A Market Day, Vol. 1*; The Love Hall Tryst *Songs Of Misfortune*; Steeleye Span *Commoner's Crown*.

# LORD RANDAL (LORD RENDLE) (CHILD 12; ROUD 10)

"Where have you been all the day, Henery my son?
Where have you been all the day, you're a pretty one."
"Out in the green fields, out in the green fields.
Make my bed quick, a pain in my head,
And I want to lie down, I want to lie down."

"What have you been eating of, Henery my son?
What have you been eating of, my pretty one?"
"Eels, mother, eels, mother.
Make my bed quick,"
etc.

"What will you leave your father, Henery my son?
What will you leave your father, my pretty one?"
"Land and houses, mother, land and houses, mother.
Make my bed quick,"
etc.

"What will you leave your mother, Henery my son?
What will you leave your mother, my pretty one?"
"Coals and horses, mother, coals and horses, mother.
Make my bed quick,"
etc.

"What will you leave your brother, Henery my son?
What will you leave your brother, my pretty one?"
Hen and chicken, mother, hen and chicken, mother.
Make my bed quick,"
etc.

"What will you leave your sister, Henery my son?
What will you leave your sister, my pretty one?"
"A rope to hang her, mother, a rope to hang her, mother.
Make my bed quick,"
etc.

Another classic murder ballad, with an astonishingly large record of collection throughout the English-speaking world, 'Lord Randal' is also remarkable for its enigmatic story. The reason why Randal's true-love should have poisoned him invariably remains obscure, and the occasional introduction into the plot of a criminal relative – sister (as in Mrs Bond's version), brother-in-law, father, grandmother, or wicked stepmother – does nothing to clarify the motive behind it.

In the absence of an explanation, the song can be taken as a fine example of the narrative compression characteristic of the Child ballads. The name Randal, Ronald, Rendal, Randolph, Tiranti, Henry, varies more than anything else. The ballad has, however, given rise to various comic burlesques – including versions along the 'O mother be quick, I want to be sick, and lay me down to die' pattern – as well as a 'nursery branch' of the story in 'The Little Wee Croodin Doo'. It is also (possibly) the model for the comic song 'Billy Boy', which has proved nearly as popular with singers as 'Lord Randal' itself. Even the melodies that are recognizably variants of the 'Villikins and Dinah' tune are, according to Bronson, part of an overall tune family, although the 'Croodin Doo' and 'Billy Boy' tunes appear to be distinct.

'Lord Randal' has several European analogues and an Italian broadside of 1629 suggests that the ballad story was known at an early date. However, there is no clear record of it in English prior to the 19th century, although Scottish versions of 'Billy Boy' appear in the late 18th century. A rather unconvincing attempt has, however, been made to relate Randal to Randal III, sixth Earl of Chester (d1232) (*JFSS*, 3.1 (1907), 44).

Ray Driscoll sang what appears to be a unique song, 'The Wild, Wild Berry', which tells more of a story and is sung to a version of the 'Dives and Lazarus'/'Star of the County Down' tune. 'The Wild, Wild Berry' has the name Randal and is undoubtedly related to the ballad, but it is equally certainly a distinct song in its own right.

This version was collected by Cecil Sharp from Mrs Bond at Barrington, Somerset, on August 23rd, 1904. It is recorded as 'Lord Rendle', and is one of those puzzling cases in which the words written down under the musical notation do not match the words apparently collected at the same time. Nor are the words easy to fit to the tune. It also omits parts of the narrative. In *One Hundred English Folksongs* Sharp used a version "compiled from different sets", which makes things clearer:

"Where have you been all the day, Rendal my son?
Where have you been all the day, my pretty one?"
"I've been to my sweetheart, mother,
I've been to my sweetheart, mother.
Make my bed soon,
For I'm sick to my heart and I fain would lie down."

"What have you been eating, Rendal my son?
What have you been eating, my pretty one?"
"Oh eels and eel broth, mother,"
etc.

"Where did she get them from, Rendal my son?
Where did she get them from, my pretty one?"
"From hedges and ditches, mother,"
etc.

"What was the colour of their skin, Rendal my son?
What was the colour of their skin, my pretty one?"
"Oh spickit and sparkit, mother,"
etc.
"What will you leave your father, Rendal my son?
What will you leave your father, my pretty one?"
"My land and houses, mother,"
etc.

"What will you leave your mother, Rendal my son?
What will you leave your mother, my pretty one?"
"My gold and silver, mother,"
etc.

"What will you leave your brother, Rendal my son?
What will you leave your brother, my pretty one?"
"My cows and horses, mother,"
etc.

"What will you leave your lover, Henery my son?
What will you leave your lover, my pretty one?"
"A rope to hang her, mother,"
etc.


**Recordings** Battlefield Band *Out For The Night*; Martin Carthy *Shearwater*; Mary Delaney *The Voice Of The People, Vol. 17*; Johnny Doughty *Up In The North And Down In The South*, as 'Billy Boy'; Ray Driscoll *A Century Of Song*, as 'The Wild, Wild Berry'; George Dunn *Chainmaker*; Gordon Hall *Good Things Enough*; John MacDonald *The Voice Of The People, Vol. 13*; The Prodigals *Dreaming In Hell's Kitchen*; Paddy Reilly *From Puck To Appleby*; Jean Ritchie *Ballads From Her Appalachian Family Tradition*; Jeannie Robertson *Classic Ballads Of Britain And Ireland, Vol.1*; Buffy Sainte-Marie *Fire & Fleet & Candlelight*.

# POISON IN A GLASS OF WINE (OXFORD CITY)
(ROUD 218)

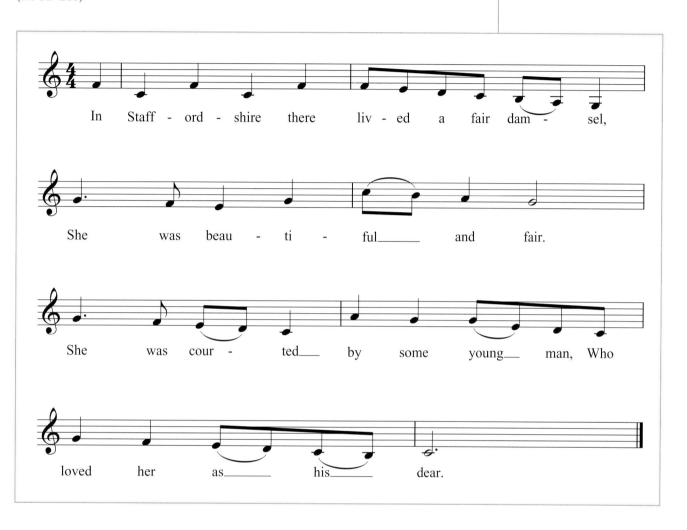

In Staffordshire there lived a fair damsel,
She was beautiful and fair,
She was courted by some young man,
Who loved her as his dear.

He says, "My dear, come let us marry,
Marry without more delay.
I will work both late and early,
If you my wedded wife will be."

She says, "My dear, come let us tarry,
Tarry for the space of a year or two,
And by that time we shall see,
How the cares of life doth go."

There was a ball of dancing given,
This young man was to be there,
And quickly his true love followed after,
Soon to prove her ruin there.

He saw her dancing with some other,
Jealous thoughts came in his mind,
How to destroy his own true lover,
In his heart he could not find.

In his pocket he concealed,
Poison strong he did conceal,
This in a glass of wine he gave her,
Soon to prove her overthrow.

"Take me home to my mother,
Take me home, my dear," she cried.
"It was that glass of wine you gave me,
Made me ill as ill can be."

"It was poison that I gave thee,
I took some of the same myself,
So in each other's arms we will die together,
Come all young men, don't jealous be.

"Jealous young men, jealous old men,
Jealous as all men be,
So in each other's arms we will die together,
Come all young men, don't jealous be."

This widespread song is a classic tale of jealousy, with a hint of class tension in some versions where it is a servant who is in love with a lady. It goes by various titles, including 'Down the Green Groves, 'Young Maria', and 'Oxford City' – and other places may substitute for Oxford, as here. Although particularly well represented in England, 'Poison in a Glass of Wine' has also been collected in Scotland, Ireland, North America, and Tristan da Cunha.

The song may have originated with the broadside trade. Certainly the number of extant imprints testifies to its lasting popularity. They include Jackson, Pratt (Birmingham), Walden (Gloucester), Birt, Catnach, Fortey, Hodges, Pitts (London), Livsey, Wheeler (Manchester), Fordyce (Newcastle), Harkness (Preston). Although singers have often held that it tells a true story, there is no known factual basis.

There are many recordings. In 1908, the great Lincolnshire singer Joseph Taylor made a 78rpm recording of the song, under the title 'Worcester City', for the Gramophone Company, which can also be heard on the LP *Unto Brigg Fair*. Recordings of more recent English singers are quite common, and there are also a few recordings from America, such as that by Norah and Garrett Arwood, who also play the tune on the fiddle. Bluegrass pioneers The Stanley Brothers, who came from the southern Appalachians, recorded the song in 1948, as 'A Little Glass Of Wine', helping to turn it into a bluegrass standard.

This version, recorded as 'Oxford City', was collected from James Hiscock at Bartley, Hampshire, in September 1908, by George Gardiner.

**Recordings** Garrett and Norah Arwood *Far In The Mountains*; Louie Fuller *The Voice Of The People, Vol. 13*; Fred Jordan *A Shropshire Lad*; Magpie Lane *Oxford Ramble*, as 'Oxford City'; George 'Pop' Maynard *Just Another Saturday Night*, as 'Oxford City'; Freda Palmer *Up In The North And Down In The South*; Pentangle *One More Road*; Ralph Stanley & The Clinch Mountain Boys *Featuring Keith Whitley And Ricky Skaggs*, as 'Little Glass Of Wine'; Alex, Belle, Cathie and Sheila Stewart *The Stewarts Of Blair*; Joseph Taylor *The Voice Of The People, Vol. 3*, as 'Worcester City'.

# THE THREE BUTCHERS (JOVIAL BUTCHERS) (ROUD 17)

It's of two jolly butcher boys, as I have heard men say,
A-going to some market, some money for to pay.
As they were riding along the road, as fast as they could ride,
"Oh stop, oh stop," says Johnson, "For I hears some woman cry."

"I will not stop," says William. "I will not stop," says he.
"Then I will stop," says Johnson, "For I never was afraid of thee."
Then Johnson lightened from his horse, and viewed the place all round.
He spied some naked woman with her hair pinned down to the ground.

"How came you here?" said Johnson, "How came you here fast bound?
How came you here stark naked with your hair pinned down to the ground?
"'Twas of three highway robbers, my hands and feet they bound.
They left me here stark naked with my hair pinned down to the ground."

Then Johnson being a valiant man, of courage stout and bold,
He pulled his coat from off his back to shelter her from the cold.
Then Johnson took her up behind him and so gently rode along
Until he came to some lonesome place where this woman she jumped down.

She put her fingers to her ears so loudly screeched and squalled,
When out jumped three highway robbers all from those bushes and boughs,
Then Johnson fired and killed two and the other he did not mind,
Until this wicked woman she stabbed him from behind.

She shall be hung in chains so strong, in chains of iron strong,
She killed the finest butcher boy that ever the sun shone on.

'The Three Worthy Butchers of the North' (*Roxburghe Ballads*, VII, 59) or 'A New Ballad of the Three Merry Butchers' (*Pepys Ballads*, II, 176; *Roxburghe Ballads*, VII, 62) was printed on London broadsides of the 17th century, and the ballad continued to enjoy a healthy life in broadside print. Imprints include Wright (Birmingham), Bennett and Boyes (Brighton), Marshall (Bristol), Ford (Chesterfield), Hoggett, Walker (Durham), Andrews, Beaumont (Leeds), Batchelar, Catnach, Hodges, Pitts, Such (London), Bebbington (Manchester), Marchbank (Newcastle), Williams (Portsea), Forth (Pocklington), Harkness (Preston), Johnson (York). As might be expected, the song has been frequently collected in England, Scotland, and North America.

It is not clear that there was any factual basis to the story, even in the 17th century. The names of the butchers vary – Ips, Gips, and Johnson, or Gibson, Wilson, and Johnson, and occasionally they are huntsmen or sportsmen – but that of the hero, Johnson, usually remains constant. Occasional versions collected from singers have the butchers bravely fight off their assailants, but generally the story is one of treachery and cruel murder perpetrated against honest, respectable tradesmen.

This version was collected by George Gardiner from F. Osman in Hampshire, who called it 'Jovial Butchers'. There are only two butchers in his version.

**Recordings** Damien Barber *The Furrowed Field*; Harry Cox *The Bonny Labouring Boy*; Mary Drain *Ozark Folksongs*, as 'Dixon And Johnson'; Gryphon *Gryphon*; Walter Pardon *A World Without Horses*; Tony Rose *Young Hunting*; Pete Seeger *American Ballads*; Wiggy Smith *Band Of Gold*.

A broadside version of 'The Three Butchers', printer unknown but probably 18th century.

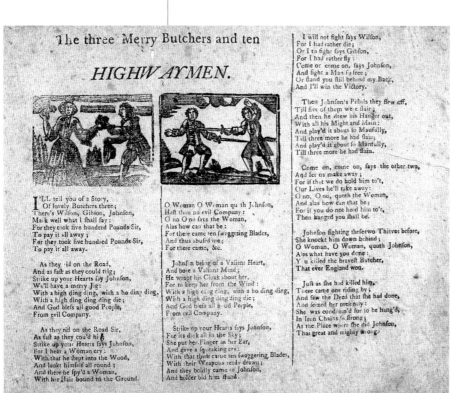

# THE WEXFORD GIRL (THE MILLER'S APPRENTICE)
(ROUD 263)

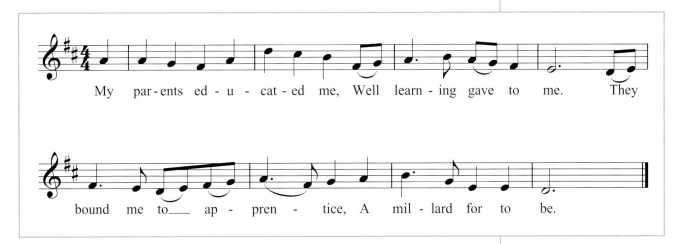

My par-ents ed-u-cat-ed me, Well learn-ing gave to me. They bound me to__ ap-pren-tice, A mil-lard for to be.

My parents educated me,
Well learning they gave to me,
They bound me to a prentice,
A millard for to be.

Till I fell in love with a pretty girl,
With a dark and rolling eye,
I promised her that I would marry her,
If she would with me lie.

I courted her for six long months
A little now and then,
Till I thought it a shame to marry her,
My being so young a man.

I went unto her father's house,
The hour if it were night,
I asked her that we might walk,
And sit and talk about her wedding-day.

I caught her by her curly locks,
And I dragged her through the green,
Until I came to the river-side,
And I throwed her body in.

I went unto my master's house,
The hour of twelve that night,
My master rose and let me in,
By the striking of a light.

He asked me, he questioned me,
What stained my hands and clothes.
The only answer I thought fit,
Was the bleeding of my nose.

I got into bed that night,
But there no rest could take,
For the drowning of my own true love,
A-hanged I shall be.

... so many days after
I was down at William Jones house,
And her body came floating,
Down by the tide.

A broadside version, called
'Bloody Miller', printer and
date unknown.

## Bloody Miller

My parents educated me, good learning gave to me,
They bound me prentice to a miller with whom I did agree
I fell a courting a lass with a black and rolling aye,
I promised to marry her if she would with me lie.

I courted her for six long months a little now and then,
I was ashamed to marry her I being so young a man,
Till at length she proved with child by me she thus to me did say
Ah Johnny do but marry me or else for love I die.

I went unto her sisters house at eight o'clock at night
And little did the fair one know I owed her any spite
I ask'd her if she'd take a walk down though the meadows walk
And there we'd sit and chat awhile and fix the wedding day.

I took a stick out of the hedge and hit her on the crown,
The blood from this young innocent came trickling on the ground
She on bed bended knees did fall and loud for mercy call,
Saying Johnny dear dont murder me for I am big with child.

I took her by her yellow locks & dragged her to the ground
And we came to a river side where I threw her body down,
With blood from this young innocent my hands & feet dyed
If you'd seen her in her in bloo n she might have been my bride

I went unto my masters house at ten o'clock at night,
My master getting out of bed and striking up a light,
He asked me and questioned me what dyed my hand & feet,
I made him a fll answer I'd been bleeding at the nose.

I then took up a candle to light myself to bed,
And all that blessed long night my own true love lay dead
And all that blessed long night no rest I could find,
For the burning flames of torment round my eyes did play.

In two or three days after this fair maid she was missed,
I was taken on suspicion and into prison cast,
Her sisters prosecuted me for my awful doubts
Her sister prosecuted me for asking of her out,

In 2 or 3 days after this fair maid she Was found,
Came floating by her mother's door near to Waterford town,
The Judge and Jury the quickly did agree,
For the murder of my troo love that hang &, I must be.

A classic example of the 'murdered-sweetheart' ballad, 'The Wexford/Oxford/ Lexington/Knoxville Girl' – the titles vary greatly – can be traced back to 18th-century broadsides entitled 'The Berkshire Tragedy; or, The Wittam Miller'. Later broadsides, with imprints including Cheney (Banbury), Pratt, Taylor, Wrighton (Birmingham), Whinham (Carlisle), Turner (Coventry), Fordyce (Hull), Catnach, Disley, Evans, Pitts (London), Fordyce (Newcastle), and Sefton (Worcester) give the title as 'The Cruel Miller' or 'The Bloody Miller' and tell the story in a more concise, episodic manner, closer to the versions collected from singers.

The earlier broadsides include much circumstantial detail, including the murderer's strategy of advertising in *The Post-Boy*, a genuine early-18th-century periodical, and offering a reward for the discovery of his sweetheart's body. Nevertheless, this particular ballad has not been tied to any identified event. There is, though, a broadside of the late 17th century, also titled 'The Bloody Miller', among the *Pepys Ballads* (II, 156), which tells a closely similar story, albeit in a poetically rather more crude manner, and which relates to the real-life murder of one Anne Nicols by Francis Cooper which took place near Shrewsbury on February 10th, 1684.

'The Wexford Girl', under its various titles, has been widely collected in England, Scotland, and North America, with one record from Tristan da Cunha. Although it is unwise to read too much into such things, there appear to be a large number of extant recordings of this ballad from female singers.

This version was collected by Cecil Sharp from William Spearing at Isle Brewers, Somerset, England, on April 6th, 1904. Question marks on the typescript suggest that whoever typed them out (probably Maud Karpeles) couldn't make sense of Sharp's record of the last verse. "Millard" is a regional variant of "miller". Spearing called the song 'The Miller's Apprentice'.

**Recordings** Carter Family *In The Shadow Of Clinch Mountain*, as 'Never Let The Devil Get The Upper Hand Of You'; Nick Cave & The Bad Seeds *B-Sides And Rarities* as 'Knoxville Girl'; Mary Delaney *From Puck To Appleby,* as 'Town Of Linsborough'; Mary Ann Haynes *Here's Luck To A Man*; The Lemonheads *Car Button Cloth* as 'Knoxville Girl'; The Louvin Brothers *Tragic Songs Of Life* as 'Knoxville Girl'; Ewan MacColl *Scots Street Songs* as 'Knoxville Girl'; The Outlaws *The Outlaws* as 'Knoxville Girl'.

William Spearing

# Songs of sailors and the sea

Songs about sailors and the sea are well represented among English folk songs. The sea was, of course, an important occupation over a long period of time, for fishing and trade, as well as the military. The sailor's occupation, involving parting and lengthy absences, also provides an ideal plot line for songs of several quite different kinds. 'The Dark-Eyed Sailor', for example, included among the love songs in this book, provides an ideal setting for a 'broken-token' song dealing with the reunion of long-parted lovers.

While songs such as 'The Greenland Whale Fishery' describe the sailor's life, 'Adieu Sweet Lovely Nancy' is another tender song about parted lovers, and 'The Female Cabin Boy' is representative of a class of cross-dressing ballads which see resourceful females take on male roles in order to stay with their lovers. 'Admiral Benbow' celebrates a naval hero; there was also a whole raft of songs concerning the death of Nelson, though few seem to have survived among singers.

'The Mermaid' and 'The Golden Vanity' are two sea songs with an estimable pedigree (the earliest printed texts of 'The Golden Vanity' mention Sir Walter Raleigh), both of which have been frequently collected among sailors. Although sea shanties represent a rather different kind of song, often with quite unstable texts, and space prohibits their inclusion here, it is worth noting that songs like 'The Golden Vanity' were sometimes adapted to such use. Shanties were used on board sailing ships to provide a rhythmic accompaniment to work involving hauling on the ropes, and were common in merchant shipping during the days of sail.

Old sailors like Captain Lewis (right), of Minehead, Somerset, were among the most fruitful sources of songs for the early collectors.

Captain Lewis

# ADIEU, SWEET LOVELY NANCY (ROUD 165)

Here's adieu my lovely Nancy, ten thousand times adieu,
I'm just now going for to leave you in search of something new.
Come and change your ring with me, my love, come and change your ring with me,
Let that be as a token, whiles I am on the sea.

Whiles I am on the sea, my loves, who knows not where I am,
Kind letters I will write to you from every foreign land.
Kind letters I will write to you with best of my goodwill,
Oh let my body be where he will, my heart be with you still.

You see a storm arising and we are all confound,
Looking out every moment that we shall all be drown'd,
Cheer up, never be fainthearted, we shall see our girls again,
In spite of all our danger, we'll plough the raging main.

There's tailors, tinkers, shoemakers, lies snoring fast asleep,
Whiles we poor jolly sailors bold lies ploughing on the deep,
Not a hedge nor bush to shelter us nor keep us from the cold,
But on the seas we must abide like jolly sailors bold.

Our officers command us, for them we must obey,
Expecting every moment that we shall be cast away,
So now the war's all over, and we are safe ashore,
We'll sing and we'll dance my boys and we'll do as we done before.

'Adieu, My Lovely Nancy' is as much love song as sea song, telling of faithful love between a sailor and his sweetheart, made more poignant by the inevitable departures that the sailor's life entails. It should not be confused with 'Farewell Nancy' (Roud 527), also known as 'The Sailor's Farewell', which shares the theme but has a quite different story and tune. Both have been popular with singers in England, as well as Ireland, Canada, the USA, with 'Adieu, My Lovely Nancy' collected as far away as Australia and Tristan da Cunha.

Broadside imprints of 'Adieu, My Lovely Nancy' (some with the title 'The New Sailor's Farewell') include Jackson, Pratt, Russell, Wright (Birmingham), Ford (Chesterfield), Walker (Durham), Ward (Ledbury), Thompson (Liverpool), Catnach, Fortey, Pitts (London), Pearson, Swindells (Manchester), Fordyce (Newcastle), Henson (Northampton), Williams (Portsea), Harkness (Preston), Sefton (Worcester).

Printings of 'Farewell Nancy' appear to be fewer. Imprints include Bebbington (Manchester), Jennings, Pitts (London), as well as Baird (Cork), and Birmingham (Dublin). It also appears in the *Vocal Library* (1820).

This version of 'Adieu, My Lovely Nancy' was collected by Henry Hammond from Joseph Elliott at Todber in Dorset, in September 1905. The original notation superimposes two slight variants of the tune on top of each other, probably reflecting the fact that it was sung differently each time. By way of compromise, we have used one version for the first time through the tune and another for the second. Most versions of the song have "token of true love" at the end of the first verse, which makes the meaning more clear.

**Recordings** Altan *Local Ground*; Blue Murder *No One Stands Alone*; Boys Of The Lough *Lonesome Blues And Dancing Shoes*, as 'Farewell, My Lovely Nancy'; Nora Cleary *The Voice Of The People, Vol. 12*, as 'Farewell, My Lovely Nancy'; The Copper Family *A Song For Every Season*; Tim Hart & Maddy Prior *Folk Songs Of Olde England Vol.1*; Martin Simpson *Kind Letters*; Waterson:Carthy *Fishes & Fine Yellow Sand*, as 'Farewell, My Lovely Nancy'.

## ADMIRAL BENBOW (ROUD 227)

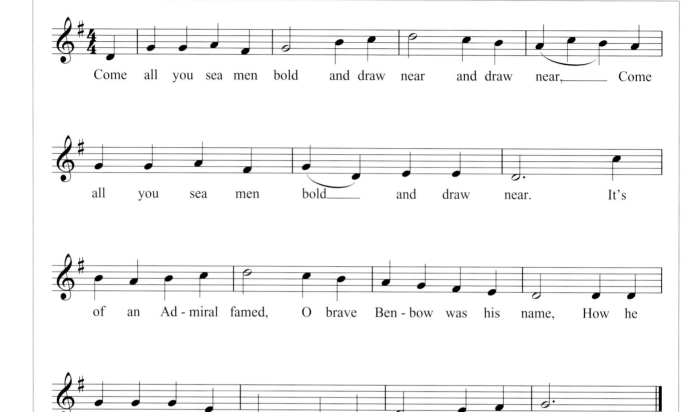

Come all you seamen bold and draw near and draw near,
Come all you seamen bold and draw near.
It's of an admiral famed, Oh brave Benbow was his name,
How he fought all on the main you shall hear, you shall hear.

It was Reuben and Benbow fought the French, fought the French,
It was Reuben and Benbow fought the French.
They fought them up and down till the blood came trickling down,
Till the blood came trickling down where they lay, where they lay.

Said Scrooby unto Webb: "We will run, we will run,
For I value no disgrace nor the losing of my place,
But the enemy I won't face, nor their guns, nor their guns,
But the enemy I won't face, nor their guns, nor their guns."

Brave Benbow lost his legs, by chain-shot, by chain-shot,
Brave Benbow lost his legs, and all on his knees he begs:
"Fight on my English lads, 'tis our lot, 'tis our lot.
Fight on my English lads, 'tis our lot, 'tis our lot."

The doctor dressed his wounds, Benbow cried, Benbow cried,
"Let a cradle now in haste on the quarter-deck be placed,
That the enemies I face till I die, till I die.
That the enemies I face till I die, till I die."

The *Oxford Dictionary of National Biography* has an extensive entry detailing the career of John Benbow (1653–1702). Having entered the navy as a master's mate, he served in the Mediterranean and elsewhere, subsequently leaving the navy and acquiring his own merchant vessel. He is said to have staged a successful defence against Moorish pirates, cutting off their heads and salting them down in order to claim prize money against them. After the Glorious Revolution he rejoined the navy and served in action against the French, gaining a reputation for fearlessness. In 1698 he was appointed commander-in-chief in the West Indies, and engaged the French off Cape Santa Marta. It was here that his right leg was broken by chain shot. At this point his captains jointly recommended that their force withdraw, to Benbow's annoyance. On their return to Jamaica, Benbow had them court-martialled and two of them were shot in consequence. Benbow died in Jamaica as a result of his wounds on November 4th, 1702.

Subsequently, the engagement off Santa Marta spawned a controversy in print which ran through the first half of the 18th century, with writers on different sides either defending the captains or praising Benbow's fighting spirit. Nevertheless, Benbow emerged in legend as a naval hero. A monument erected by public subscription in St Mary's Church, Shrewsbury, in 1843 hails him as "the Nelson of his times", and the Royal Navy named three different ships after him. There is an Admiral Benbow inn in *Treasure Island*, and it has been claimed that Tennyson's poem 'The Captain' alludes to the legend. Naval historians have tried to reassess Benbow's reputation, pointing out that he achieved no remarkable successes over the enemy. A modern view is that his reputation grew out of the complex and confusing circumstances of early naval battles, and no doubt the press and the circulation of the ballad itself played an important part.

Rather surprisingly, there does not appear to be much in the way of a record of early 18th century broadsides of the 'Admiral Benbow' ballad. The earliest known example seems to be one printed by Fowler of Salisbury around 1784/5. Later imprints include Ford (Chesterfield), Armstrong (Liverpool), Davenport, Jennings, Pitts (London), Kendrew (York). Some of these lack the familiar "Come all you sailors bold, lend an ear" opening and tell Benbow's story in a rather more wordy manner. A reproduction of the Armstrong version is available online in Oxford University's Bodleian Library Broadside Ballads collection (www.bodley.ox.ac.uk/ballads).

Often associated with the Copper family, 'Admiral Benbow' has also been collected from a number of other singers, but apparently only in England. It was known to the poet John Clare, for example; and Cecil Sharp collected it from Captain Lewis in Minehead, who had a substantial repertoire of songs, many of them with nautical themes.

This version was collected from Captain Lewis on January 13th, 1906. "Rueben" appears to be a corruption of The Ruby, one of the ships under Benbow's command, though not his flagship. Scrooby and Webb, the two captains who fled and were later shot, were actually called Kirby and Wade. Sharp amended the names in his printed version of the song to match the historical facts.

**Recordings** The Copper Family *Coppersongs 3: The Legacy Continues*; June Tabor With Martin Simpson *A Cut Above*.

# THE BOLD PRINCESS ROYAL (PRINCESS ROYAL)
(ROUD 528)

On the fourteenth day of February we sailed from the land,
In the bold Princess Royal bound for Newfoundland.
We had fifty bright seamen for our ship's company,
And boldly from the eastward to the westward steered we.

We had not been sailing past days two or three,
When a man from our masthead a ship he did see.
As soon as this pirate she hoved alongside,
With a loud-speaking trumpet "Whence came you?" he cried.

"Good Lord," cried our captain, "What shall we do now?
Here comes a bold pirate to rob us I know."
"Oh no," cries our chief mate, "That never shall be so,
We will shake out our reefs and from her we'll go."

As soon as this pirate she hoved alongside,
With a loud-speaking trumpet, "Whence come you?" he cried.
Our captain being aft when he answered them so,
"We've come from fair London and bound for Cairo."

"Come back up your topsails and heave your ship to,
For I have some letters to send on by you."
"We'll back up our topsails and heave our ship to,
But it will be in harbour alongside of you."

Then they fired and shot after us but could not prevail,
And the bold Princess Royal soon showed them her tail.
"Go down to your grog, boys, and be of good cheer.
We've escaped the bold pirate, brave boys, never fear."

One of the most popular of sea songs, 'The Bold Princess Royal' has been widely collected in England and North America, and less frequently in Scotland and Ireland. It appeared on English broadsides with imprints including Hodges, Disley, Fortey, Pitts, Such (all London), Ross (Newcastle), Dalton (York). It is not known whether the story of the song has any basis in real events, although it has been claimed that it dates from the American War of Independence or shortly before.

'The Bold Princess Royal' was the only song that Ned 'Wintry' Adams, coxswain of the Hastings lifeboat, sang. Bob Copper, who recorded him, tells the extended story of how he eventually persuaded the reluctant Ned to sing it, in the bar of the London Trader pub, in *Songs and Southern Breezes* (pp60–66).

This version was collected by Cecil Sharp from Joseph Laver in Bridgwater, Somerset, on August 13th 1906. The first line of Sharp's notation did not fit the words; he compromised by changing "fourteenth" to "fourth". We have reinstated the correct word, but have not amended the written rhythm to match.

**Recordings** Blue Epitaph *Ode By...*; Velvet Brightwell *Good Order!*; Harry Cox *The Voice Of The People, Vol. 12*; Robin & Barry Dransfield *Lord Of All I Behold*; Walter Pardon *A World Without Horses*; Bob Roberts *Sea Songs And Shanties*.

# CAROLINE AND HER YOUNG SAILOR BOLD
(ROUD 553)

It's of a nobleman's daughter, so comely and handsome we hear,
Her father possessed a great fortune of thirty-five thousand a year,
He had but one only daughter, Caroline was her name we are told,
One day from her drawing-room window she admired a young sailor bold.

His cheeks appeared like two roses, his hair was as black as a jet,
Young Caroline watching the portals walk, round them William she met,
She said, "I'm a nobleman's daughter, possessed of ten thousand in gold.
I'll forsake both my father and mother to wed with my young sailor bold."

Said William, "Young lady remember, your parents you're bound for to mind.
On sailors there is no dependence when their lover is left far behind,
Be advised stay at home with your parents, and do as by them you are told,
And never let anyone tempt you to wed with a young sailor bold."

Caroline she went straight to her father, in her jacket and trousers so blue,
He received her and momently fainted, when first she appeared to his view,
She cried, "My dear father forgive me, and deprive me for ever of gold,
Grant me my request I'm contented to wed with my young sailor bold."

Her father admired young William, and vowed that in sweet unity,
If life did them spare till the morning, together they married should be,
They were married on Caroline's fortune, 'twas thirty-five thousand in gold,
So now they lives happy and cheerful, Caroline and her young sailor bold.


Collected from singers in England, Scotland, Ireland, and North America, 'Caroline and her Young Sailor Bold' usually includes the motif of the woman who dresses as a sailor to follow her true-love, in the face of here parents' opposition. Here she is much more faithful lover than bold female warrior. Her sailor reminds her of her duties to her parents. She goes, dressed in the blue uniform of a sailor, to tell her father of her intentions. But her father gives his consent to the marriage, so she doesn't need to go.

'Caroline and her Young Sailor Bold' is particularly well represented in 19th-century broadside print, with imprints ranging through Russell (Birmingham), Spencer (Bradford), Phillips (Brighton), Brown, Jefferies (Bristol), Whinham (Carlisle), Willey (Cheltenham), Clift (Cirencester), Ford (Chesterfield), Keys (Devonport), Walker (Durham), Sanderson (Edinburgh), Stone (Exeter), Chilcott (Leominster), Ringham (Lincoln), Catnach, Disley, Fortey, Hillatt and Martin, Pitts, Such, Taylor (London), Wheeler (Manchester), Fordyce, Walker (Newcastle), Reed (Newport), Henson (Northampton), King (Oxford), Williams (Portsea), Harkness (Preston), Burridge (Truro), Robertson (Wigton), as well as Haly (Cork), Birmingham (Dublin).

This version was collected by George Gardiner from Moses Blake of Lyndhurst in Hampshire, in 1906. The second line of the second verse is garbled. In the broadside versions it reads, "Young Caroline watched his departure, walked round and young William she met."

Blake's version also omits two crucial verses necessary to tell the story as found in the broadside versions. They should appear between verses three and four above. These words are from the version printed by Fortey in London:


She said, "There's no one shall persuade me, one moment to alter my mind,
But I'll ship and proceed with my true love, he never shall leave me behind."
Then she dressed like a gallant young sailor, forsook both her parents and gold,
Four years and a half on the salt seas, she ploughed with her young sailor bold.

Three times with her love she was shipwrecked, and always proved constant and true,
Her duty she done like a sailor, went aloft in her jacket so blue.
Her father long wept and lamented, from his eyes tears in torrents long rolled,
When at length they arrived safe in England, Caroline and her young sailor bold.


**Recordings** Andrea Corr *Rogue's Gallery: Pirate Ballads, Sea Songs & Chanteys*; George Dunn *Chainmaker*; Gordon Hall *When The Wind Blows*; Tony Harvey *Songs Sung In Suffolk*; Joe Heaney *The Road From Connemara*; Sarah Makem *Sea Songs And Shanties*; Maggy Murphy *Linkin' O'er The Lea*; Walter Pardon *Put a Bit of Powder On It, Father*.

# THE FEMALE CABIN BOY (ROUD 239)

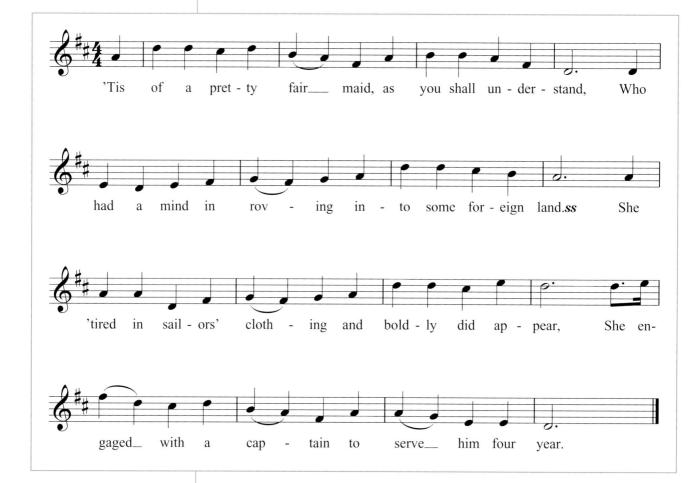

'Tis of a pretty fair maid, as you shall understand,
Who had a mind in roving, into some foreign land.
She 'tired in sailors' clothing, and boldly did appear,
She engaged with a captain to serve him four year.

She engaged with the captain, his cabin boy to be.
The wind being in favour, they soon put out to sea.
The captain's lady being on board, she seemed overjoyed,
To think the captain had engaged such a handsome cabin boy.

Quite nimble was this pretty maid, and did her duty well,
But mark what followed after, the song itself will tell,
In eating captains' biscuits, her colours did destroy.
The waist did swell of pretty Nell, the handsome cabin boy.

'Twas through the Bay of Biscay, this gallant ship did plough.
One night among the sailors, there was a pretty row.
They bundled from their hammocks, which did their rest destroy,
And they sweared about the groaning of the female cabin boy.

"Oh doctor, Oh doctor," the cabin boy did say,
The sailors sweared by all that's good the cabin boy will die,
The doctor hung with all his might and smiled at the fun,
To think a cabin boy could have a daughter or a son.

When the sailors heard the joke they all began to stare,
The child belonged to none of them, they solemnly did swear.
The lady to her captain said, "My dear I wish you joy!
'Tis either you or me betrayed the female cabin boy."

They all took up a bumper and drinked success to trade.
Here's a health unto the cabin boy that's neither man nor maid,
And if the wars should rise again some seamen to employ,
We ship some other sailors like the female cabin boy.

'The Female Cabin Boy' has proved popular with singers in England and Scotland, with a few records from the USA and Canada. It is well represented on broadsides, too, with imprints including Merry (Bedford), Pratt (Birmingham), Talbot (Cambridge), Willey (Cheltenham), Clift (Cirencester), Walker (Durham), Lindsay (Glasgow), White (Liverpool), Catnach, Disley, Fortey, Hillatt and Martin, Hodges, Pitts, Such (London), Bebbington, Pearson, Swindells (Manchester), Fordyce (Newcastle), Forth (Pocklington), Williams (Portsea), Harkness (Preston), Jones (Sheffield). There are also several Irish imprints, although the song does not appear to have been collected from singers in Ireland.

Like 'Caroline and her Young Sailor Bold', 'The Female Cabin Boy' draws on the female warrior motif, and the setting is at sea, but the song has much less to do with sailors and female courage than with sex and sexual identity. Dianne Dugaw (*Warrior Women And Popular Balladry*, p84) writes of 'The Female Cabin Boy', "Among its laughter, it warns of the deep confusions and implicit dangers in such gender masquerading."

This version was collected by Henry Hammond from Mrs Rowsell at Taunton in Somerset, in 1905. Hammond's manuscript comments, "The D in the 10th bar sounds to my unskilled ear wrong, but she sang it, and I had to note it." The phrase "she 'tired in sailors' clothing" means she "attired" or dressed in sailor's clothing.

**Recordings** Kate Bush *This Woman's Work*, as 'The Handsome Cabin Boy'; Martin Carthy *Martin Carthy*, as 'The Handsome Cabin Boy'; Jerry Garcia & David Grisman *Shady Grove*, as 'The Handsome Cabin Boy'; Bob Hart *A Broadside*; Ewan MacColl & Alf Edwards *Sea Songs & Shanties*, as 'The Handsome Cabin Boy'; Roger McGuinn *McGuinn's Folk Den Vol.1*, as 'The Handsome Cabin Boy'; Walter Pardon *A World Without Horses*, as 'The Handsome Cabin Boy'; Jeannie Robertson *The Queen Among The Heather*, as 'The Handsome Cabin Boy'; Frank Zappa *The Lost Episodes*, as 'The Handsome Cabin Boy'.

## THE GOLDEN VANITY (CHILD 286; ROUD 122)

O I had a ship in some for-eign coun - try, And she was call - ed aft - er the Gold - en Van - i - ty. I fear she will be ta - ken by some proud young en - em - y, And then she'll be sunk at the bot - tom of the sea. So we sinked here in the low - lands low, low - lands low, So we sinked her in the low - lands low.

Oh I had a ship in some foreign country,
And she was called after the Golden Vanity.
I fear she will be taken by some proud young enemy,
And then she'll be sunk at the bottom of the sea.
So we sunked her in the lowlands low, lowlands low,
So we sunked her in the lowlands low.

The first spoken up was the little cabin boy,
Saying, "Master what will you give me, if her I do destroy?"
"Oh, I will give you gold and I will give you store,
And you shall have my daughter if I return on shore."
So he sinked her in the lowlands low, lowlands low,
So we sinked her in the lowlands low.

The little boy looked overboard and swam to her ship's side,
The one was at the cards, the other at the dice,
So he took two borers in his hand, he bored two holes at once,
So the waters flowed so strong they couldn't work the pumps.
So he sinked her in the lowlands low, lowlands low,
So he sinked her in the lowlands low.

So the little boy swum round till he came to his ship's side,
Saying, "Master pick me up or I shall go along with the tide."
"I will not pick thee up, my daughter shan't be thy bride,
You can't swim no further, you must go along with the tide."
So he sunk her, in the lowlands low, lowlands low,
So he sunk her in the lowlands low.

The little boy swum round till he came to the other side,
Saying, "Shipmates pick me up or I shall go along with the tide."
So the shipmates picked him up and on the deck he died.
They throwed him overboard so he went along with the tide.
So he sunked her in the lowlands low, lowlands low,
So he sinked her in the lowlands low.

'The Golden Vanity' first appears on 17th-century broadsides as 'Sir Walter Raleigh Sailing in the Lowlands' and has subsequently been collected a vast number of times from singers in England, Scotland, and North America. It has not often been published as a shanty, but Stan Hugill states that he and his shipmates sang it both at the capstan and the pumps.

Subsequent versions lose sight of Sir Walter Raleigh. The main point of variation lies in the fate of the cabin-boy, who is sometimes rescued and sometimes drowned. On occasion, the cruel captain is punished, either directly by the crew who throw him overboard, or else by the cabin-boy's ghost which returns to haunt him and/or causes the ship to sink. Among the names given for the ship are the *Mary Golden Tree* and the *Golden China Tree*.

Later broadside imprints include Brueton, Pratt (Birmingham), Bennett (Brighton), Sharman (Cambridge), Willey (Cheltenham), Batchelar, Catnach, Fortey, Hodges, Pitts, Such (London), Cadman (Manchester), Williams (Portsea), Pierce (Southborough).

Cecil Sharp collected this version from Alfred Emery (aged 78) at Othery, Somerset, on April 6th, 1908. He noted down two versions of the start of the tune to fit the wording of the second verse. Pedants will observe that Emery is recorded as using every variant of the past tense of the verb "to sink" (sinked, sunk, sunked), with the exception of the standard English "sank".

**Recordings** The Almanac Singers (including Woody Guthrie, Pete Seeger) *Deep Sea Chanteys And Whaling Ballads*; Dodie Chalmers *Classic Ballads Of Britain And Ireland, Vol. 2*, as 'Golden Victory'; Lonnie Donegan B-side of 'My Old Man's A Dustman' single; Johnny Doughty *Hidden English*; Burl Ives *Ballads*; Frank Proffitt *Her Bright Smile Haunts Me Still, Vol. 2*; Almeda Riddle *Bad Man Ballads, Vol. 7*, as 'Merry Golden Tree'; Jean Ritchie *Ballads From Her Appalachian Family Tradition*, as 'The Merry Golden Tree'; Pete Seeger *American Ballads*; Steeleye Span *The Best Of British Folk Rock*; Duncan Williamson *Traveller's Tales, Vol. 2*

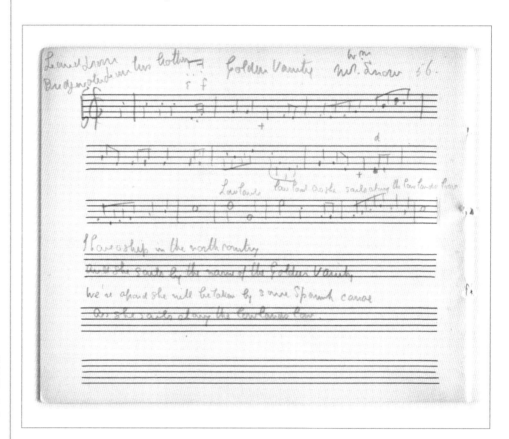

This is Cecil Sharp's notebook entry for a different version of 'The Golden Vanity', collected from William Snow at Somerton, Somerset, on January 18th, 1906.

# THE GREENLAND WHALE FISHERY (ROUD 347)

It was on the fourteenth day of March,
Or February the twenty-third,
When we hoisted our top sails to our mast-head,
For to face the storm and cold, brave boys,
For to face the storm and cold.

Our bo'sun went unto the masthead,
With a spy-glass in his hand,
"There's a whale, there's a whale, there's a whalefish," he cried,
"And she blows a devilish span, my boys,
And she blows a devilish span."

Our Captain on the quarter deck
Gave orders to obey.
"Over all, over all your davit tackle falls,
And launch you a boat to the sea, brave boys,
And launch you a boat to the sea."

Then overboard our boats we tossed,
And the whale fish was in view,
"Pull away, pull away, my jolly tars,
And soon we'll bring her to, brave boys,
And soon we'll bring her to."

The whale was struck and the line let go,
And he gave a splash with his tail,
Capsized the boat and we lost five men.
 So we did not catch that whale, my boys,
So we did not catch that whale.

The losing of that whale, brave boys,
It grieved our hearts full sore.
But the losing of our five ship-mates
It grieved us ten times more, my boys,
It grieved us ten times more.

One of the most widespread of occupational songs, 'The Greenland Whale Fishery' has been collected in England, Scotland, North America, with records also from the Bahamas and the Channel Islands. The record in print likewise testifies to the song's wide currency, with imprints including Peach (Birmingham), Spencer (Bradford), Brown, Collard, Marshall (Bristol), Wilson (Cambridge), Whinham (Carlisle), Keys (Devonport), Menzies (Edinburgh), Stone (Exeter), Armstrong (Liverpool), Birt, Catnach, Fortey, Pitts, Such (London), Swindells (Manchester), Fordyce (Newcastle), Reed (Newport), Harkness (Preston), Pierce (Southborough), Burridge (Truro).

A.L. Lloyd wrote at some length about this song in *The Penguin Book of English Folk Songs*:

"Until 1830, the whaling ships put out each spring from London, King's Lynn, Hull, Whitby, bound for the right-whale grounds of Greenland. The best of our whaling ballads are about the Greenland fishery. After 1830, the fleets moved to Baffin's Bay, and subsequently to the grounds off Hawaii and Peru, but still most of the songs the whalermen sang were of the Greenland days."

Most of the collected versions of this song include a date in the first verse, with 1784, 1794, and 1802 among the earliest listed in Roud, although all the known broadsides are of the 19th century. 'The Greenland Voyage; or, The Whale Fisher's Delight' included in *A Collection of Old Ballads* (1725) is a quite different song, though there is evidently some continuity of subject.

The *Penguin Book* text notes that the two sources of the captain's grief (the loss of crew members and the loss of the whale) are sometimes placed in reverse order, so as to make him seem more interested in profit than in his men's well-being. This has been criticized as an ideological interference to make this more of a protest song, but versions with this emphasis have been collected from singers.

This version comes from the collection of George Gardiner. The tune was taken down by his collaborator, C.F. Guyer, from the singing of Frederick White (aged 68) of Southampton, on June 21st, 1906.

**Recordings** Judy Collins & Theodore Bikel *Live At Newport 1959–1966*; Harry Cox *Songs And Stories From East Coast Fishermen, Voice Of Suffolk, No. 6*; The Dubliners *At Home With*; Philip Hamon & Hilary Carre *The Folk Songs Of Britain, Vol.6*; Ewan MacColl & A.L. Lloyd *The Singing Sailor*; Van Dyke Parks *Rogue's Gallery: Pirate Ballads, Sea Songs & Chanteys*; The Pogues *Red Roses For Me*; The Watersons *Sea Songs & Shanties*; The Weavers *Traveling On With*.

# HENRY MARTIN (CHILD 250; ROUD 104)

There was___ three broth-ers in mer-ry Scot-land,___ In mer-ry Scot-

land there was three, and they did cast lots which should sail O! and rob, Which should

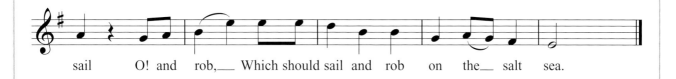

sail O! and rob,___ Which should sail and rob on the___ salt sea.

Bars 11, 12, 13 are as follows in verses three and four:

a rich mer-chant ship a___ rich mer-chant sh-ip
of old En - ge - land of___ old En - ge - la - nd

There was three brothers in merry Scotland,
In merry Scotland there was three.
So they did cast lots which should sail Oh! and rob,
Which should sail Oh! and rob,
Which should sail and rob on the salt sea.

Now the lot then did fall on young Henry Martin,
The youngest of all then the three.
So he turned a robber all on the salt seas,
The salt seas, the salt seas,
To maintain his two brothers and he.

He had not been sailing one long winter's night
One cold winter's night before day.
Before that he spied a rich marchant ship,
A rich marchant ship,
Come bearing down straight that way.

"Oh who are you? Oh who are you?" says Henry Martyn,
"Oh who are you? Oh who are you?" said he.
"Oh I am a rich merchant of Old England,
Of Old England;
If you please, will you let me pass by?"

"Oh no, Oh no," says Henry Martyn,
"Oh no, Oh no," says he,
"For I've turned a robber all on the salt seas,
The salt seas, the salt seas,
To maintain my two brothers and me."

The swashbuckling ballad of 'Henry Martin' has been widely collected from singers in England and North America, and is represented in Wales by the singing of Phil Tanner; but, surprisingly, there is just a single record from Scotland, where the hero is given the name of Robin Hood!

Child noted that the ballad must have derived from the earlier, and much longer, 'Andrew Barton' (Child 167), which was included in the Percy Folio Manuscript of *circa* 1650 and printed on broadsides of the later 17th and 18th centuries. Child has a wealth of historical comment on the matter. In brief, in 1476 the Portuguese seized a Scottish ship commanded by John Barton, in consequence of which the Scottish king granted Barton's sons, Andrew, Robert, and John, licence to take reprisals. The Bartons, however, appear to have grossly exceeded their remit and effectively became pirates, harassing not just the Portuguese but also English merchantmen. They are said to have sent three barrels of salted Flemish seamen's heads as a present to King James IV of Scotland, and the ballad describes Barton's mysterious 'beams', apparently a special kind of weapon that gave him increased firepower. Their activities caused Henry VIII to order action against them, and in 1511 Barton's ship was captured and the pirate beheaded.

In its shorter, 'Henry Martin' form, the ballad appeared in print under various imprints, such as Collard (Bristol), Andres, Baines, Beaumont (Leeds), Armstrong (Liverpool), Batchelar, Birt, Catnach, Phair, Pitts, Ryle (London), Cadman, Pearson, Swindells (Manchester), Kendrew (York).

This version was collected by Henry Hammond from William Bartlett at Wimborne in Dorset, in 1905. Hammond included detailed observations about Bartlett's complicated repetitions. In verses two, three, and four, he repeated the first two lines; in verses three, four, and five, he repeated the last two lines. "This repetition or doubling back can I imagine be done at the will of each singer," Hammond observed.

**Recordings** Joan Baez *Joan Baez*; Donovan *HMS Donovan*; Bob Green *Songs And Stories From East Coast Fishermen, Voice Of Suffolk, No. 6*; Bert Jansch *Jack Orion*; Sam Larner *Now Is The Time For Fishing*; Phil Tanner *The Voice Of The People, Vol. 2*.

# THE LOSS OF THE RAMILLIES (THE RAM-BE-LAY)
(ROUD 523)

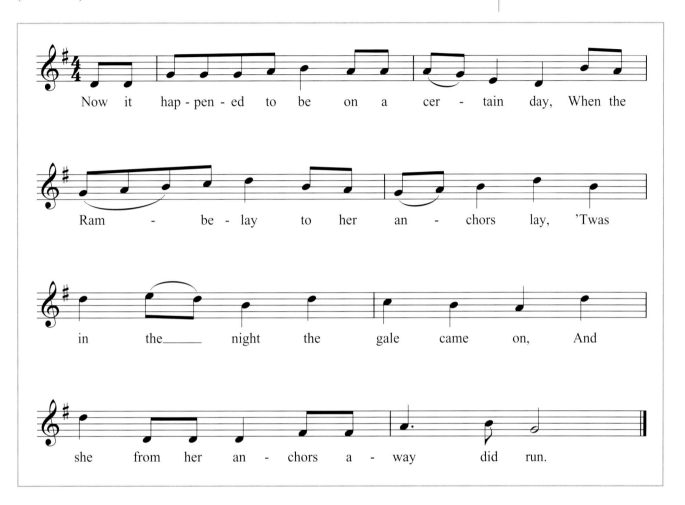

Now it happened to be on a certain day,
When the Ram-be-lay to her anchors lay,
'Twas in the night the gale came on
And she from her anchors away did run.

The wind poured down a dreadful chop,
Oh the seas wash over our maintop,
'Twas all in vain our eyes do see,
For the seas tonight our graves will be.

(Two lines omitted)
And when we could not better do,
We let our cables run right through.

Our bosun cried out "My hearties all,
(One line omitted)
Come launch your boat your lives to save,
Or the seas this night will be our grave."

Overboard, overboard our long boats being tossed,
And so many got in that the most was lost,
There was only but me to tell the tale,
How our ship behaved all in the gale.

Sad news, sad news to Plymouth town,
That the Ram-be-lay was lost and most was drowned,
For Plymouth town will float with tears,
In hearing of her sad affairs.

HMS *Ramillies* was wrecked on the Devon coast on February 15th, 1760. A total of 734 lives are said to have been lost, with only 26 men saved from the wreck. At least two different songs were written about the disaster, presumably close to the time, although there are no known 18th-century records of either.

'The Loss of the Ramillies' has been collected several times in England, Scotland, Canada, but it does not appear to have been printed on broadsides. 'The Fatal Ramillies' (Roud 1266), a different song on the same theme, has been collected a few times in England, and appeared on broadsides under various imprints, including Bennett (Brighton), Brown (Bristol), Sharman (Cambridge), Keys (Devonport), Stone (Exeter), Catnach, Pitts, Such (London), Reed (Newport), Pierce (Southborough).

Broadsides commemorating shipwrecks are common, often with titles beginning 'The Loss of …' or 'The wreck of …'. Another example is 'The Loss of the Royal Charter' (Roud 3327; 9040), which has been collected occasionally from singers in England and Ireland and appeared on broadsides with imprints including Pearson (Manchester) and Sanderson (Edinburgh). The *Royal Charter* was wrecked off Anglesey in 1859 with the loss of more than 400 lives and Charles Dickens wrote an account of the disaster. Interestingly, due to the location of the wreck, ballads were also printed in Welsh.

This version was collected by Henry Hammond from Joseph Elliott at Todber, in Dorset, in September 1905. Hammond wrote it down as 'The Ram-be-lay'. Elliott provided only two lines for verse three and three for verse four.Many versions of the song exist, with considerable variations, particularly in the nautical language. The version that follows was collected by George Gardiner from Frederick White, a former seaman, at Southampton on June 21st, 1906.

It was on one day, one certain day,
When the Ramillies at her anchor lay,
That very night a gale came on,
And our ship from her anchorage away did run.

The rain pouring down in terrible drops,
The sea broke over our fore-top,
Our yards and our canvas neatly spread,
We were thinking to weather the old Ram's Head.

Our bo'sun cries "My good fellows all,
Listen unto me while I blow my call,
Launch out your boats your lives for to save,
Or the seas this night will be our grave."

Then overboard our boats we tossed,
Some got in but soon were lost;
There were some in one place, some in another,
The watch down below, they all were smothered.

When this sad news to Plymouth came,
That the Ramillies was lost and all her men,
Excepting two that told the tale,
How that ship behaved in that dreadful gale.

Come all you pretty maidens and weep along with me,
For the loss of your true lovers and the Ramillie;
All Plymouth town it flowed with tears,
When they heard the news of that sad affair.

The Ram's Head is the Rame peninsula in Cornwall. The bosun's "call", mentioned in verse three, is his whistle.

**Recordings** Jumbo Brightwell *Songs From The Eel's Foot*; Walter Pardon *A World Without Horses*.

# THE MERMAID (CHILD 289; ROUD 124)

'Twas nine o' clock by the bells, And we were not far from land, When we saw a mer-maid sit-ting on a rock, With a glass and a comb in her hand.

'Twas nine 'o clock by the bells,
And we were not far from land,
When we saw a mermaid on a rock,
With a glass and a comb in her hand.

Chorus:
And the raging waves did roar,
And the stormy winds did blow,
And the sailor climbed to the top gallant mast,
While the land-lubber lay down below.

Then up spoke the captain of the ship
And a fine old man was he,
"Oh I have a wife in Bristol town,
And tonight she a widow will be."

Then up spoke the captain's mate,
And a brave young man was he,
"Oh I have two sons in Bristol town,
And tonight they orphans will be."

Then up spoke the little cabin boy,
And a good little boy was he,
"Oh I have a mammy in Bristol town,
And tonight she'll be weeping for me.

But I've heard my mammy say,
That there's One who rules the waves,
And He can if He please bring us all to land,
And save us from watery graves."

Then the captain went home to his wife,
And the mate to his sons ne'er to part,
But none were so happy as the little cabin boy,
When his mammy clasped him close to his heart.

The idea of the mermaid (or merman) as a sign of bad luck for seafarers can be traced back to the sirens of classical antiquity – in Homer's *Odyssey*, for example. It seems to have become established in Britain in the Middle Ages, and mermaids sometimes turn up in church iconography. The comb and glass, which are prominent in the ballad, are not known in classical art and probably attached themselves to the alluring female figure as symbols of vanity, which could then be exploited by moralists and preachers. The mermaid does seem to have been taken as a natural, if freakish, creature, not as a supernatural being, and belief in mermaids persisted over many centuries. Travellers' tales from the 16th century onwards record sightings and even captures of mermaids, and fakes created out of parts of monkeys and fish have regularly turned up. It has been

187

suggested that sailors' sightings of marine mammals such as the manatee and dugong contributed to the belief in the existence of mermaids.

Child's earliest text of 'The Mermaid' is from a Newcastle collection tentatively dated 1765, titled 'The Seamen's Distress'. It appeared on many 19th-century broadsides, with imprints including Wright (Birmingham), Marshall (Bristol), Wilson (Cambridge), Clift (Cirencester), Lindsay (Glasgow), Armstrong, McCall, Thompson (Liverpool), Birt, Catnach, Disley, Fortey, Hodges, Pitts (London), Swindells, Wheeler (Manchester), Ross, Walker (Newcastle), Plant (Nottingham) Williams (Portsea), Harkness (Preston), as well as Baird (Cork), and in various north American songsters and newspapers. Comical versions also appeared in American college glee books, and Mike Yates suggests that some of the American folk versions may be serious reinterpretations of these. A hillbilly version features a lamenting girl, though she is not on board the ship or among those about to die.

With its memorable tune and "landlubbers lying down below" chorus, 'The Mermaid' has been frequently collected from singers in England, Scotland, and North America. At least some of these sources have been sailors or had connections with the sea. Some American versions are quite localized; for instance, a text from Cape Cod, Massachusetts, gives the name of the ship as the *Maid O' Home* and closes with a stanza about the church in Plymouth, MA, where "many a woeful wife" mourns. On the other hand, the song's popularity is very much wider than its seafaring subject might suggest.

Collected by Cecil Sharp from Sister Emma (aged 71), an Anglican nun at a convent in Clewer, in Berkshire, on February 27th, 1909.

**Recordings** Martin Carthy & Dave Swarbrick *Straws In The Wind*; The Clancy Brothers & Tommy Makem *The First Hurrah!*; Johnny Doughty *Round Rye Bay For More*; Bob Hart *A Broadside*; William Howell *Classic Ballads Of Britain And Ireland, Vol. 2*; Peggy Seeger *Folksongs And Ballads*; The Spinners *Folk At The Phil!*.

Cecil Sharp's notebook entry for a different version of 'The Mermaid', collected from John Haste of Enmore, Somerset, on January 15th, 1906.

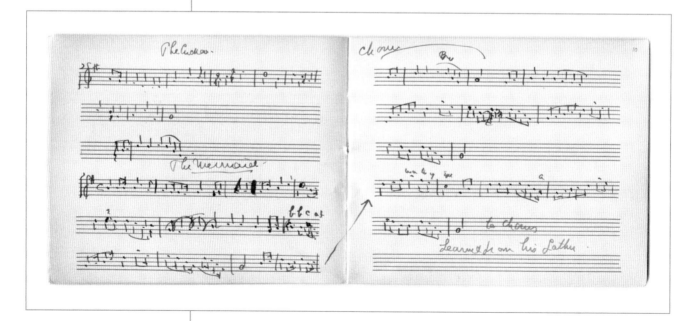

# SPANISH LADIES (ROUD 687)
## (FAREWELL AND ADIEU TO YOU SPANISH LADIES)

Farewell and adieu to you Spanish ladies,
Farewell and adieu to you ladies of Spain,
For we've received orders to sail for Old England,
And I hope in a short time for to see you again.

We'll rant and we'll roar like true British heroes,
We'll rant and we'll roar all on the salt seas,
We'll drink and be merry and drown melancholy,
So here's a good health to all true-hearted souls.

The first land we made was called the Deadman,
The Ramhead at Plymouth, Start, Portland, Isle of Wight,
Then we sailed in by Beachy, Fairlee and Dungeness, my boys,
Until we arrived at the South Foreland Light.

Now orders were given for the grand fleet to anchor,
All in the downs that night for to lay,
And it's let go your stoppers, stand by your shank painters,
Haul up your clew garnets, stick out tacks or sheets.

Let every man toss off his full bumper,
Let every man toss off his full bowl,
Oh we'll drink and be merry and drown melancholy,
So here's a good health to our sweethearts and wives.

'Spanish Ladies' appears to have started life as a naval song, probably in the 18th century, and subsequently become very popular with sailors of all kinds as a homeward-bound song, with various adaptations to different nationalities and home-ports. Stan Hugill, who knew the song as a capstan shanty, notes that it has two different tunes, with later generations of sailors preferring the livelier and faster one. Ushant is Ouessant, the most westerly of the small islands off the coast of France, about 14 miles from Finisterre.

'Spanish Ladies' has been widely collected in England, Ireland, North America (especially Newfoundland), and Australia. Broadside imprints from the 19th century include Whinham (Carlisle), Fordyce (Hull), Catnach, Hodges, Pitts, Such (London), Fordyce (Newcastle), Williams (Portsea), Harkness (Preston). Both Captain Marryat in *Poor Jack* (1840) and Melville in *Moby-Dick* (1851) have sailors singing 'Spanish Ladies'; and in *White Jacket* (1850) Melville observed that it was a favourite on board British men-of-war.

Australian drovers adapted 'Spanish Ladies' as 'Brisbane Ladies'; Pacific whalermen remade it as 'Talcahuano Girls'; and 'The Ryans And The Pittmans', a Newfoundland adaptation, employs the shanty as a chorus to a rollicking tale of a young fisherman's love affairs.

Collected by Henry Hammond from Mr Felt at Poole Union, a workhouse, in Dorset, in October 1906. His notation of the tune included very minor variants in eighth and twelfth bars. The words, especially the list of landmarks, are very similar to those used in the broadsides. According to Roger McGuinn, who has recorded the song for his *Folk Den* project on the Internet and on CD, "Deadman" is Dodman Point, near Plymouth, and "Fairlee" is Fairlight Hill, near Hastings, both navigation points visible from the English Channel.

**Recordings** Cadgwith Fishermen *Sea Songs And Shanties*; Johnny Doughty *Round Rye Bay For More*; Walter Pardon *When The Wind Blows*.

# Songs of sex
## and seduction

A whole series of bawdy songs celebrate sex in its various forms. Songs such as 'The Cunning Cobbler' and 'The Molecatcher' involve various kinds of trickery, and can be related to songs of outwitting. 'The Game Of All Fours', 'The Thrashing Machine' and the like exploit metaphors from the everyday world that readily lend themselves to descriptions of sexual acts. This need not be understood as a form of euphemism, since there is no real attempt at concealment. Rather, the enjoyment of metaphor, which is transparent to everyone hearing the song, is an important part of its pleasure. The sheer number of folk songs that employ sexual metaphors reinforces this reading.

Neither are such songs descriptions of the common experience of 'frolicking peasants'. Vic Gammon, in his article on 'Song, Sex, and Society in England, 1600–1850', argues cogently that these are songs that reproduce the gender relations of their society and thus mark the boundaries of acceptable behaviour. To be sure, there is an element of sexual fantasy, but there is also a marked contrast with what social historians have revealed about the way in which communities over a long period of time policed themselves in relation to sex and the maintenance of the social order.

Yet they are also songs to be enjoyed. Neither is the sexual fantasy just crudely male-directed; witness 'My Husband's Got No Courage in Him'. For the female, though, the potential consequences of sexual encounters are always more dangerous, as 'The Bedmaking' reveals. That is why women need their wits about them, and songs of outwitting like 'Bonny Kate' and 'The Oyster Girl' could belong here as well.

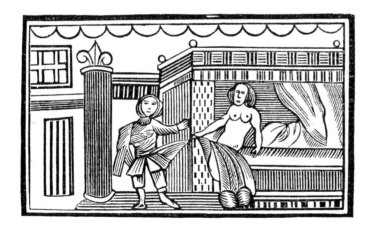

## THE BEDMAKING (MY MOTHER SENT ME TO SERVICE)
(ROUD 1631)

My mo-ther sent me to ser-vice, When I was young. My mis-sus and me could

ne-ver not ag-ree, Be-cause my mas-ter he did kiss me. Fal the

dal, fal the did-dle dal, Fal the did-dle dad-dle dee.

The first verse, being one line short, was sung as above.
The ensuing verses, all of which have four lines, were sung as below:

My mis-sus sent me up a-loft, To make her beds up nice and soft. My

mas-ter fol-lowed af-ter with a gay gold ring, "You had bet-ter take that for the

bed-mak- ing." Fal the dal, fal the did-dle dal, Fal the did-dle dad-dle dee.

My mother sent me to service, when I was young.
My missus and me could never agree,
Because my master he did kiss me.
Fal the dal, fal the diddle dal,
Fal the diddle daddle dee.

My missus sent me up aloft,
To make her beds up nice and soft,
My master followed after that with a gay gold ring,
"You had better take that for the bed-making."

My missus followed after in great haste,
She caught master's arms all around my waist.
From the top to the bottom she did give a sling,
"You had better take that for the bed-making."

My missus turned me out of doors,

She called me a dirty (word omitted) whore.
She bid me to walk till my shoes grow thin,
And then to remember the bed-making.

When six months was over and seven months come,
This pretty damsel grew thick in the waist.
She longed for mutton, veal and beef.
Her stomach grew little and belly grew big.

When eight months was over and nine months past,
This pretty fair damsel delivered her son.
She had him christened and his name was Dan.
She sent him home to the gay old man.

Included in Peter Buchan's (often rather disappointing) collection of racy songs, *Secret Songs of Silence*, which presumably means it had some currency in Scotland in the early 19th century, 'The Bedmaking' is subsequently only known from English singers. Cecil Sharp, the Hammond brothers, and George B. Gardiner all collected versions.

This version was collected by Cecil Sharp from Mrs Lizzie Welch at Hambridge, Somerset, on April 5th, 1904. She called it 'My Mother Sent Me To Service'. We have included a note by Sharp explaining why he provided two tunes. The first is for the first verse, which is one line short. The remaining verses are sung to the second tune. Singers may prefer to stretch Mrs Welch's short first line so that the first verse becomes a four-line verse like the others, which will permit using the same tune (the second tune) all the way through the song – as well as being more comfortable to sing. Fitting the words to the tune is a challenge elsewhere in the song, particularly in verse three. Note also that the typed words for the second line of verse one differ from those taken down with the music. The redundant B-naturals in the notation are in Sharp's original: they are there to make clear that the tune has a major rather than minor sixth, and thus that it is in D Dorian.

**Recordings** Frankie Armstrong *Out Of Love, Hope And Suffering*; Martin Carthy *Crown Of Horn*.

## THE CRABFISH (TOMMY DODDLER) (ROUD 149)
As sung by Charlie Stringer.

**CD TRACK 8**

1. I went a-fish-ing by the lit-tle brook; I

caught two fish on one lit-tle hook, Tom-my Dodd-ler.

2. I took one home, thought it'd make a fright;

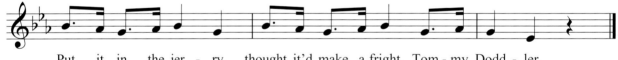

Put it in the jer-ry, thought it'd make a fright, Tom-my Dodd-ler.

I went a-fishing, by the little brook,
I caught two fish on one little hook,
Tommy Doddler.

I took one home, thought it'd make a fright,
Put it in the jerry, thought it'd make a fright.
Tommy Doddler.

And when the old maid got out to widdle,
That little codfish had a hold of the middle,
Tommy Doddler.

Oh mother, oh mother, as sure as you're born,
The devil's in the jerry, a-sticking up his horn,
Tommy Doddler.
Tommy Doddle-oddle all the day

Father got the poker, mother got the broom,
Chased the little codfish all around the room,
Tommy Doddler.

They chased the poor fish till the poor beggar died,
Tommy Doddler,
Tommy Doddle-oddle all the day.

'Tommy Doddler' is a version of a song called 'The Crabfish', widely collected in England, Scotland, Ireland, North America, and Australia. 'The Crabfish' can also be found as 'The Sea Crabb' in the Percy Folio Manuscript (*c*1650). The story, though, can be traced back farther than that: in Italian prose retelling by Franco Sacchetti (*c*1330–1400), in a French jest book of *c*1620, as well as in a lengthy, sophisticated narrative poem by Charles Churchill dating from the early 1760s. Indeed, as a tale the narrative has been found in Turkey, India, Indonesia, Korea, Finland, Norway, Germany, to name just a few. The song's absence from broadside print is presumably explained by its bawdy nature (and the opportunities for explicitness which are not always fully realised), but its appeal is nonetheless assured. Roger Renwick's *Recentering Anglo/American Folksong* (2001) has a fine chapter exploring the ramifications of this ubiquitous little narrative.

Charlie Stringer's version captures the essence of the story. Cecil Sharp collected a version from Mrs Overd at Langport, in Somerset, in August 1904. It presented a considerable challenge to his Edwardian sense of decency, and his typescript of the words – reproduced verbatim here – is notable for its omissions.

There was a little man and he had a little wife,
And he loved her as dear as he loved his life.
Mash a row dow dow dow diddle all the day
Mash a row dow dow dow diddle all the day.

One hour in the night, my wife fell sick,
And all that she cried for a little crabfish.

Then her husband arose and put on his clothes,
And down to the seaside he followed his nose.

"Oh fisherman, Oh fisherman, can'st thou tell me,
Has thou a little crabfish thou'st could sell me?"

"Oh yes, Oh yes, I've one, two and three,
And the best of them I will sell thee."

So they had no pot to boil him in
So he whipped him to the pot when his wife used to ...

"Oh husband, Oh husband, I pray thee come hither,
For the devil's in the pot and he's got me by the leather."

And the baby was born, etc.

The line beginning "So he whipped him to the pot…" is left unfinished, as it is here, with a note to "check with notebook". The last verse also ends exactly as it does here: it is not uncommon for this song to end with the wife pregnant. Sharp subsequently published a bowdlerised version of the song in which "up got the crabfish and nipped her by the nose", noting that "some of the words have been altered". The nonsense chorus seems to have been sung at the end of every verse.

**Recordings** Cyril Barber *Songs Sung In Suffolk*; The Cecil Sharp Centenary Collective: Simon Care, Ashley Hutchings, Emily Salde, Roger Wilson *As I Cycled Out On A May Morning*; Norah Cleary *The Voice Of The People, Vol. 7*; Charlotte Renals *Catch Me If You Can*; Charlie Stringer *Who Owns The Game?*.

Charlie Stringer

# THE CUNNING COBBLER (ROUD 174)
## (THE COBBLER AND THE BUTCHER)

A story, a story to you I will tell,
Concerning a butcher in London did dwell.
The butcher was possessed of a beautiful wife,
And a cobbler he loved her as dear as his life.
Fal de diddle di do,
Fal de diddle dee.

The butcher he went to market, to purchase an ox,
And then the little cobbler, as sly as a fox,
He put on his Sunday clothes, a-courting he did go,
'Twas to the jolly butcher's wife because he loved her so.
Fal de diddle di do, etc.

It was early the next morning, the cobbler slipped in the butcher's shop.
The butcher asked him what he meant and bid him here for to stop.
He pinned a paper on his back and on it was the news:
"The cobbler in the bedroom goes to mend the lady's shoes."
Fal de diddle di do, etc.

Oh then he went unto the house, inquiring for a job,
He says, "My darling have you got a job for me?"
The butcher's wife knew what he meant:
"I'll go upstairs and see."
Fal de diddle di do, etc.

And then she came downstairs and gave the man a call,
Saying, "I have got a job for you if you have got your awl,
And if you do it work meanwhile some cash to you I'll pay."
"Oh yes," says the cobbler and began to stitch away.
Fal de diddle di do, etc.

As he was working in the shop, a rap came at the door.
The cobbler crept beneath the bed and lay upon the floor.
"Lie still," says the butcher's wife. "What will my husband say?"
And he let in the policeman along with her to play.
Fal de diddle di do, etc.

The butcher threw his drenching horn in underneath the bed,
And then he broke the chamber mug and cracked the cobbler's head.
The cobbler hollered murder, he says "Who are you?
I am the little cobbler that mends the lady's shoe."
Fal de diddle di do, etc.

"Oh if you're the little cobbler, come go along with me,
And I will pay before you go for mending the lady's shoe."
He locked him in the bull's stall, the bull began to roar,
The butcher laughed to see the bull to roll him on the floor.
Fal de diddle di do, etc.

It was early the next morning, the people were about,
The butcher rubbed his face in blood and then he let him out.
The people were affrighted as up the street he ran,
His coat and breeches were so torn that he almost showed his bum.
Fal de diddle di do, etc.

His wife was affrighted as in the house he came,
He run and knocked her on the floor,
And says, "You butcher, I'll never go mending any more."
Fal de diddle di do, etc.

With its farcical action worthy of Georges Feydeau, 'The Cunning Cobbler' was extremely popular with singers and broadside printers alike, but apparently only so in England. Broadside imprints include Merry (Bedford), Jackson (Birmingham), Stewart (Carlisle), Willey (Cheltenham), Forth (Hull), Birt, Catnach, Disley, Fortey, Goode, Hodges, Such (London), Butterworth, Wheeler (Manchester), Ross, Walker (Newcastle), Harkness (Preston), Dalton (York).

Collected by Cecil Sharp from William Nott at Meshaw, Devonshire, on January 12th, 1904. The manuscript gives the song two titles: 'The Little Cobbler' and 'The Cobbler And The Butcher'. Sharp also records a rather different tune that Nott used when he repeated the song: we have used the first version. We have taken the nonsense syllables of the chorus from the version used in the music notation rather than the lyrics typescript. In verse five, "work meanwhile" would make more sense as "workmanlike", which appears in other versions.

Other versions of the song have a more logical plot. The version Henry Hammond collected from J. Hansford in Bridport, Dorset, in May 1906 makes more sense. He called it 'The Shoemaker And The Butcher'.

A story, a story to you I will tell,
Concerning of a butcher, near London did dwell.
This butcher was possessed of a beautiful wife,
And the cunning little cobbler, he loved her as his life.
To my fal the dal the dido, fal the dal the dee.

The butcher went to market to purchase an ox,
The cunning little cobbler is so sly as a fox,
He put on all his Sunday clothes and a-courting he did go,
Unto the jolly butcher's wife, he dearly loved her so.

He stepped into the butcher's shop,
The butcher's wife she knew what he meant and bid him for to stop,
Says he, "My little darling, have you got a job for me?"
The butcher's wife so cunning said, "I'll go upstairs and see."

She went into her bedroom and give the snob a call,
"I've found an easy job for you if you have found your awl,
And if this work you'll do for me, some cash will I you pay."
"Oh thank you," said the cobbler and began to work away.

And while the cobbler was at work, a rap come at the door,
The cobbler crawled beneath the bed and lied upon the floor,
Says he, "My little darling, what will your husband say?"
But she let the policeman in the room along with her to play.

Oh the butcher came from market and put them in a fright,
The policeman scrambled down the stairs and soon was out of sight.
The butcher's wife so nimble she locked the bedroom door,
And in her fright she forgot the cobbler on the floor.

Oh the butcher being drowsy, he started off for bed,
Says he, "There's something very hard and very [word omitted] inside."
Says she, "It is my rolling pin." The butcher did but laugh,
And said, "My dear, you've rolled your bread all with the policeman's staff."

Then he looked out the windows and underneath the bed,
And there he broke the mimber mug and cracked the cobbler's head,
The cobbler cried out "Murder!" He said, "What man are you?"
"I am the little man that do mend the lady's shoe."

"And if you am the little man, you come along with me,
I'll pay you well before you go for mending shoes with me."
He locked him in the bullock's pen, the beasts begin to roar,
The butcher laughed to see the fun, they turned him o'er and o'er.

So early next morning, when the people was about,
The rubbed the cobbler's face with blood and then he turned him out.
He pinned a paper to his back and on it was the news,
"The cobbler in the bedroom goes to mend the ladies' shoes."

A note on the typescript provides a helpful definition of "snob" from a dictionary of English dialect: "a vulgar person, a journeyman shoemaker". The "mimber mug" is not explained, but in context it is probably a chamber-pot.

**Recordings** Chris Foster *Jewels*; Walter Pardon *A World Without Horses*; George Spicer *Just Another Saturday Night*.

William Nott

# THE GAME OF ALL FOURS (THE PACK OF CARDS)
(ROUD 232)

As I walked out one midsummer morning,
It happened to be on a sunshiny day,
Oh there I beheld a most beautiful damsel,
As she was walking along the highway.

I stepped up to her thinking to woo her:
"Good morning to you, my pretty maid.
Where are you going so early this morning?"
"I'm going to Glasgow, sir," she said.

"Shall I go with you, my fair pretty maid,
All for to bear your sweet company?"
She looked and she aisied and at me she gazed.
"Oh yes, kind sir, you are welcome from me."

We walked together for a space of three weeks or more,
Till a little further acquainted became.
"Come sit you down by me, my pretty fair maid,
Then I will show you a curious fine game."

He took out the cards and he dealt them out gaily,
A trump to himself he had but poor Jack,
And she had the ace and the deuce for to play me,
These was the very best cards in the pack.

She threwed out her ace and took poor Jack from me,
And then she was high low Jack and the game.
He said, "Pretty fair maid, call this way tomorrow,
Then we will play the game over again."

A song that has been collected widely in England, 'The Game of All Fours' appears to have been particularly popular with Gypsy and traveller singers. Broadside imprints include Walker (Durham), Birt, Disley, Pitts (London), as 'The Cards' or 'The Game of All Fours' ('The Game of Cards' on Irish broadsides is a quite different song altogether). The maid's destination varies among singers, with Windsor appearing on a number of broadsides. It seems redundant to point out that the song is not really about a card game at all, but Maud Karpeles placed it in the sports and pastimes section of her edition of *Cecil Sharp's Collection Of English Folk Songs* (1974)!

All Fours is a genuine card game, though, one of a family of games in which the ace is high and the jack low. Various sources state that it has been played in fairly recent times in Cornwall and the Black Country. Among the earliest records is in Charles Cotton's *Compleat Gamester* (1674), and it became particularly popular in 19th-century America, where it was known as Seven-Up or Old Sledge. Anyone really wanting to know more about card games than about sex will be able to find plenty of information on the World Wide Web.

Collected by Cecil Sharp from Charles Ash at Crowcombe, in Somerset, on September 16th, 1906. In the manuscript it is called 'The Pack Of Cards'. Again, Sharp recorded a slight variation on the tune, which we have omitted for clarity. The word "aisied" in the third verse is puzzling. Some variant of "smiled" would fill the gap.

**Recordings** Brass Monkey *Flame Of Fire*; George Dunn *Chainmaker*; John Kirkpatrick *Shreds And Patches*; Sam Larner *Now Is The Time For Fishing*; Patterson Jordan Dipper *Flat Earth*; Sarah Porter *Just Another Saturday Night*; Betsy Renals *Catch Me If You Can*; Kate Rusby *The Girl Who Couldn't Fly*; Phoebe Smith *The Yellow Handkerchief*; Norma Waterson *Bright Shiny Morning*.

# THE MOLECATCHER (ROUD 1052)

I am a jol-ly mole-cat-cher by my trade. I goes_ in the fields with my trap and my spade. From morn-ing to night, from morn-ing to night, Whilst the young far-mer is play-ing with my wife. To my fol le rid-dle fol le rid-dle li___ do, Ri-te fol le ro le did-dle lol le day.

I am a jolly molecatcher by my trade,
I goes in the fields with my trap and my spade.
From morning to night, from morning to night,
Whilst the young farmer is playing with my wife.

Chorus:
To my fol le riddle fol le riddle li do,
Ri te fol le da ro le diddle lol le day.

The molecatcher he being jealous of the thing,
He waited on the banks to see him go in.
He had not been there but a very little while
Before he saw the farmer get over the stile.

He goes to the door and knocked at the ring,
"I pray then good woman is your husband within?'
"Oh no, he's gone a-molecatching, you need not have fear."
Little did she think, her husband was so near.

He goes upstairs with their best design,
The molecatcher followed after a little ways behind,
The very first stroke sat down in his lap,
"Oh," then says the molecatcher, "I've got you in my trap."

"Damn it," said the molecatcher, "I'll make you pay your ground.
The money that I'll ask you, it shall be fifty pound."
"Damn it," said the farmer, "That money I don't mind.
That'll only cost me a sixpence at a time."

Another tale of bawdy trickery, popular with singers but, surprisingly perhaps, not printed on broadsides – perhaps it was a little too explicit? James Reeves (*The Everlasting Circle*, p191) finds fornication implied even in the name of the inn, 'The Plough', which appears in some versions.

Collected by George Gardiner from George Digweed at Micheldever in Hampshire in 1906. The rhythm at the start of the second line of the chorus has been adjusted to fit the words ("Ri te").

**Recordings** Heather Alexander *Festival Wind*; Peter Bellamy *Wake The Vaulted Echoes*; Gordon Hall *In Horsham Town*; Vic Legg *I've Come To Sing A Song*; Ewan MacColl *Solo Flight*.

## MY HUSBAND'S GOT NO COURAGE IN HIM
### (OH DEAR NO) (ROUD 870)

As I walked out one summer's morning,
To view the fields and the leaves were springing,
I saw two maidens standing by,
And one of them her hands was wringing,
And all of her conversation were,
"My husband got no courage in him,
Oh dear no, Oh dear no,
My husband got no courage in him,
Oh dear no.

"All sorts of meat I do preserve,
All sorts of drink that is fitten for him,
Both oyster pies and rhubarb too,
But nothing will put courage in him.
Oh dear no, Oh dear no,
My husband got no courage in him,
Oh dear no.

"Come all you pretty maidens wherever you may be,
Don't have a man before you try him,
Lest you should sing a song with me,
My husband got no courage in him.
Oh dear no, Oh dear no,
My husband got no courage in him,
Oh dear no.

"Seven long years I've made his bed,
And six of them I've laid by the side of 'm,
And this morning I rose with my maidenhead,
That shows he got no courage in him.
Oh dear no, Oh dear no,
My husband got no courage in him,
Oh dear no."

A rather more feminine perspective on male sexual performance than, say, 'The Nutting Girl', 'My Husband's Got No Courage in Him' has been collected in both England and Scotland – not from large numbers of singers but with some women represented among them. There are a few broadside imprints as well, including Jackson, Pratt, Watts (Birmingham), Paul (London), Harkness (Preston). There are also some unascribed sheets. The apparent preponderance of Birmingham imprints is surely no slur on the menfolk of that city! "Courage" has been a euphemism for sexual potency since the 16th century.

Collected by Cecil Sharp from John Vincent (aged 72) at Harptree Lodge, Priddy, on August 29th, 1906, as 'Oh Dear No'. The words here do not entirely fit the tune collected at the same time. There are two extra lines in the first verse of the typescript, which the music notation omits. Melodic material from the verse or chorus can be adapted to supply the extra lines or they can be dropped.

**Recordings** Maddy Prior & June Tabor *Silly Sisters*.

Cecil Sharp's original notebook entry for 'Oh Dear No', collected from John Vincent in August 1906.

# THE NUTTING GIRL (ROUD 509)

It's of a brisk young damsel, she lived down in Kent.
She arose one summer's morning and she to nutting went.
There was a brisk young farmer a-ploughing of his land,
He called to his horses and bid them gently stand.

Popular with English singers, 'The Nutting Girl' has also been collected in Scotland, and there is just a single record from the USA. Most of the singers seem to have been men, and it is difficult to read the song as much more than a rather male-oriented celebration of sex. It is also used, with or without some words, as a morris dance tune.

It was popular on broadsides, too, mostly as 'The Nut Girl', with imprints including Jackson (Birmingham), Boyse (Brighton), Collard, Marshall (Bristol), Ford (Chesterfield), Forth (Hull), Batchelar, Catnach, Disley, Fortey, Hodges, Pitts, Such, Taylor (London), Jacques (Manchester), Ross, Walker (Newcastle), Henson (Northampton), Forth (Pocklington), Williams (Portsea), Harkness (Preston), Price (St Clement's), Peirce (Southborough), Johnson (York).

This version was collected by George Gardiner from Charles Chivers at Basingstoke, Hampshire, in August 1906. The typescript includes only a first verse. Gardiner also collected some words for the song, but no tune, from Richard Read, at Bishop's Sutton, also in Hampshire, in June 1905. Read's words will fit Chivers' tune:

Come all you brisk young fellows that loves to hear a song,
Come listen to my ditty, I'll not detain you long,
'Tis of a brisk young lady that lived down in Kent,
She rose one summer's morning and she to nutting went.

It's of a brisk young farmer, a-ploughing of his land,
He called to his horses and bid them gently stand.
He sat himself upon his plough, a song for to begin.
His voice was so melodious he made those valleys ring.

It's of a brisk young damsel, a-nutting in the wood,
His voice was so melodious it charmed her as she stood.
She got no longer power in that lonely wood to stay,
But what few nuts she got, poor girl, she threw them all away.

She went unto her Johnnie, as he sit on his plough,
She says, "Young man, I finds myself I'm sure I can't tell how."
He says, "My pretty fair maid, I'm glad to meet you here,
Come sit you down by the side of me, I'll keep you out of fear."

Young Johnnie left his horses, likewise he left his plough.
He took her to some shady grove, her beauty for to show.
He took her by the middle so small and then he set her down.
"Oh John," says she, "And I seems to see the world go round and round."

Young Johnnie went unto his plough, all for to finish his song.
He said, "My pretty fair maid, your mother will think it wrong."
That as they tripped along the plain, she on his breast did lean,
"Oh John," said she, "And I longs to see the world go round again."

Come all you brisk young maidens, a warning take by me,
If you should go a-nutting, I pray get home in time,
For if you should stay too long to hear that ploughboy sing,
Oh perhaps a burden you might have all in your arms in spring.

**Recordings** Tony Harvey *Songs Sung In Suffolk*; Arthur Howard *Merry Mountain Child*; Morris On *Morris On*; Will Noble *In That Beautiful* Dale; Cyril Poacher *Plenty Of Thyme*.

# THE THRASHING MACHINE (ROUD 1491)

It's of a young farm-er near Lon-don 'tis said, He kept_ a ser-vant, a

bloom-ing young maid. Her name it was Mol - ly, she was scarce-ly six - teen, She would

work ve - ry well at the thrash-ing mach - ine. Fal de dal did - dle di,

fal de dal dee, fal de dal did - dle, fal de dal dee.

It's of a young farmer near London 'tis said,
He kept a servant, a blooming young maid.
Her name it was Molly, she was scarcely sixteen,
She would work very well at the thrashing machine.

Chorus:
Fal di dal diddle di, fal di dal dee,
Fal di dal diddle, fal did al dee.

"Oh Molly," said master, "The times are hard,
Will you go with me into the farm yard?
You harness young Dobbin, you know what I mean.
I think we can manage the thrashing machine."

"Oh master," says Dolly, "What will missus say?"
"Never mind," says master, "She's making of hay.
And while she is spreading the grass that is green,
We can be working the thrashing machine."

So the barn doors were open, young Dobbin stood and sighed.
The farmer got on the machine for to ride.
"Oh master," says Molly, "You thresh very clever.
I think we can manage the threshing machine."

So young Dobbin he got tired of going round,
He hangs to the traces, he bows to the ground,
Although once in good order, he's now got a wen,
Through working so hard at the threshing machine.

Oh Molly says smiling, "We have had a loss.
I think it require a much stronger horse.
If Dobbin was strong as before he has been,
I think why we would keep working the thrashing machine."

Six months it passed over,
Molly's front parlour began for to swell,
And that shortly after she had got a wen,
The fruits of her labour with his thrashing machine.

William Nott

'The Thrashing Machine' is a typical example of the kind of English bawdy song that makes play with the tools of a particular trade or occupation. Mechanical thrashing was introduced into English agriculture in the first part of the 19th century and the machines would have been a familiar sight to rural singers from that time on.

The song has been collected from singers in England, Canada, Ireland, and Australia, though not in large numbers. It also turns up on broadsides under such imprints as Pratt (Birmingham), Hodges, Paul (London), Walker, Williamson (Newcastle), Harkness (Preston).

It is often said that singers were reluctant to sing bawdy songs like this for collectors, or that collectors were reluctant to take them down, but it might be more simply the case that collectors were not so often present on the sort of social occasions when such songs were sung. 'The Long Peggin' Awl' is a similar song, known from Harry Cox of Norfolk, and there are a handful of other records from Canada and the USA.

'The Thrashing Machine' is virtually always sung to the ubiquitous 'Villikins And Dinah' tune. 'Villikins And Dinah' was a mid 19th-century music hall parody of an earlier, highly sentimental broadside ballad, 'William And Dinah': the tune went on to be used for hundreds of different songs, most of them comic in intent. This is the tune:

Our version, however, uses a different melody. It was collected by Cecil Sharp from William Nott at Meshaw, Devonshire, on January 9th, 1904. The typed words have been amended slightly to match those on the music manuscript: "farmer" has become "young farmer" and the chorus is different. A "wen" is a swelling.

**Recordings** Lehto & Wright *The Thrashing Machine And Other Stories*; Ewan MacColl *The Wanton Muse*; Annie O'Neil *Songs of Seduction*; George Spicer *Down In The Fields*; The Yetties *Our Friends*.

Ewan MacColl

# Songs of trickery and outwitting

There is a significant strain in English folk song that depicts various ways in which characters get the better of one another. At one end of the spectrum are comic tales, like 'Marrow Bones', which are akin to the medieval *fabliaux* – comic stories about trickery and sex in which the viewpoint is seemingly largely amoral and the respectable tend to suffer at the hands of the disreputable (Chaucer's *Miller's Tale* and *Reeve's Tale* are fine examples of the genre). Other songs involve robbers being beaten at their own game. At the most serious end of the spectrum are songs in which women in particular have to rely on their native wit in order to save themselves from various kinds of unpleasant fate, including becoming victims of the Devil.

It is perhaps not immediately obvious that the slapstick comedy of 'The Farmer's Curst Wife' is very far along the spectrum towards seriousness but, however lightly told, the fact is that the 'heroine' of the ballad does defeat the Devil and so escapes from hell. 'The Outlandish Knight' and 'The Broomfield Wager' are threatening and mysterious ballads, with heroines who at moments recall those of Shakespeare.

The battle of the sexes is a constant theme running through many of these songs of trickery and outwitting, and at least some of them could be thought of as women's songs. Yet there is also a crossover here, evident in songs like 'Bonny Kate' and 'The Oyster Girl', with the more overtly bawdy folk songs such as 'The Molecatcher' and 'The Cunning Cobbler', and it is not at all clear that English folk song resolves the battle of the sexes any more definitively than do the tales of Chaucer or the plays of Shakespeare. Female characters, as might be expected, seem more likely to win by using their wits than through sheer strength. But, as in Shakespeare, their triumphs are often contained within a conventional social framework; clever women win, for example, exemplary husbands.

As Vic Gammon ('Song, Sex, And Society in England, 1600–1850') has demonstrated in relation to the more overtly sexual songs, folk songs reproduce and contribute to the maintenance of the durable principles underpinning a social system – what sociologists, following Pierre Bourdieu, term *habitus*. After all, conflict, and its resolution, are at the heart of all social systems, and one can reasonably expect folk songs to mirror this, though in an artistic and not necessarily realistic manner.

# THE BAFFLED KNIGHT (NEW MOWN HAY)
(CHILD 112; ROUD 11)

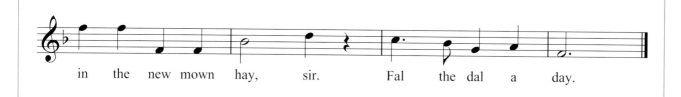

As I walked out one May morning,
To view the fields all round, sir,
And there I spied a pretty little maid,
All on the new mown hay, sir.
Fol the dol a day.

I asked if she to wed with me
All on the new mown hay,
And answer that she gave to me,
"I'm afraid it will not do, sir."
Fol the dol a day.

"And if you go to my father's yard
When it's walled all around, sir,
And there you shall have the will of me
And thirty thousand pound, sir."
Fol the dol a day.

When he came to her father's yard,
Where it's all walled around, sir,
She whipped inside her father's door
And barred this young man out, sir.
Fol the dol a day.

"When you met me in that field
You thought you met a fool, sir,
Go take your bible in your hand,
Go a little more to school, sir."
Fol the dol a day.

"There is a shrub in my father's yard,
It's called the merry girl, sir,
If young men want to when they can,
They shall not when they will, sir."
Fol the dol a day.

"There is a cock in my father's yard,
He will not tread the hen, sir,
And I really believe in all my heart
That thou are the same, sir."
Fol the dol a day.

'The Baffled Knight' can be traced back to Thomas Ravenscroft's *Deuteromelia* of 1609, with several subsequent 17th-century broadside printings and appearances in influential publications such as Thomas Durfey's *Pills to Purge Melancholy* (1719–20) and Thomas Percy's *Reliques of Ancient English Poetry* (1765). Some of the 17th-century broadsides capitalized on the popularity of the ballad with second, third, and fourth parts, which relate further encounters in the course of which the maid continues to outwit her libidinous suitor. Later broadside imprints include Lane (Durham), Dicey and Marshall, Pitts (London), Harkness (Preston), and Baird (Cork), and the ballad has been widely collected in England and, less often, in Scotland and North America.

'The Baffled Knight' is essentially an illustration of the proverb 'He that will not when he may, when he would he shall have nay' – in other words, take your opportunities while you have the chance – which the *Oxford Dictionary Of English Proverbs* records as far back as an Anglo-Saxon *Homily* of the 10th century, with later references as diverse as Robert Burton's *Anatomy Of Melancholy* (1638) and Robert Louis Stevenson's *Catriona* (1893). The proverb finds garbled expression in the sixth verse of this version. The broadside printed by Lane in Durham includes a verse that states it more clearly:

> There's crowing cocks in our town,
> We'll make a capon of you, sir;
> We have a flower in our garden,
> Some call it a marigold, sir.
> And he that would not when he might,
> He shall not when he would, sir.

The verse also includes a taste of the quasi-proverbial material that is more apparent in the longer versions: a horse that dare not help itself to corn; the cock that does not tread the hen; and the marigold. This last has never been satisfactorily explained, though 'To Marygolds' by Robert Herrick (1591–1674) ought to be pertinent (Reeves, *The Idiom of the People*, p43):

> Give way, and be ye ravisht by the Sun,
> (And hang the head when as the Act is done)
> Spread as He spreads; wax lesse as he do's wane;
> And as he shuts, close up to Maids again.

A phonograph recording was made in December 1907 by Cecil Sharp of (probably) Alfred Edgell singing 'Among The New Mown Hay', which has often been considered as the same song as 'The Baffled Knight', although it is now generally distinguished as a different song (Roud 2941). With its strong melody and resourceful heroine, 'The Baffled Knight' invites comparison with 'The Broomfield Wager' (p216).

This version of 'The Baffled Knight', was collected by Cecil Sharp from John Dingle at Coryton, in Devon, on September 12th, 1905, as 'New Mown Hay'.

**Recordings** Emily Bishop *Country Songs & Carols*; Sam Larner *Now Is The Time For Fishing*; William Rew *Songs Of Seduction*.

## BONNY KATE (ROUD 1633)

'Twas of Newmarket you shall hear,
There did dwell a damsel fair.
'Twas of Newmarket you shall hear
There did dwell a damsel fair.
Some they called her Bonny Kate,
Going to, coming from Newmarket late.

Oh, oft times a lawyer she did meet,
Who enticed her with kisses sweet.
Oh, oft times a lawyer did she meet,
Who enticed her with kisses sweet.
He enticed her more and more,
Shewed her gold and silver store.

"Oh, if it's you will sleep in town,
These five guineas I'll put down.
Oh, if it's you will sleep in town,
These five guineas I'll put down."
She took him then to the sign of 'The Bell'
Where in service she did dwell.

"Can I have a bed," said he,
"For my wedded wife and me?"
"Can I have a bed," said he,
"For my wedded wife and me?"
"Oh yes, kind sir," the landlord said,
No, nor he did not own his maid.

"Can I have a supper dressed,
Fish and fowl of the best?
Can I have a supper dressed,
Fish and fowl of the best?
And a bottle of wine to drink a while,
For young Kate has walked a dozen mile."

After supper the glass went round,
Until the score came to one pound.
After supper the glass went round,
Until the score came to one pound.
That the lawyer freely paid.
"Now to bed, young Kate," he said.

Young Kate she was handed on before,
And at the top there was a door.
Young Kate she was handed on before,
And at the top there was a door.
Young Kate she went straightway through,
That's where she bid the lawyer adieu.

Lord, how this lawyer stamped and swore,
When he found he'd lost his dear.
Lord, how this lawyer stamped and swore,
When he found he'd lost his dear.
And young Kate's heart was crowned with joy,
To think she'd got five yellow boys.

This delightful song about a clever maid is very rare, in spite of the satirical appeal of a story that involves outwitting a lawyer. George B. Gardiner collected a version in Hampshire in 1907 and Cecil Sharp found one in Devon in 1905, and that seems to be it. Neither survives as a sound recording, but the song became well known to the folk revival from the singing of Shirley Collins, and the tune is also well known as a fiddle tune or reel.

Collected by George Gardiner from William Burgess at Titchfield, Hampshire, in September 1907. The music was taken down by J.T. Guyer. "He did not own his maid", in verse four, means he did not acknowledge her. The "five yellow boys" in the final verse are the five guineas.

**Recordings** Shirley Collins *Amaranth*; John Doherty *Johnny Doherty*; The Etchingham Steam Band (includes Shirley Collins) *The Etchingham Steam Band*.

## THE BROOMFIELD WAGER (BROOMFIELD HILL)
(CHILD 43; ROUD 34) As sung by Gordon Hall.

CD TRACK 9

1. As I was a-walk-ing one morn-ing at ease, A-
view-ing those leaves as they hung on the trees, They were
all in full mo-tion ap-pear-ing to be, And
those that were wi-thered,___ they fell from the tree.
Then what is the life of a man, a-ny more___ than the leaves? A
man has his sea-son, and why should he grieve? Although in this wide world he ap-pears bright and
gay, Like the leaves he will wi-ther___ and soon fade a-way.

"One wager, one wager, I will lay unto thee,
One hundred bright nobles to your ten,
That you will ne'er me follow to the bonny Broomfield Hill,
And a maiden you never shall return."

"One wager, one wager, I will lay unto thee,
Your hundred bright nobles to my ten,
That I will go a maiden to the bonny Broomfield Hill,
And will come back a maiden once again."

There was a knight and a lady so bright
Had a true tryst at the broom,
The one to go ride early on the May morning,
And the other in the afternoon.

The maiden sat at her mother's bower door,
And there she made her moan,
Saying, "Whether shall I go to the bonny Broomfield Hill,
Or shall I bide me at home?"

"For if I shall go to the bonny Broomfield Hill,
Then my maidenhead is gone,
But if I bide me at my mother's bower door,
Then my true love will call me forsworn."

Then up then spake an old witch-woman,
All from her lofty room,
Saying, "Well you may go to the bonny Broomfield Hill,
And yet come a maiden home.

"For when you reach the bonny Broomfield Hill,
You will find your love asleep,
With a costly silver belt about his neck,
And its brother about his feet.

"Then take the blossom from off the green broom,
The blossom that smells so sweet,
And lay it down at his white collarbone,
There and place the twigs at his feet.

"Then take the ring from off your soft white hand
And place it on your true love's right thumb
That this will be of a token to your true love when he wakes
He will know that you have been at his command."

"One wager, one wager, I will lay unto thee,
Your hundred bright nobles to my ten,
Then I will go a maiden to the bonny Broomfield Hill,
And will come back a maiden once again."

The knight jogged on to the bonny Broomfield Hill,
The weather being very mild and warm,
As he became quite weary, why he sat him down to rest,
And he fell fast asleep on the green lawn.

Now when the maiden reached the bonny Broomfield Hill,
She found her love asleep,
With a costly silver belt about his neck,
And its brother about his feet.

Then took she the blossom from off the green bloom,
The blossom that smelled so sweet,
And laid it at his white collar bone,
Then placed the twigs at his feet.

Then three times she danced around the soles of his shoon,
And stroked down the hair of his head,
And three times she kissed his ruby ruby lips,
As he lay fast asleep on his green bed.

Then the ring from her finger she instanter withdrew,
And placed it on her true love's right thumb,
Saying, "This will be a token to my true love when he wakes,
He will know that I have been at his command."

Now when the knight woke from out of his long sleep,
And espied the maiden's ring on his right thumb,
He knew that the fair maid had been at his command,
And the tryst wager she had won.

"Oh where were ye, my milk white steed,
That I have cost so dear,
That would not watch and waken me,
When there was a maiden here?"

"I stamped with my feet, master,
Which made my bright bridle ring.
But no kind of thing would waken ye
Till the maiden was past and gone."

"And where were you, my gay goshawk,
That I have loved so dear,
That would not watch and waken me
When there was a maiden here?"

"I flapped with my wings, master,
Which made my bright bell to ring,
But nothing of this earth would waken ye,
Till the maiden was past and gone."

217

"And where were ye, my addle-pated page,
As draws my meat and fee,
That would not watch and waken me,
Till the maiden skipped over the lea?"

"I prodded and shook, master,
Now have I this to say,
That if you lay still when laid abed at night,
Then you would not sleep through the day."

"One wager, one wager, I did lay unto thee,
Your hundred bright nobles to my ten,
I did go a maiden to the bonny Broomfield Hill,
And did come back a maiden once again."

"If I had been awake, when I was fast asleep,
Of you I would have had my will,
Or it's you I would have killed and your red blood would have spilled,
And the small birds would all have had their fill."

"You hard-hearted young man, how can you say so?
Your heart must be hard as any stone,
For to think to murder one that has loved thee so long,
And has danced on the green and mossy lawn."

"One wager, one wager, I did lay unto thee,
Your one hundred bright nobles to my ten,
And I did go a maiden to the bonny Broomfield Hill,
And did come back a maiden once again.

"Yes, I did go a maiden to the bonny Broomfield Hill
And did come back a maiden once again."

This song is usually known as 'The Broomfield Wager', but it was sung and recorded by Gordon Hall as 'Broomfield Hill'. 'The broom' in folk songs is often a place for sexual liaisons. Some earlier texts of this ballad have an aura of magic and witchery, but the collected versions tend to recount a more straightforward wager on a woman's chastity, which led Child to comment on the "pungent buckishness" of the broadside text. The terms of the wager vary and the exact sum is probably not of great import. Rather, the point is that the woman stands to lose everything; the man, on the other hand, stands to enjoy either just a good long sleep or the woman's virginity.

'The Broomfield Wager' has been widely collected in England, and also in Scotland, Ireland, and the USA, and it was printed on various broadsides of the 18th and 19th centuries, with imprints including Russell (Birmingham), Turner (Coventry), Disley, Pitts (London), and White (Newcastle). Hugh Shields mentions a Dublin broadside in which a girl for a wager deceives a local Don Juan by dressing up as a man dressed up as a girl (*Narrative Singing In Ireland*, p94).

On the one hand, the ballad perpetuates the double standard of sexual morality that has perhaps always characterized English society. Quite a number of collected versions, moreover, include a stanza that contains a real threat of violence:

If only I had her fast in my arms
And I could but have my will,
All the birds in the wood should drink of her blood
Until they had all had their fill. (JFSS (1910), 110–11)

Is he threatening to rape her, or to kill her if she does not yield to him? Or does he mean that he will injure or kill her if she *does* surrender to him and thus devalues herself? On the other hand, the ballad provides us with another resourceful heroine, and in the end it mocks at the man's laddishness and over-confidence.

**Recordings** George Dunn *Chainmaker*; Jo Freya *Traditional Songs Of England*; Gordon Hall *When The May Is All In Bloom*; Walter Pardon *Hidden English*; Cyril Poacher *Plenty Of Thyme*; John Roberts & Tony Barrand *Dark Ships In The Forest*; June Tabor *At The Wood's Heart*.

Gordon Hall

## THE FARMER'S CURST WIFE (DEVIL AND FARMER)
(CHILD 278; ROUD 160)

There was an old farmer in Yorkshire did dwell,
(Whistle)
He had an old wife and he wished her in hell.
Sing fa la la la, fa la la la, sing fal la la liddle la day.

Oh the devil came in when he was at plough,
Saying, "One of your family I will have now."

"Now, Oh Mr Devil, and which do you crave?"
"Your ugly old wife, and she I will have."

So they bundled the old woman into a sack
The devil he lugged her away on his back.

So when Mr Devil he came up to his door,
You must go in there , you infernal old whore.

There she saw three young devils a-hanging in chains,
She took off her pattens, got smashing their brains.

So they to the Devil for mercy did call,
"This infernal old whore she will kill us all."

So they bundled the old woman out over the wall
She fell on her arse a most hell of a fall.

So the women they're ten times worse than the men,
For they've been into hell and got kicked out again.

Child's title for this ballad, 'The Farmer's Curst Wife', emphasizes its connection with misogynistic literature more than do some of the other titles by which it is known, such as 'The Devil And The Farmer's Wife' or 'The Devil And The Ploughman'. But the fact remains that the farmer's wife gets the better of the Devil and his imps by virtue of her sheer obstreperousness.

In some versions the devils are found dancing in chains or on a wire, and this has prompted the suggestion that there is a connection with medieval mystery plays. The ballad cannot be shown to go back that far in time. The earliest extant record probably lies in the 19th-century broadsides printed by Pitts (London), but Robert Burns rewrote the ballad as 'Kellyburnbraes', so it must have been around in the 18th century. In addition, 17th-century broadsides of 'The Devil and the Scold' (*Roxburghe Ballads*, II, 366–71) tell a very similar story, where the wife's scolding and drunken debauchery are depicted even more graphically, and she gives the Devil an equally rough ride (literally, for he appears in the form of a horse to take her to hell). Certainly, though, the serio-comic treatment of the theme of damnation is comparable to its treatment in medieval popular drama.

The misogynistic element in the ballad cannot be readily explained away. The farmer's wife is stereotyped as a 'scold' even if she can defeat the Devil. Suffice it to say, however, that there is more than one way to inflect lines such as:

> You see the women is worse than the men,
> If they get sent to Hell, they get kicked back again.
> (*JFSS* 1906, 184–85)

or:

> The women they are so much better than men,
> When they go to hell they're sent back again.
> (Sharp, *English Folk Songs from the Southern Appalachians*, I, 277–78)

'The Farmer's Curst Wife' has proven extremely popular with traditional singers in England, Scotland, Ireland, and especially North America. No doubt some of this popularity can be attributed to a catchy tune and, in this version, a whistling chorus (whistling has been believed to be unlucky and to risk precipitating evil).

Collected by Henry Hammond from Sam Dawe at Beaminster, in Dorset, in June 1906. The song is recorded as 'Devil And Farmer (Curst Wife)'. It is the only tune in this book with a whistled refrain after the first line of each verse. The handwritten lyrics have the words "Loose & humorous" written above them. Each subsequent verse follows the pattern of the first, with the whistled line interpolated and the nonsense chorus sung twice at the end.

**Recordings** Horton Barker *Anglo-American Ballads, Vol. 1;* E2K *Shift;* Texas Gladden *Ballad Legacy*, as 'The Devil And The Farmer's Wife'; Spider John Koerner *Raised By Humans;* Thomas Moran *Folk Songs Of Britain, Vol 5;* Tim O'Brien & The O'Boys *Oh Boy! O'Boy!;* Walter Pardon *A World Without Horses*, as 'The Devil And The Farmer's Wife'; Pete Seeger *American Ballads*.

## THE GYPSY LASS (ROUD 229)

My father is the king of the gypsies, 'tis true,
My mother she learned me some cabinet to do.
With my pack on my back and they all wish me well,
I started off for London some fortunes for to tell,
Some fortunes for to tell, some fortunes for to tell,
I started off to London some fortunes for to tell.

As I was a-walking through fine London streets,
A handsome young squire I chanced for to meet.
When he viewed cheeks and it pleased him so well,
He says, "My little gypsy lass, can you my fortune tell?"

Oh yes, kind sir, give me hold of your hand,
Oh you have got riches, both houses and land,
And all these pretty lasses you must put them aside,
For it's this little gypsy lass that will be your bride.

Adieu to the meadows and shady groves,
No more with my sisters accompanying I'll go.
For the bells they shall ring merrily and the sweet music play,
And we'll crown the glad tidings of that lucky day.

Oh once I was a gypsy lass, but now a squire's bride;
I've servants now to wait on me and in my carriage ride.

'The Gypsy Lass' or 'The Gypsy's Wedding-Day' is first known on an 18th-century broadside. Imprints in the 19th century include Jackson, Pratt, Russell, Taylor (Birmingham), Hook (Brighton), Stewart (Carlisle), Lindsay (Glasgow), Birt, Catnach, Disley, Hillatt and Martin, Paul, Pitts, Ryle, Such (London), Wheeler (Manchester), Forth (Pocklington), Williams (Portsea), Harkness (Preston), Ford (Sheffield), Sefton (Worcester). It was also printed in America.

The song has been widely collected in England and the USA. Again, a young woman gets the better of a man, with the predicted reward of marriage, and on this occasion her social status is substantially elevated too. Though collected from Gypsy singers, as might be expected, the song is by no means restricted to any particular group, with plenty of male as well as female performers.

Collected by Cecil Sharp from William Nott at Meshaw, in Devon, on January 9th, 1904. The "some cabinet" that the girl learns in line two is a garbled version of a reference to camping in the broadsides. It seems likely that each verse had a chorus, constructed on the same pattern as that of the first verse.

**Recordings** Eliza Carthy *Anglicana*; Shirley Collins *No Roses*; Burl Ives *Sings His Favourites*; Esma Redzepova & Usnija Jasarova *Songs Of A Macedonian Gypsy*; Jasper Smith *The Voice Of The People, Vol. 11*, as 'The Squire And The Gypsy'; Joseph Taylor *The Voice Of The People, Vol. 1*; Percy Webb *Songs From The Company Of The Butley Oyster*.

# THE HIGHWAYMAN OUTWITTED (ROUD 2638)

In Surrey there lived an old farmer,
And his daughter to market do go,
And she swore that no one would hurt her,
But still she kept going to and fro.

One night as she was a-walking,
A highwayman met her on the highway,
And he clapped his pistol up to her,
And soon he did 'blige her to stay.

He stripped this damsel stark naked
And gave her the bridle to hold;
And she stood shivering and shaking
Just ready to perish with the cold.

She hitched her right foot in the stirrup,
"Here's adieu to all false highwaymen"
And, as she was gently galloping,
She says, "Catch me, kind sir, if you can."

This highwayman soon followed after,
Which made him to puff and to blow.
When he found he could nowise overtake her,
He said, "Stop, and I'll give you your clothes."

"My clothes I don't value, it's nothing,
You can keep it, kind Sir, if you please."
Then he found he could nowise overtake her,
For his boots they encumbered his knees.

She rode through woods and through valleys,
Till she came to some place that she knowed,
And the first that she met was her father,
Saying, "Damsel, Oh where is your clothes?"

"I've been robbed all by some highwayman,
I've been robbed all on the highway,
And he clapped a pistol up to me,
And soon he did 'blige me to stay."

He pulled a portmantel all from the horse,
And laid it on the ground floor,
Saying, "Damsel, here is your portmantel,
To keep the cold wind from the door."

Typical of a group of songs in which the tables are turned on robbers, this one has a resourceful and resilient young woman in the role of heroine, and in spite of being left to return home on horseback stark naked, she usually comes off decidedly the richer. Collected in England, Canada, and Tristan da Cunha, 'The Highwayman Outwitted', also known as 'The Farmer in Cheshire' (and other counties may substitute), appeared on broadsides from various printers including Pitts (London) and Harkness (Preston).

Two other songs are sufficiently closely related as to be at times virtually indistinguishable. One is 'The Yorkshire Bite', or 'The Crafty Ploughboy' (Roud 2637), in which a farmer's boy outwits a highwayman. The other is 'The Crafty Farmer' (Child 283; Roud 2640), it is the farmer himself who tricks a thief. 'The Crafty Farmer' can be traced rather further back in time than either of the other two songs, to the 18th century, and it is likely that this is the period in which they all have their origins. All three are commonly sung to a 17th-century tune known as 'The Rant', or 'Give Ear To A Frolicksome Ditty'..

'The Box Upon Her Head', or 'The Undaunted Female' (Roud 289) is another comparable song, with a particularly strong record in broadside print, which sees a servant girl defeat a series of robbers, less by her wits than through sheer physical courage.

Collected by George Gardiner from Daniel Newman (aged 65) at Axford, in Hampshire, in September 1907. The tune was noted by Charles Gamblin. A note on the music manuscript by Frank Purslow, who edited the tune for the *Marrow Bones* series of songbooks, comments, "This is an exact copy of Gamblin's original notation, but the tune does not fit the text. There seems to be a bar missing." A suggestion is made for the missing bar, and we have adopted it. The broadside version printed by Pitt makes the young woman's cunning more explicit. She climbs on the horse while the highwayman is counting her money:

> She rode over hedges and ditches,
> And places she knew very well.
> And she left him with a parcel of farthings,
> The sum of five shillings to tell.

She and her father do rather better:

> They searched this thief's portmantel,
> And they searched his budget all round,
> And they found as much gold in treasure,
> As 'mounted to five thousand pound.

Both "portmantel" and "budget" are leather bags or purses, although the former seems also to mean a coat.

**Recordings** Alec Bloomfield *Good Order!*, as 'The Farmer From Cheshire'; Packie Byrne *Donegal & Back!*; The Copper Family *Coppersongs 2*, as 'The Farmer In Cheshire'; Magpie Lane *English Songs And Dances*; Jimmy McBeath *Up In The North And Down In The South*, as 'The Farmer In Cheshire'; Harry Scott *The Leaves Of Life*, as 'The Box Upon Her Head'; Charlie Stringer *Songs Sung In Suffolk*, as 'The Farmer From Cheshire'; Jane & Amanda Threlfall *Gown Of Green*.

## MARROW BONES (ROUD 183)
### (THERE WAS AN OLD WOMAN or THE RICH OLD LADY)

There was a woman in Crewkerne town,
In Crewkerne town did dwell,
She loved her husband dearly,
But another man (word omitted) as well.

Chorus:
To my diddle fol la,
Hi diddle dee,
Hi diddle fi diddle day.

The old man being weary,
(Line missing.)
He swored he go and drown himself,
If he could find the well.

And unto her did say,
She went unto the doctor,
To see what she could find,
You get some dozen o' marrow.

The old woman being tender-hearted,
She led him to the stream,
And the old man nimbly popped aside,
And the old woman tumbled in.

The old woman being struggling,
And getting near the brim,
With a jolly great long pole,
He shoved her further in.

The old woman being gone to the bottom,
And could no more be seen,
The old man he went laughing home,
And gained his sight again.

So there's an end to my song, sir,
And I can sing no more.
And they that say that I can, sir,
Be a liar and a son of a whore.

With my to meri fa la
Tiddi fal la
Fal the la tiddi fal la.

This is one of two, very similar, ditties quite frequently collected in England, Scotland, Ireland, and North America. Both this song and 'Johnny Sands' employ the comic but nonetheless misogynistic theme of the 'scolding' wife (she is so described in the titles of certain versions of 'Johnny Sands') being 'duly' punished. 'Marrow Bones' was printed (under the title 'There Was an Old Woman in Yorkshire') by Pitts (London) and in an Edinburgh chapbook. Nevertheless, the record in print is perhaps rather sparse, considering the evidence of the popularity of both songs with traditional singers.

Collected by Cecil Sharp from Mr Warren, at Haselbury Plucknett, Somerset, on August 23rd, 1905. The song is recorded as 'There Was An Old Woman' or 'The Rich Old Lady'. This is obviously a very incoherent and truncated set of words.

Sharp only collected one other version in England, from Thomas Taylor at Ross workhouse, in Herefordshire, in 1921. Here the story is much more complete:

There was an old woman in our town,
In our town did dwell,
And she loved her old husband dearly,
But another man twice as well.

(Chorus)
Sing whip she la-rey, tid-i-foo la-rey,
Whip she la-rey O.

Now she went and got six marrow-bones
And she made him suck them all,
And that made the old man blind
Till he couldn't see any at all.

The old man said he'd drown himself
If he could find the way.
The old woman quickly answered:
Oh I'll show you the way.

She led him to the water
And took him to the brim.
And he said he'd drown himself
If she would push him in.

The old woman she went to give a run,
To push the old man in,
And he popped to the one side,
And the woman went tumbling in.

She plunged about in the water,
A-thinking she could swim,
But the old man went and got a puthering prop,
And he propped her further in.

So now my song is ended,
You may pen it down in ink,
I won't bother my head to sing any more
If you don't give me some drink.

**Recordings** Seamus Ennis *The Bonny Bunch Of Roses*; John Kirkpatrick *Shreds And Patches*, as 'Johnny Sands'; Jimmy Knights *The Voice Of The People, Vol. 6*; Red Mick McDermott *The Hardy Sons Of Dan*; Will Noble *In That Beautiful Dale*, as 'Johnny Sands'; Steeleye Span *Ten Man Mop, Or Mr Reservoir Butler Rides Again*.

### THE OUTLANDISH KNIGHT (CHILD 4; ROUD 21)
As sung by Vic Legg.

CD TRACK 10

1. There was a young man came from the north lands, He came here one day un-to me. He said that he'd take me back to the north lands, And that's where he would mar-ry me, mar-ry me, And that's where he would mar-ry me.

2. "You get me some of your mo-ther's food, and some of your fa-ther's gold. You take me to-night to your fa-ther's sta-ble, where nags do stand thir-ty and three, Where nags do stand thir-ty and three. You take me to-night to your fa-ther's sta-ble, Where nags do stand thir-ty and three."

There was a young man came from the north lands
He came here one day unto me.
He said that he'd take me back to the north lands
And that's where he would marry me, marry me,
And that's where he would marry me.

"You get me some of your mother's food,
And some of your father's gold,
You take me tonight to your father's stables,
Where nags do stand thirty and three,
Where nags do stand thirty and three.
You take me tonight to your father's stables
Where nags do stand thirty and three."

I got him some of my mother's food,
And some of my father's gold.
I took him that night to my father's stable,
Where nags do stand thirty and three.

"Mount on, mount on, my pretty Polly,
Mount on mount on," cried he.
We rode till we came to the wide river side,
These words then he shouted to me.

"Pull up, pull up, my pretty Polly,
Pull up, pull up," cried he.
"For six pretty maidens I have a-drowned here,
The seventh now you shall be, shall be,
The seventh now you shall be."

"And take me off your fine silk gown,
And give it on over to me.
For it seems such a pity, such a fine gown as that,
To be rotted all in the salt sea."

"You turn your back to the facing of me,
In viewing those flowers so gay.
For it isn't fitting such a ruffian as you,
For a naked young woman to see."

He turned his back to the facing of her,
In viewing those flowers so gay,
She wrapped her arms around his waist,
And bundled him in the salt sea, the salt sea.
And bundled him in the salt sea.

"Oh take me out, my pretty Polly,
Oh take me out," cried he.
"Oh take me out, my pretty Polly,
My bride then you shall be."

"Stay there, stay there, you false-hearted man,
Stay there instead of me.
For six pretty maidens you have a-drowned here,
The seventh hath drownded thee."

She mounted on the milk-white steed,
And led the dapple grey,
She rode till she came to her father's house,
Three hours before it was day.

The parrot up in the window so high,
A-viewing the lady did say,
"I'm afraid that some ruffian has led you astray,
That you tarried so long away."

"Oh don't you flitter or flatter Polly,
Nor tell your tales upon me,
And your cage shall be made of the glitters of gold,
And the door of the best ivory, ivory,
And the door of the best ivory."

Astonishingly popular among traditional singers in the English-speaking world, 'The Outlandish Knight', or 'Lady Isabel And Elf-Knight', as Child called it, offers a kind of serious counterpart to 'Marrow Bones', at least as far as the drowning motif is concerned. Here, though, the woman triumphs: a young woman who has allowed herself to be seduced by a stranger's promises of marriage, nonetheless proves sufficiently resourceful to save herself once she becomes aware that her 'suitor' is in fact a serial killer. Moreover, she still has the wit to keep her own counsel, with the assistance of her faithful parrot, when her father's suspicions are aroused by her return home while it is still night.

The ballad of 'The Outlandish Knight' has counterparts right across Europe, and this whole body of European balladry is sometimes referred to by the title of the Flemish/Dutch ballad, 'Heer Halewijn', which may represent the earliest form of the story. It is though to have entered England from France, with additional dissemination into Scotland from Scandinavia. Vargyas (*Researches into the Mediaeval History of Folk Ballad*, pp129–57) describes the progress of the ballad across Europe, with reproductions of iconographic representations of the story from sources such as wall paintings in European churches.

Although truth-telling turtle doves alert the heroine to her imminent danger in some of the German ballads (and Child took these birds to be the spirits of earlier victims), the episode with the parrot is unique to the English-language ballad. Talking birds are not unknown in other English-language ballads; for example, 'Young Hunting' (Child 68; Roud 47), which has remained current with traditional singers in America. But as a talking bird, the parrot of 'The Outlandish Knight' is much more remarkable for what it does *not* say than for what it *does* say; in short, it keeps the heroine's secret. So the parrot, and its supposed escape from the intrusive cat, provides a disturbing image of the ballad heroine. Having been awakened to her own sexuality and learned a sharp lesson from the experience, she, like the parrot, finds herself confined once again to her domestic environment. Resourceful though she may be, a bird in a gilded cage is a highly pertinent emblem (which can be seen in art works of various kinds, especially Flemish and Dutch genre paintings of the 16th and 17th centuries) for a social system that places a high value on female chastity.

Notwithstanding Child's title, and the illusion that no time at all has passed in those versions that repeat, both at the heroine's departure and on her return home, the phrase 'Three hours before it was day', this is not a supernatural ballad. The title 'The Outlandish Knight', by which the song is almost exclusively known to English singers, employs what was until recently a common English word, meaning no more than "a stranger". Shirley Collins recalls a conversation with her neighbours, Fanny and Will Eastwood, in Etchingham, Sussex, in the 1970s: "Talking one day to Fanny, who was then in her eighties, about her early life, she told me she'd been courted by another man before she married Will, but couldn't marry him 'because he was too outlandish'. 'What was so outlandish about him?' I asked, intrigued. 'Oh, he came from a village about three miles away,' she replied!" (Shirley and Dolly Collins, *Love, Death & the Lady*.) In America the song is sometimes known as 'Pretty Polly', in Scotland as 'May Colvin', and in Ireland as 'False Sir John'.

In spite of its European pedigree, the ballad cannot easily be traced back to a very early date. Although there are numerous broadsides extant, most bear 19th-century imprints, including Johnson (Beverley), Marshall (Bristol), Ford (Chesterfield), Catnach, Dever, Disley, Fortey, Hill, Pitts, Such, Taylor (London), Williams (Portsea). A broadside without imprint in the *Roxburghe Ballads* (VII, 383), however, is probably of the 18th century.

Vic Legg's version omits a passage, found in the broadsides, in which the parrot, having been overheard by the father, explains away why he is making a noise.

> The king being in his chamber so high,
> And hearing the parrot did say,
> "What ails you, what ails you my pretty polly,
> That you prattle so long before day?"

"It's no laughing matter," the parrot did say,
"But so loudly I call unto thee,
For the cats have got into the window so high,
And I'm afraid that they'll have me."

The parrot is then rewarded for his ingenuity by being given the gold cage with the ivory door.

**Recordings** Bellowhead *Burlesque*; May Bradley *Garners Gay*; Martin Carthy *Shearwater*; Shirley Collins *Love Death & The Lady*; Fred Jordan *Hidden English*; Vic Legg *I've Come To Sing A Song*; Sarah Porter *Just Another Saturday Night*; Jean Ritchie *Ballads From Her Appalachian Family Tradition*, as 'False Sir John'; Spriguns *Revel Weird & Wild*; Lisa Theriot *A Turning Of Seasons*, as 'Lady Isabel & The Elf Knight'; Waterson:Carthy *A Dark Light*.

One of many 19th-century broadsides of 'The Outlandish Knight', printer unknown.

# THE · OUTLANDISH Knight

AN Outlandish Knight came from the North
And he came a wooing to me. [land,
*He* told me he'd take me unto the North lands
And there he would marry me,

Come fetch me some of your father's gold,
And some of your mother's fee.
And two of the best nags out of the stable
Where they stood thirty and three

She fetched him some of her father's gold
and some of her mother's fee,
And two of the best nags out of the stable,
Where they stood thirty and three,

She mounted on her milk white steed,
He on the dapple grey,
They rode till they came unto the sea side,
Three hours before it was day,

Light off, light off thy milk white steed,
And deliver it unto me,
Six pretty maids have I drowned here,
And thou the seventh shall be,

Pull off, pull off thy silken gown,
And deliver it unto me.
Methinks it looks too rich and too gay,
To rot in the salt salt sea,

Pull off pull off thy silken stays,
And deliver them unto me.
Methinks they are too fine and gay,
To rot in the salt salt sea,

Pull off, pull off, thy Holland smock,
And deliver it unto me,
Methinks it looks too rich and too gay.
To rot in the salt salt sea,

If I must pull off my holland smock.
Pray turn back unto me,
For it is not fitting that such a ruffian,
A naked woman should see,

He turned his back towards her,
and viewed the leaves so green,
She catched him round the middle so small
And tumbled him into the stream

He dropped high and he dropped low,
Until he came to the side,
Catch hold of my hand my pretty Polly,
And I will make you my bride,

Lie there, lie there, you false hearted man,
Lie there instead of me,
Six pretty maidens have you drowned here,
and the seventh has drowned thee,

she mounted on her milk white steed
And led the dapple grey,
She rode till she came to her own father's hall
Three hours before it was day,

The parrot being in the window so high
And hearing the lady did say,
I'm afraid that some ruffian has led you astray.
That you have tarried so long away,

Don't prittle nor prattle my pretty parrot,
Nor tell no tales of me,
Thy cage shall be made of the glittering gold
Although it is made of a tree,

The King being in the chamber so high,
and hearing the parrot did say,
What ails you what ails you my pretty parrot
That you prattle so long before day,

Its no laughing matter the parrot did say,
But so loudly I call unto thee.
For the cats have got into the window so high,
And I am afraid they will have me

Well turned, well turned, my pretty parrot,
Well turned, well turned for me,
Thy cage shall be made of the glittering gold
and the door of the best ivory

## The Wandering Boy,

Written by Henry Kirk White and sung by Master Hyde, at the London Concert
WHEN the winter winds whistle along the
wild moor,
And the cottager shuts on the beggar his door
When the chilling tear stands in my comfortless
How hard is the fate of the Wandering Boy (eye

The winter is cold I have place of rest
and my heart is as cold as it blows in my face
No father, no mother no kindred have I,
For I am a parentless Wandering Boy.

Yet I had a home and I once had a sire,
A mother who granted each infant desire
Our cottage it stood in a wood embower'd vale
When the Ring Dove would warble its sorrowful
tale,

But my father and mother were summon'd away
and they left me to hard hearted strangers a prey
I fled from their rigour with many a sigh
and now, I am left a poor little Wandering Boy
The wind it is keen and the snow loads the gale
And no one will list to my innocent tale
I'll go to the grave where my parents both lie
And death shall befriend the poor Wandering Boy

Pitts printer Wholesale Toy and Marble ware
house 6 Great st Andrew street 7 dials

## THE OYSTER GIRL (ROUD 875)

As I was go-ing through one of the Lon-don streets, A pret-ty lit-tle oy-ster girl I chanced there for to meet, And a-cross to her bas-ket so nim-bly I did trip, "Oh have you a-got a-ny oy - sters?" "Oh yes sir, oh yes sir, oh yes sir," says she, "I've some of the fi - nest oy - sters that ev-er you did see, And I sell them by one, by two, and by three, And then I will bar-gain for my bas-ket of oy - sters."

As I was going through one of the London streets,
A pretty little oyster girl I chanced there for to meet,
And across to her basket so nimbly I did trip,
"Oh have you got any oysters?"
"Oh yes sir, Oh yes sir, Oh yes sir," said she,
"I've some of the finest oysters that ever you did see,
And I sell them by one, or by two and by three,
And then Oh will you bargain for my basket of oysters?"

So I went unto the landlord, "O landlord," says I,
"Oh have you got a spare-room for the oyster girl and I,
That we may go in and so merry, merry be,
To bargain for her basket of oysters?"
"Oh yes sir, Oh yes sir, Oh yes sir," says he,
"I have got a spare room for the oyster girl and thee,
That you may go in and so merry, merry, be,
To bargain for her basket of oysters."

So I had not been in the room scarcely but an half an hour,
Before she picked my pocket of fifty pounds and more,
And out of the doorway so nimbly she did trip,
And she leaved me with her basket of oysters.
So I went unto the landlord; "Oh landlord, says I,
Oh have you seen that oyster girl that comes along with I?
She has picked my pocket of all my money,
And she's leaved me with her basket of oysters."

"Oh yes, sir, oh yes, sir, oh yes, sir," says he.
"I have seen that oyster girl that comes along with thee.
She has paid me your reckoning and you may go free,
And return unto your basket of oysters."
I've travelled through England, through Scotland and France,
But never in my life was I led to such a trance.
So now the English girl took the Frenchman in at last,
And she leaved him with her basket of oysters.

---

'The Oyster Girl' has been collected in England, Wales (where it was sung by the great Phil Tanner), Scotland, Ireland, and North America. Oysters have long had a reputation as an aphrodisiac, so the girl's trade gives a clue to the plot right from the start.

The earliest appearance in print seems to be 'The Eating of Oysters' in a collection published of the end of the 18th century or the beginning of the 19th, entitled *A New Patriotic Song*, with the imprint of Randall (Stirling) (c1794–1812). Later broadside imprints include Russell (Birmingham), Birt, Fortey, Goode, Hodges, Such (London), Bebbington, Pearson (Manchester). (Some 19th-century broadside printings with the same title, but beginning 'Many a knight and lady gay', are of a completely different song.) The text printed by Hodges, incidentally, is paired with 'God Save the Queen'!

Collected by Cecil Sharp from Alfred Willy at Hambridge, Somerset, on January 6th, 1904. Sharp notes that only in the first verse is the penultimate bar ("then I will bargain …") irregular, in that it has five beats. He also says that the last two lines of every verse may be repeated ad lib.

**Recordings** George Dunn *Chainmaker*; Mary Ann Haynes *Here's Luck To A Man*; Phil Tanner *The Gower Nightingale*; Duncan Williamson *Put Another Log On The Fire*.

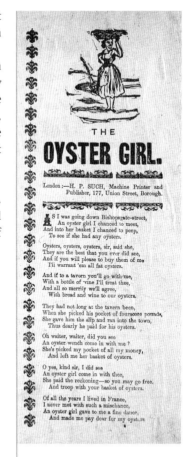

A 19th-century broadside of 'The Oyster Girl', printed by Such in London.

## THE POOR OLD COUPLE (ROUD 491) Sung by Manny Aldous.
## ("CLEVERLY DONE," SAID HE)

CD TRACK 11

There was an old couple and they were poor,
Artful, artful, dinner all day,
There was an old couple and they were poor,
They lived in a house with only one door.
Oh, what a rum couple were they,
Oh what a rum couple were they.

The good old man he went out one day,
Artful, artful, dinner all day,
The good old man he went out one day,
He left his old woman at home to stay.
Oh, what a bad woman was she,
Oh, what a bad woman was she.

The clerk of the parish passed by that way,
Artful, artful, dinner all day,
The clerk of the parish passed by that way,
She called him in by the wink of her eye.
Oh, what a bad woman was she,
Oh, what a bad woman was she.

The good old man he came home at last,
Artful, artful, dinner all day,
The good old man he came home at last,
He tried the door and found it barred.
"Oh, my poor wife," cried he,
"Oh, my poor wife," cried he.

"Now I've been sick since you've been gone,
Artful, artful, dinner all day,
I've been sick since you've been gone,
If you'd been in the garden you'd have heard me groan."
"Oh, my poor wife," cried he.

"One favour I'll ask you to do for me,
Artful, artful, dinner all day,
One favour I'll ask you to do for me,
Go fetch me an apple off yonder tree."
"Oh, that will I do," cried he.
"Oh, that will I do," cried he.

As he was climbing up of the tree,
Artful, artful, dinner all day,
As he was climbing up in the tree,
She let the clerk out and away ran he.
"That's cleverly done," cried he.
"That's cleverly done," cried he.

As he was climbing up of the tree,
Artful, artful, dinner all day,
She pulled the ladder and down fell he,
"That's cleverly done," cried he.

Another variation on the battle of the sexes theme: this time the woman gets to enjoy her lover and to outwit her husband too. Not known to have been printed on broadsides, 'The Poor Old Couple' (also known as 'Cleverly Done Said He') has been collected a number of times from singers in rural England and occasionally in the USA. It also appears, under the title 'The Absent Farmer', in Peter Buchan's enticingly titled, but ultimately slightly tame, collection, the *Secret Songs of Silence*, compiled in the early 19th century, and this might be the earliest record.

**Recordings** Sam Friend, Alf Peachey & Jimmy Knights *The Contented Countryman*.

Manny Aldous

## SCARBOROUGH FAIR (THE LOVER'S TASKS)
(CHILD 2; ROUD 12)

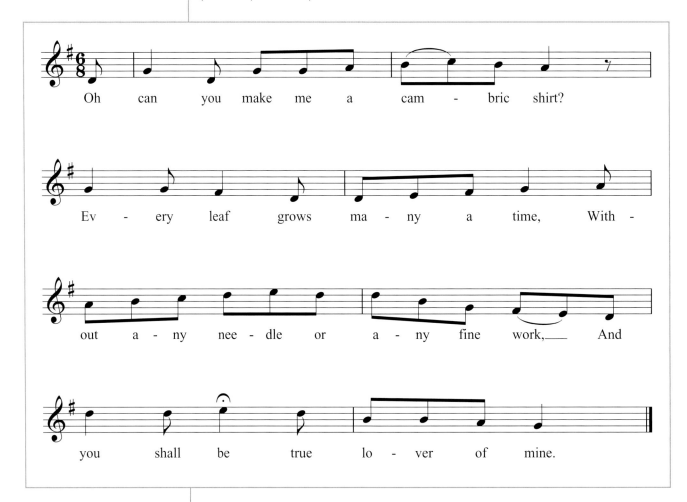

Oh can you make me a cam - bric shirt?

Ev - ery leaf grows ma - ny a time, With -

out a - ny nee - dle or a - ny fine work,___ And

you shall be true lo - ver of mine.

Oh can you make me a cambric shirt?
Every leaf grows many a time,
Without any needle or any fine work.
And you shall be a true lover of mine.

And wash it down in yonder well,
Every leaf grows many a time.
Where neither springs water nor rain ever fell.
And you shall be a true lover of mine.

And dry it off on yonder thorn,
Every leaf grows many a time.
Where there grew no leaf since Adam was born.
And you shall be a true lover of mine.

Oh can you buy me an acre of land,
Every leaf grows many a time.
Betwixt the salt water and the sea sand?
And you shall be a true lover of mine.

And plough it all over with a snail's horn.
Every leaf grows many a time.
And sow it throughout with one barleycorn.
And you shall be a true lover of mine.

Then gather the crop in a no-bottom sack,
Every leaf grows many a time.
And send it to mill on a butterfly's back.
And you shall be a true lover of mine.

Made famous for the folk revival by Martin Carthy and Simon and Garfunkel, 'Scarborough Fair' straddles the duality of supernatural and secular encounters between a woman and a man, a woman and the Devil, or a woman and some other kind of supernatural being (hence Child's title of 'The Elfin Knight'). The oldest text comes from a broadside of about 1670 (perhaps Scottish) but there is subsequently only a single broadside known, under the title 'The Humours of Love', probably of the late 18th or early 19th century, although it was also included in a 19th-century collection. Nevertheless, the song has been frequently collected from singers in England, Scotland, Ireland, and North America.

The idea seems to be that by posing 'impossible' tasks, a woman can keep an unwelcome lover or, interchangeably, the Devil, at arm's length. Yet Barre Toelken (*Morning Dew and Roses*, pp104–25) has argued that a trail of allusions to sex and death is woven through the dialogue, and that while the woman may be heard to say no through setting the tasks, she may be understood to mean yes from the sexual metaphors she employs in her answers. On the other hand, the same allusions can make any potential sexual relationship seem sterile if not downright dangerous. The song is certainly highly ambiguous.

'The Elfin Knight' has given rise, especially in England, to songs, under titles such as 'An Acre Of Land' or 'Sing Ivy', that lack any real narrative framework but retain some reference to the tasks of 'The Elfin Knight', and also to a nursery rhyme, 'My Father Left Me Three Acres Of Land'. These are perhaps more common among singers nowadays than the more comprehensive 'Scarborough Fair' versions. Although they are near-nonsense pieces, often sung to an upbeat tune, the kind of allusions that Toelken has read into the tasks may render even items such as these less innocent than they might at first appear.

The herbs of the refrain that accompanies some of the 'Scarborough Fair' versions – notably the one found in *Gammer Gurton's Garland*, an 1810 anthology of nursery rhymes – are, as is often the case with plants in folklore, amenable to different interpretations. Rosemary, for example, was believed to protect against evil but was also associated with funerals and death. Sage was used in identifying lovers, but was also held to grow best where the wife was dominant in a marriage. They can only serve to reinforce the deep-rooted ambiguity of the song.

Collected by W. Gilbert, possibly in Cornwall, and passed to Cecil Sharp. The song is recorded as 'The Lover's Tasks'. The line "Every leaf grows many a time" mirrors lines in the Scottish versions noted by Child: "Sober and grave grows merry in time" and "Every rose grows merry wi' thyme". The music notation has "true lover", as shown here, rather than "a true lover".

**Recordings** Peck Allmond *Kalimba Collage*; Martin Carthy *Martin Carthy*, as 'Scarborough Fair'; The Copper Family *Come Write Me Down: Early Recordings*, as 'An Acre Of Land'; Marianne Faithfull *Go Away From My World*, as 'Scarborough Fair'; Herbie Hancock *New Standard*, as 'Scarborough Fair'; Justin Hayward (with Mike Batt and The London Philharmonic Orchestra) *Classic Blue*, as 'Scarborough Fair'; Bert Jansch *Rosemary Lane*, as 'Rosemary Lane'; Liz Jefferies *The Voice Of The People, Vol. 15*, as 'Rosemary Lane'; Fred Jordan *A Shropshire Lad*, as 'An Acre Of Land'; Ewan MacColl & Peggy Seeger *Classic Scots Ballads*; Thomas Moran *Folk Songs Of Britain, Vol 4*; Tom Newman *Up In The North And Down In The South*, as 'Sing Ovy, Sing Ivy'; Charlie Potter *The Voice Of The People, Vol. 14*, as 'Sing Ivy'; Simon & Garfunkel *Parsley Sage Rosemary & Thyme*, as 'Scarborough Fair'.

Art Garfunkel and Paul Simon

# Songs of war and army life

Like most European – and, for that matter, North American – nations, the people of Britain have endured more or less continuously the experience of war. Through one form or another of conscription, or the opportunities offered by the army and navy as a career, war has affected the whole population; and songs about war – about the lives of soldiers and sailors, grief at loss, joy at victory, celebrated military leaders – have unsurprisingly been popular with singers of all kinds. Moreover, while some of these songs can be tied to particular wars, the underlying sentiments of a song such as 'The Bonny Light Horseman' resonate well beyond the immediate context and, allied to a good tune, ensure its continued currency. In addition, a number of songs, such as 'The Deserter' and 'Muddley Barracks', reflect in various ways – from the heartfelt to the sardonic – on the army life that a large proportion of the population must have experienced in one form or another, voluntarily or not.

English songs range over a variety of conflicts from Elizabethan times ('The Young Earl Of Essex's Victory Over The Emperor Of Germany' [Child 288; Roud 123]) to World War II ('D-Day Dodgers' [Roud 10499]). Neither should patriotic songs like 'The British Grenadiers', which are not generally classed as folk songs, be overlooked. However, as Gavin Greig observed, "The 20 years that ended with Waterloo have left more traces on our popular minstrelsy than any other period of our history has done." Indeed, songs concerning the French Revolutionary and Napoleonic Wars do seem to have become assimilated into folk tradition in a remarkable way. That might be because that period of warfare involved the entire nation in an unprecedented manner, though the impact of previous conflicts should not be minimized.

Napoleon Bonaparte is a particularly enigmatic figure in this regard. There is no shortage of broadside street ballads that mock Napoleon and denigrate the French. Yet, especially after Waterloo, there appeared folk songs in which Napoleon was depicted as hero: 'The Bonny Bunch Of Roses', 'The Grand Conversation On Napoleon', 'The Deeds Of Napoleon'. Frank Kidson thought that all the songs that depict Napoleon as hero were of Irish origin and envisage Bonaparte as a potential liberator. Certainly there are examples that do appear to be Irish, but for others there is no such evidence (and presumably the reference to the Act of Union in 'The Bonny Bunch Of Roses' would militate against any potential Irish nationalistic sentiment). Moreover, as Vic Gammon has pointed out ('The Grand Conversation'), their continued popularity in England still has to be explained.

In fact, songs like 'The Bonny Bunch Of Roses' successfully blend English patriotism with admiration for Bonaparte. Gammon concludes: "Some may have seen Napoleon as a radical hero, the defender of the Revolution of progress and liberation, others may simply have been impressed with the epic and heroic quality of his story."

## BOLD GENERAL WOLFE (ROUD 624)

One Monday evening as we set sail,
The wind did blow a pleasant gale.
For to fight the French it was our intent,
Through smoke and fire, through smoke and fire,
And it was dark and a gloomy night.

Now the French was landed on the mountains high,
And we poor hearts in the valleys lie.
"Never mind, my lads," General Wolfe did say,
"Brave lads of honour, brave lads of honour,
Old England shall win the day."

Then the very first broadside we give to them,
We killed seven hundred and fifty men.
"Well done, my lads," General Wolfe did say,
"Brave lads of honour, brave lads of honour,
Old England shall win the day."

Then the very first broadside they give to us,
They wounded our general in his right breast.
Then out of his tender breast loving blood did flow,
Like any fountain, like any fountain,
Till all his men were filled with woe.

"Now here's a hundred guineas all in bright gold,
Take it and part it for my blood's quite cold.
And use your soldiers, as you did before,
Your soldiers own, your soldiers own,
And they will fight for ever more.

"Oh when to old England you do return,
Pray tell my friends that I am dead and gone.
Pray tell my tender old mother dear,
That I am dead Oh, that I am dead Oh,
And I shall never see her no more."

'Bold General Wolfe' has been frequently collected, but mostly in England, with a few records from Canada. The song commemorates Wolfe's victory over the French at Quebec, which ensured British control of Canada. Leading his troops by a secret path to the Heights of Abraham overlooking the town, Wolfe stormed the stronghold but was mortally wounded in the hour of victory. Wolfe (1727–59) had already served with distinction at Culloden, in the Rochefort expeditionary force, and at the siege of Louisbourg, and his youthful death on September 13th, 1759 ensured that he would be remembered as a military hero. He is also remembered for having stated that he would rather have written Gray's *Elegy* than conquered Quebec.

The earliest known broadsides carry 19th-century imprints, including Marshall (Bristol), Walker (Durham), Birt, Catnach, Pitts, Phair, Ryle, Such (London), Ryle (London and Portsea), Pierce (Southborough), and Haly (Cork).

This version was collected by Henry Hammond from William Bartlett in Wimborne Union workhouse, in Dorset, in 1905. Hammond notes: "This is what I made of Bartlett's singing. I found the lyrics difficult to catch."

**Recordings** Martin Carthy *Waiting For Angels*; The Copper Family *Come Write Me Down: Early Recordings*; Bob Hart *A Broadside*; Cyril Poacher *Plenty Of Thyme*; Bob Scarce *The Folk Songs Of Britain, Vol. 8*.

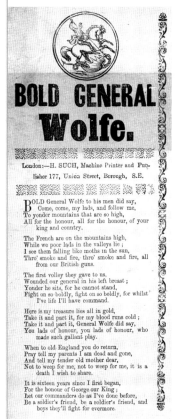

A broadside of 'Bold General Wolfe', printed by Such of London towards the end of the 19th century.

# THE BONNY BUNCH OF ROSES (ROUD 664)

By the dangers of the ocean, one morning in the month of June,
Oh the feathered warbling songster, the charming note so sweet a-tune,
There I beheld a female, seemingly in grief and woe,
Conversing with young Bonyparte concerning the bonny bunch of roses, O.

Oh then said young Napoleon and graspt his mother by the hand:
"Oh mother do have patience until I'm able to command.
I will raise a mighty army and through tremjus dangers go,
In spite of all the universe I'll gain you the bonny bunch of roses, O.

"When you saw great Bonyparte you fell down on your bended knees,
And asked your father's life of him and he granted it right manfully.
It was there he took an army and likewise kings to join his throne.
He was so well provided, enough to sweep the world all through.

"But when he came near Moscow, near overpowered by driving snow,
Moscow was a-blazing, there he lost all the bonny bunch of roses, O."
"Adieu, adieu for ever, and now I'm on my dying bed,
If I had lived I should have been clever, now droop my youthful head."

For while our bones doth moulder and weeping willows over us grow,
By the deeds of bold Napoleon, concerning the bonny bunch of roses, O.

'The Bonny Bunch of Roses' is framed as an imaginary dialogue between Napoleon's widow, Marie Louise of Austria, and his son, Napoleon II (François Charles Joseph Bonaparte, the titular King of Rome). Since the song, in some versions, refers to the death of Napoleon I on Saint Helena in 1821, it must have been written after that time. The sickly Napoleon II, born in 1811, died in 1832.

'The Bonny Bunch of Roses' is a fine example of the capacity of Napoleonic ballads to combine admiration for Bonaparte as a military leader with patriotic sentiment. The 'bonny bunch of roses' refers both to the redcoats of the British army and symbolically to the union of England, Wales, Scotland, and Ireland, sealed by the Act of Union of 1801 which brought Great Britain and Ireland under a single parliament.

The song, combining a fine lyricism with stirring sentiment, proved immensely popular with both singers and broadside printers. It has been collected throughout Britain and Ireland and North America. Broadside and songster imprints include Russell, Taylor (Birmingham), Talbot (Cambridge), Stewart (Carlisle), Willey (Cheltenham), Clift (Cirencester), Oliver (Darlington), Horsley (Derby), Walker (Durham), Lindsay (Glasgow), Elliott (Hereford), Birt, Catnach, Disley, Edwards, Fortey, Hill, Hillatt and Martin, Paul, Pitts, Sharp, Such, Taylor (London), Bebbington, Pearson, Swindells, Wheeler (Manchester), Ross (Newcastle), Ordoyno, Plant (Nottingham), Forth (Pocklington), Williams (Portsea), Harkness (Preston), Dalton (York), as well as unascribed sheets, and Irish and American imprints.

A few of the London sheets ascribe the song to the authorship (presumably) of one George Brown, to whom 'The Grand Conversation on Napoleon' is also credited.

Collected by Cecil Sharp from Tom Sprachlan at Hambridge, in Somerset, in September 1903. This is a severely truncated version of the story. We have added speech marks in an attempt to clarify the conversation. We have also retained the original spelling of "Bonyparte". "Tremjus" is a corruption of "tremendous".

The Harkness broadside (see over) provides much more detail.

By the dangers of the ocean,
One morning in the month of June,
The feathered warbling songsters,
Their charming notes so sweet did tune,
There I espied a female,
Seemingly in grief and woe,
And conversing with young Bonaparte,
Concerning the bonny bunch of roses, O.

O then said young Napoleon,
And grasp'd his mother by the hand,
Do mother pray have patience,
Until I am able to command;
I will raise a terrible army,
And through tremendous dangers go,
And in spite of all the universe,
I will gain the bonny bunch of roses, O.

When first you saw great Bonaparte,
You fell upon our bended knee,
And asked your father's life of him,
He granted it most manfully.
'Twas then he took an army,
And o'er the frozen realms did go,
He said, I'll conquer Moscow,
Then go to the bonny bunch of roses, O.

He took three hundred thousand men,
And likewise kings to join his throng,
He was so well provided,
Enough to sweep this world along,
But when he came near Moscow,
Near overpowered by driven snow,
All Moscow was a-blazing,
Then he left the bonny bunch of roses, O.

Now son ne'er speak so venturesome,
For England is the heart of oak,
England, Ireland, and Scotland,
Their unity can ne'er be broke.
And son, look at your father,
In St Helena his body lays low,
And you will follow after,
So beware of the bonny bunch of roses, O.

Oh mother, adieu for ever!
Now I am on my dying bed;
If I'd liv'd I should have been clever,
But now I droop my youthful head.
But while our bones do moulder,
And weeping willows o'er us grow,
The deeds of bold Napoleon,
Will sing the bonny bunch of roses, O.

**Recordings** Shirley & Dolly Collins *Snapshots*; Harry Cox *The Bonny Labouring Boy*; Seamus Ennis *Bonny Bunch Of Roses*; Fairport Convention *The Bonny Bunch Of Roses*; John Wesley Harding *Trad. Arr. Jones*; Fred Jordan *A Shropshire Lad*; Ewan MacColl *Scots Street Songs*; Walter Pardon *Put a Bit of Powder On It, Father*; Cyril Poacher *Plenty Of Thyme*; Bill Porter *Just Another Saturday Night*; Phil Tanner *The Gower Nightingale*.

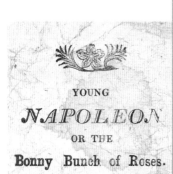

A broadside of 'The Bonny Bunch Of Roses', printer and date unknown.

# THE BONNY LIGHT HORSEMAN (ROUD 1185)

Ye fair maids and widows I pray give attention,
It's of a fair maiden I'm just going to mention.
It's of a fair maiden who was going to wander,
To apply to King George for the loss of her lover.
Broken-hearted I'll wander for the loss of my lover,
For my bonny light horseman in the wars he was slain.

The dove she does mourn for the loss of her lover,
"Oh where shall I wander?" this fair maiden said,
"Oh where shall I wander..."

One of the more consciously poetic but also one of the tenderest of the songs about the wars, with its haunting chorus, 'The Bonny Light Horseman' evidently relates in a slightly generalized way to events of the French Revolutionary and Napoleonic Wars. The song appeared in print early in the 19th century, if not before, and English imprints include Pratt, Whiting (Birmingham), Batchelar, Catnach, Evans, Goode, Pitts, Such (London), Swindells (Manchester), Cooper (Newcastle under Lyme), Forth (Pocklington), Harkness (Preston). It was also printed in American broadsides and songsters, with imprints such as Locke and Bubier (Boston), De Marsan, Nafis and Cornish (New York).

The song has been less often collected from singers, although versions are known from England, Ireland, Scotland, the USA, and Canada. Some of these are rather pared down, concentrated around the lines of the chorus. In Scotland, 'Broken-hearted I Wander' has in some instances become a children's singing game.

From the collection of George Gardiner. The manuscript ends: "The rest is wanting." It also notes that the singer and locality are unknown, but "may be in Scotland". To make more sense of the song, you might wish to consult the broadside versions. This one was printed by Swindells in Manchester:

Maids, wives and widows, I pray give attention,
Unto these few lines I am going to mention,
I'm a maid in distress, and now going to wander,
For my bonny light horseman who was slain in the wars;
Broken hearted I will wander,
For the loss of my lover who was slain in the wars.

Three years and six months since he left England's shore,
My bonny light horseman 'tis him I adore,
He was mounted on horseback, so gallant and free,
And through the whole regiment respected was he.
Broken hearted I will wander,
For the loss of my lover who was slain in the wars.

If I'd wings like an eagle, so swift would I fly,
Unto the same spot where my true love did die,
Over his grave would I flutter my wings,
I would kiss his cold lips over again.
Broken hearted I will wander,
For the loss of my lover who was slain in the wars.

Like a dove I will moan for the loss of its mate,
Soon I will die for my true lover's sake,
No man upon earth my affection will gain,
I'll a maid live and die for my love that is slain.
Broken hearted I will wander,
For the loss of my lover who was slain in the wars.

**Recordings** Cherish The Ladies *Threads Of Time*; Jacquey Gabriel *The Birds Upon The Tree And Other Traditional Songs And Tunes*; Steve Gillette & Cindy Mangsen *The Light Of The Day*; Martin Howley *The Voice Of The People, Vol. 8*, as 'The Young Horseman'; Planxty *After The Break*; Mick Ryan & Pete Harris *The Widow's Promise*; Lal & Norma Waterson *A True Hearted Girl*.

# THE DESERTER (ROUD 493, 1655, 2405)

The first time I deserted I thought myself free,
When my false-hearted comrade informed all on me.
I was quickly followed after, I was brought back with speed,
I was handcuffed and jingled heavy irons indeed.

Court-martial, court-martial, court-martial for me,
My sentence passed on me three hundred and three,
May the Lord have mercy on them for such cruelty,
Now the Queen's duty lay so heavy on me.

Now the next time I deserted I thought myself free,
When my false-hearted sweetheart informed all on me.
I was quickly followed after, I was brought back with speed,
I was handcuffed and jingled heavy irons indeed.

Court-martial, court-martial, court-martial so hot,
When my sentence passed on me I had to be shot.
May the Lord have mercy on them for such cruelty,
Now the Queen's duty lay so heavy on me.

Then up rose Prince Albert in his carriage and six,
"Now show to me the young man whose coffin is fixed,
Come loosen from his irons and now set him free,
He'll make so fine soldier for his Queen and country."

'The Deserter' (Roud 493), as sung by, for example, Wiggy Smith and Walter Pardon, is a slightly fanciful piece in which a recruit repeatedly deserts from the army and is finally about to be shot when a gentleman – Prince Albert, the Duke of York, or the King himself – rides up and orders his release, either giving him money to go home or at least stating that he will make a good soldier for his Queen and country. Mike Yates says that Wiggy Smith believed it related to a true incident that occurred during the First World War, though it must date back at least to Victorian times. The song has been collected in England and Scotland, and it appeared on broadsides under imprints including Heppel, Pratt, Watts (Brimingham), Birt, Disley, Fortey, Pitts, Ryle, Such (London), Ross, Walker (Newcastle), and Harkness (Preston).

Some of these broadsides are printed under the title 'The Deserter', but some are entitled 'The New Deserter', thus distinguishing it from another song also called 'The Deserter'. The latter begins 'Once I thought I ne'er should be . . .' or 'My parents reared me tenderly . . .' (Roud 1655) and is the lamentation of a deserter who was led astray by liquor and now finds himself on the run and fearful of even the birds in the trees. This song was printed on broadsides, under the title 'The Bold Deserter' as well as 'The Deserter', with imprints including Armstrong (Liverpool), Birt, Pitts, Such (London), Swindells (Manchester), Rosson (Middlewich), Dickinson (York), and Birmingham (Dublin). A few versions were collected in Hampshire and Dorset by George B. Gardiner and the Hammond brothers, and it was also found in Ireland.

A third song called 'The Deserter', or 'Kelly's Lamentation', (Roud 2405) tells of a young man who leaves home after disagreements with his parents, enlists, and then, finding army life miserable, deserts and returns home. Otherwise only known in Ireland, Cecil Sharp collected versions of this song in Somerset and London.

'The Deserter from Kent' (Roud 2510) has only been collected from two singers, one in Surrey and one in Kent. Sung to a variant of the 'Vilikins and Dinah' tune, this seems a more light-hearted piece than the other 'Deserter' songs.

Collected by Cecil Sharp from Jack Barnard at Bridgwater, Somerset, on December 8th, 1908. Sharp's manuscript includes two minor variants of the final phrase, which we have omitted for clarity.

**Recordings** Martin Carthy *Signs Of Life*; Fairport Convention *Liege & Lief*; Knot Fibb'n *Knot Loitering*; Walter Pardon *A World Without Horses*; Wiggy Smith *Band Of Gold*.

# THE DUKE OF MARLBOROUGH (MARLBOROUGH)
(ROUD 233)

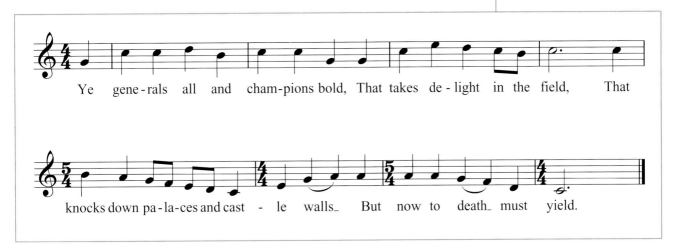

Ye generals all and champions bold,
That takes delight in the field,
That knocks down palaces and castle walls,
But now to death must yield.

I am an Englishman by my birth,
And Marlborough is my name.
In Devonshire I drew my breath,
That place of noted fame.

King Charles the second I did serve,
To face our foes in France,
And at the battle of Ramillies,
We boldly did advance.

The sun was down, the earth did shake,
So loudly did I cry,
"Fight on, my brave boys, for Old England,
We'll conquer or we'll die!"

The very day my horse was shot,
All by a musket ball,
As I was a-mounting up again,
My aide-de-camp did fall.

Now on a bed of sickness laid,
I am resigned to die,
Ye generals all, and champions bold,
Stand true as well as I.

But take no bribe, stand true to your men,
And fight with courage bold.
For I've led many's a man through smoke and fire,
But I never was bribed with gold.

I was beloved of all my men,
Kings and princes likewise,
It's many a town I've often took,
And did the world surprise.

John Churchill, First Duke of Marlborough (1650–1722) was the most successful general of his age and a prominent statesman, who made a key contribution to the suppression of Monmouth's rebellion (1685) and then to the success of the Glorious Revolution (1688) and the accession of King William III. William rewarded him by making him Earl of Marlborough. Faced with impending European war in 1700, Marlborough commanded British forces in the Low Countries. William's successor, Anne, made him Duke of Marlborough. In 1704 French armies threatened Britain's German allies, and Marlborough marched to the Danube where he won a resounding victory at Blenheim (1704), following it up with further victories at Ramillies (1706), Oudenarde (1708), and Malplaquet (1709). He was subsequently dismissed and later reinstated, and in 1715 supervised the suppression of the Jacobite rebellion.

The song can be presumed to date from not long after Marlborough's death, although there are apparently no very early records of it. Its currency with singers appears to have been restricted to England, where the Duke was a popular figure because of his military victories and his supposed integrity. The record on 19th-century (possibly some late 18th-century) broadsides attests to this enduring reputation. Imprints include Russell, Whiting (Birmingham), Bennett (Brighton), Marshall (Bristol), Ford (Chesterfield), Walker (Durham), Ward (Ledbury), Armstrong (Liverpool), Birt, Catnach, Disley, Fortey, Hodges, Phair, Pitts, Such (London), Swindells (Manchester), Angus, Fordyce, Marshall (Newcastle), Williams (Portsea), Harkness (Preston), Crome (Sheffield), Pierce (Southborough), Houghton (Worcester), Dickinson (York).

Notably, the Duke is also commemorated by his erstwhile enemies in the well-known French song 'Marlbrough s'en va-t-en guerre'.

Collected from Esther Newman (aged 90), at Andover, in Hampshire, in August 1906, by George Gardiner (with the tune noted by H. Balfour Gardiner). Gardiner's notation is very elaborate, and it is not clear how the words fitted the tune. For clarity we have added a slur on "walls" in the third line and removed numerous minor variants.

**Recordings** Home Service *Alright Jack*, as 'The Duke Of Marlborough Fanfare'; Nic Jones *Ballads And Songs*; The Old Hat Dance Band *Old Hat Dance Band*; Maddy Prior *Arthur The King*.

THE DUKE OF
**MARLBOROUGH**

YOU generals all and champions bold,
    That take delight in the fields,
That knock down palaces & castle walls,
    But now to death must yield,
I must go and face the foe,
    With sword and with shield,
I always fought with merry men,
    But now to death must yield.

I am an Englishman by my birth,
    And Marlborough is my name,
In Devonshire I drew my breath,
    That place of noted fame;
I was beloved by all my men,
    Kings and Princes likewise,
Though many towns I often took,
    I did the world surprise.

King Charles the Second I did serve,
    To face our foes in France,
And at the battle of Ramilies,
    We boldly did advance,
The sun was down, the earth did shine,
    So loudly I did cry—
"Fight on my brave boys for England,
    We'll conquer or we'll nobly die."

Now we have gained the victory,
    And bravely kept the field,
We've took a number of prisoners,
    And forced them to yield,
That very day my horse was shot,
    All by a Musquet ball,
As I was mounting up again,
My aide-de-camp did fall.

Now on a bed of sickness lay,
    I am resigned to die;
Yet generals, and champions bold,
    Stand true as well as I;
Take no bribes, stand true to your colours
    And fight with courage bold,
I have led my men thro' fire and smoke,
    But ne'er was bribed with gold.

A 19th century broadside of 'The Duke Of Marlborough', printer and date unknown.

# THE GRAND CONVERSATION ON NAPOLEON
(ROUD 1189) As sung by Gordon Hall.

'Twas o - ver that__ wild beat - en track, a friend of the bold Bo - na-parte Did

pace the sands and lof-ty rocks of St He - le na's shore. The wind__blew him in a hur-ri-cane, the

light-ning's flash a-round did dart, The sea-gulls were a-shriek-ing and the waves a-round did roar. "Oh

hush rude__ wind," the__ stran - ger__ cried, "a – while I range the drea-ry spot, Where

once a gal-lant he - ro his hea-vy eyes did close. And whilst his va - liant limbs do rot, his

fame will ne-ver be for - got." This grand con-ver-sa-tion on Na - po - le - on a-rose, This

grand con-ver-sa-tion on brave Bo - na-parte a-rose. "O Eng - land," he cried, "did

per-se - cute that he-ro bold. Much bet-ter had you slain him on the__ plains of Wa-ter-loo."

'Twas over the wild beaten track, a friend of the bold Bonaparte
Did pace the sands and lofty rocks of St Helena's shore.
The wind blew in in a hurricane, the lightning flash around did dart,
The seagulls were a-shrieking and the waves around did roar.
"Oh, hush rude wind," the stranger cried, "While I range the dreary spot,
Where once a gallant hero his heavy eyes did close.
And whilst his valiant limbs do rot, his fame will never be forgot."
This grand conversation on Napoleon arose,
This grand conversation on brave Bonaparte arose.

"Oh, England," he cried, "Did you persecute that hero bold?
Much better had you slain him on the plains of Waterloo.
Napoleon he was a friend to heroes all both young and old,
He caused the money for to fly wherever he did go.
When plans were raging night and day, that bold commander to betray,
He said 'I'll go to Moscow and that will ease my woes.
If fortune shines, without delay, then all the world will me obey.'"
This grand conversation on Napoleon arose,
This grand conversation on brave Bonaparte arose.

"Thousands of men he then did rise to conquer Moscow by surprise.
Like Hannibal he crossed the Alps, oppressed with frost and snow.
But being near the Russian land, he then began to open his eyes.
Though Moscow was a-burning and his men rode to and fro.
Napoleon dauntless viewed the plains and wept in anguish for the same.
He cried 'Retreat, my gallant men, the time so swiftly goes.'
What thousands died in that retreat, some forced their horses for to eat."
This grand conversation on Napoleon arose,
This grand conversation on brave Bonaparte arose.

"At Waterloo, his men they fought, commanded by brave Bonaparte
Attended by Field Marshall Ney, and he was bribed with gold.
When Blutcher led the Prussians in, it nearly broke Napoleon's heart
He cried 'My thirty thousand men are killed and I am sold.'
He viewed the plain and cried ''Tis lost', he there did favour a charge across,
The plain was in confusion with blood and dying woe.
The bunch of roses did advance and boldly entered into France."
This brave conversation on Napoleon arose,
This grand conversation on brave Bonaparte arose.

"Brave Bonaparte was planned to be a prisoner across the sea
The rocks of St Helena, it was the dreadful spot.
Doomed as a prisoner there to be, till death did end his misery.
His son soon followed to the tomb, it was an awful plot.
'Tis long enough have they been dead, the blast of war around is spread,
And may our shipping float again to find a daring foe.
And now my boys when honour calls, we'll boldly mount the wooden walls."
This grand conversation on Napoleon arose,
This grand conversation on brave Bonaparte arose.

'The Grand Conversation' takes the form of an imaginary monologue set on Saint Helena, where Napoleon was exiled following his defeat at Waterloo in 1815 and died in 1821, recalling the events of his career. This epic song (at least in Gordon Hall's rendition) has been collected in England, Ireland, and the USA, but not nearly as frequently as 'The Bonny Bunch of Roses', which, at least according to the attribution on some broadside sheets, was the work of the same author, George Brown.

The record in broadside print is rather stronger, with imprints including Taylor (Birmingham), Collard (Bristol), Talbot (Cambridge), Walker (Durham), Catnach, Disley, Edwards, Fortey, Hillatt and Martin, Hodges, Pitts, Such (London), Pearson, Wheeler (Manchester), Walker (Newcastle), Harkness (Preston), and Irish printers.

Gammon notes that 'The Grand Conversation' is not unique in having Napoleon cross the Alps on the way to Moscow. The popular image of the hero is more important to the ballads than historical fact. Once again, in spite of the catalogue of Bonaparte's achievements and the attribution of his defeat at Waterloo to treachery – "Field Marshal Ney… was bribed by gold" – the final stanza seems to conflate the foregoing praise of the French hero with (British) patriotic sentiment.

**Recordings** Tom Costello *The Voice Of The People, Vol. 8*; Barry Dransfield *Unruly*; Gordon Hall *When The May Is All In Bloom*; Dónal Lunny & Frank Harte *My Name Is Napoleon*; James Raynard *Strange Histories*.

## MUDDLEY BARRACKS (BUNGAY ROGER) (ROUD 1735)
As sung by Charlie Hancy.

CD TRACK 13

When I first went up to Lon - don town, They called me Bun - gay Ro - ger. They

asked I o'er and o'er a - gain, If I would be a sol - dier. They

asked I o'er and o'er a - gain 'Til I said that I was will - ing. "Cor

blast!" said I, "I'll have a try", And I signed my name and got a shil - ling. With a-

fol - a - rol - a- day, fol - a - rol - a- day, Fol - a - rol - a - lad - dy when I get home.

When I first went up to London town,
They called me Bungay Roger.
They asked I o'er and o'er again,
If I would be a soldier.
They asked I o'er and o'er again,
Till I said that I was willin'.
"Cor blast," said I, "I'll have a try",
And I signed my name and got a shilling.
With a fol-a-rol-a-day, fol-a-rol-a-day, fol-a-rol-a-laddy when I get home.

They took me out on the barrack square,
A-doing my duty manual,
They buggered I here and they buggered I there,
For doing my duty manual.
They said "Eyes right, eyes left,
Just keep your bloody great head up!"
And if you dared to answer 'em back,
They'd bugger you in the lock-up.
With a fol-a-rol-a-day, fol-a-rol-a-day, fol-a-rol-a-laddy when I get home.

They brought me home from parade that day,
I was hungry as a hunter.
We couldn't get a god-damn bite
Till that orderly bloke came around, sir.
And when they dished it up, my boys,
They dished it up on a platter,
To my surprise, in front of my eyes,
A lump of bull and a bloody tater.
With a fol-a-rol-a-day, fol-a-rol-a-day, fol-a-rol-a-laddy when I get home.

So I wish I were back home again,
A following of the plough, sir.
I wish I were back home again,
A-milking that old cow sir.
I wish I were back home again,
Behind a leg of mutton,
With a rusty old knife and a rusty old fork,
But by Christ you can keep on cuttin'.
With a fol-a-rol-a-day, fol-a-rol-a-day, fol-a-rol-a-laddy when I get home.

Charlie Hancy

Known by a variety of titles, including 'Muddley Barracks', 'Bungay Roger', and 'The Yorkshire Blinder', this song has been collected only a handful of times in England. It has been suggested that it bears some relationship to 'The Awkward Recruit', beginning 'Behold poor Will just come from drill', which mentions 'General Bonaparte' by name and was printed on broadsides with a variety of imprints. Certainly there is a similarity of tone in the catalogue of complaints listed by the recruit, but the similarity seems no closer than one of general sentiment.

Charlie Hancy uses a number of unusual words: "bull" is bully beef, a staple of army life; a "tater" is a potato; to "bugger" here means to interfere with or annoy.

**Recordings** Jumbo Brightwell *The Voice Of The People, Vol. 20*; The Cantwell Family *It Was On A Market Day, Vol. 2*, as 'The Yorkshire Blinder'; Charlie Hancy *Songs Sung In Suffolk*, as 'Bungay Roger'; Roy Harris *The Rambling Soldier*.

# Songs of work and protest

It is perhaps surprising that a relatively small number of English folk songs celebrate the lives of working men and women – though the number is rather greater if the songs about soldiers and especially sailors are included. Perhaps, when the working day was long and often hard, people preferred to sing about other things. Nevertheless, songs like 'The Painful Plough' are expressive of a certain occupational pride, perhaps because agricultural labourers were in fact often an economically disadvantaged group. Such a reading provides a link to a group of more explicit songs of protest, many of which are also based in the rural environment.

With the American War of Independence, followed by the French Revolutionary and Napoleonic Wars, and Napoleon's imposition of a ban on trade between Britain and the European mainland, Britain experienced a long period of economic hardship in the late 18th and early 19th centuries. Combined with the emotional impact of the various wars, this experience seems to be reflected in a number of forms in folk songs. Although there is not a large body of overtly political folk songs from England, songs like these that describe the suffering of ordinary men and women also convey a powerful ideological message.

Poaching, which became a crime in Norman times, long persisted in rural communities as a means of supplementing the diet, and proved a major irritant to landowners well into the 19th century. The popular image of the poacher is of a single individual or a small group of companions. In fact, it was often carried out by gangs, and with the enclosure of common land, the 'poaching wars' of the 18th and 19th centuries can be seen as an organized attack on private property that often resulted in bloody affrays. The punishments meted out were extremely severe. Poaching is generally treated sympathetically in folk songs, and there is no doubt that it was widely regarded as a 'social crime' – that is, behaviour that was illegal but was nonetheless not regarded as criminal by its perpetrators or by large sections of the community.

Transportation to the American colonies became established as a punishment for convicted criminals from around 1650, with numbers increasing during the 18th century. After the secession of the American colonies, convicts were sent to Australia, the 'first fleet' leaving England in 1787 and arriving at Botany Bay in 1788. It is estimated that, in all, some 210,000 convicts were exiled between 1650 and 1868, with 50,000 going to America and the remainder to Australia. Conditions prior to transportation, during the voyage, and in the colonies, were appalling, and transported convicts are depicted with universal sympathy in folk song, virtually regardless of their crimes prior to conviction. For this reason, songs about transportation are included here rather than in a section on crime.

## ADIEU TO OLD ENGLAND (ROUD 1703)

Oh once I could ride in my coach, And hors-es to draw me a - long, But_

now I am stir-rup and stir-rup so str-ong, In ir-ons and chains I am bound.

Here's a - dieu to Old Eng-land a - dieu, And a - dieu to some hun-dreds of pounds. If the

world had been end-ed be - fore I was born, My sor-rows I nev-er should know.

Oh once I could ride in my coach,
And horses to draw me along,
But now I am stirrup and stirrup so strong
In irons and chains I am bound.

Chorus:
Here's adieu to Old England, adieu,
And adieu to some hundreds of pounds,
If the world had ended before I was born,
My sorrows I never should know.

Oh once I could eat of the best,
The bestest of bread so brown,
But now I am glad for the hard mouldy crust,
And glad I could get it to eat.

Oh once I cold drink of the best,
The bestest of ale so brown,
But now I am glad with a cup of spring water,
That runneth from town to town.

Oh once I could lie on my bed,
My bed was the softest of down,
But now I am glad of a lock of chair straw,
To keep me up from the cold ground.

This song seems to have been largely confined to England, with one stanza from Scotland and one report from the USA. Although it has only been collected a handful of times, Baring-Gould claimed that it was common in the West Country. The story remains enigmatic, and no broadside printings are known.

Collected by Cecil Sharp from Charles Ash at Crowcombe, in Somerset, on September 16th, 1908.

**Recordings** Pete Castle *False Waters*; Shirley Collins *Adieu To Old England*; Harry Cox *What Will Become of England?*.

Harry Cox

## ALL JOLLY FELLOWS THAT FOLLOW THE PLOUGH (ROUD 346)

Early one morning, before it was day,
The cocks was a-crowing, the farmer did say,
"Come arise, my good fellows, come arise with good will,
The horses want something their bellies to fill."

When four o'clock come then up will all rise,
And unto the stable so merrily flies,
A-rubbing and scrubbing our horses I vow,
We're all jolly fellows that follow the plough.

Six o'clock came, at breakfast we meet,
And beef and bread and pork pies so heartily eat,
A piece in our pocket I'll swear and I'll vow,
We're all jolly fellows that follow the plough.

We harness our horses and away then we goes,
And trip o'er the plain, boys, as nimble as does,
And when we come there so jolly and bold,
To see which of us the straight furrow can hold.

Our master come to us and this he did say,
"What have you been doing, boys, all this long day?
You've not ploughed an acre, I'll swear and I'll vow,
You're all idle fellows that follow the plough."

I've stepped up to him and made this reply,
"We've all ploughed an acre, so you tell a lie,
We've all ploughed an acre, I'll swear and I'll vow,
We're all jolly fellows that follow the plough."

He turned himself round and he laughed at the joke,
"It's past two o'clock, boys, it's time to unyoke.
Unharness your horses and rub them down well,
I'll give you a jug of the very best ale."

Come all you brave fellows, take a warning by me,
Never fear master wherever you be.
Never fear master, I'll swear and I'll vow,
We're all jolly fellows that follow the plough.

This song has been widely collected in England, usually to this tune, a variant of 'Villikins and Dinah'. Cecil Sharp remarked, "I find that almost every singer knows it; the bad singers often know but little else." Broadside imprints include Willmor (Abingdon), Pratt (Birmingham), Stewart (Carlisle), Ford (Chesterfield), Forth (Hull), Beaumont (Leeds), Birt, Catnach, Disley, Fortey, Hodges, Pitts, Such (London), Bebbington, Pearson (Manchester), Ross, Walker (Newcastle), Williams (Portsea), Harkness (Preston), Dalton (York).

The record outside of England is very sparse, though the song has turned up a couple of times in Scotland. Gavin Greig noted the contrast between the fare accorded to English ploughmen in this song and the diet of brose (a watery dish made of oatmeal) recorded in ploughmen's songs of the Scottish North East. "If it is safe to found on a single specimen of the southern ploughman ditty, we should also say that the relations between master and servant appear to be more cordial across the Border than they are with us, judging from the general tone of our local ploughman songs." But 'All Jolly Fellows' need not necessarily be taken at face value: it can be presumed, depending on local circumstances, to have functioned as a piece of wishful thinking as much as an accurate depiction of farm life.

This version was collected by Cecil Sharp from Tom Sprachlan, at Hambridge, Somerset, in September 1903.

**Recordings** Bob Hart *A Broadside*; Fred Jordan *A Shropshire Lad*; Magpie Lane *Speed The Plough*; Bob Mills *An English Folk Music Anthology*; George Townshend *Come Hand To Me The Glass*; Jeff Wesley *Down In The Fields*.

# THE GALLANT POACHER (ROUD 793)

Come all you lads of high re-nown, that love to drink strong ale that's brown, And bring those lof-ty phea-sants down, with pow - der shot and gun. He is a gallant youth, he will tell the truth, He has crossed all life's temp tat - ious ways, No mor - tal man his life could save, He now is sleep - ing in his grave, His deeds on earth be done. He now is sleep - ing in his grave, His deeds on earth be done.

Come all you lads of high renown,
That love to drink strong ale that's brown,
And bring those lofty pheasants down,
With powder shot and gun.
He is a gallant youth, he will tell the truth,
He has crossed all life's temptatious ways,
No mortal man his life could save,
He now is sleeping in his grave,
His deeds on earth be done.

Me and five more a-poaching went,
To kill some game 'twas our intent,
Our money being gone and all was spent,
We had nothing else to try.
For the moon shone bright, not a cloud in sight,
The keeper heard us fire a gun,
And to the spot he quickly run,
And swore before the rising sun,
That one of us would die.

Now the bravest youth among the lot,
'Twas his misfortune to be shot,
His deeds shall never be forgot,
By all his friends below.
For help he cried, but was denied,
His memory ever shall be blest,
He rose again to stand the test,
While down upon his gallant breast,
The crimson blood did flow.

Now the youth he fell upon the ground,
And in his breast a mortal wound,
While through the woods the gun did sound,
That took his life away.
In the midst of life he fell, in suffering full well,
Deep was the wound the keeper made,
No mortal man his life could save,
He now lies sleeping in the grave,
Until the judgement day.

His case it makes our hearts to mourn,
Our comrades were to prison sent,
It being our enemies' intent,
That there they should remain.
But fortune changed her mind, and unto us proved kind,
No more locked up in midnight cells,
To her the turnkey ring the bells,
And bid those ponderous bells adieu,
And the rattling of their chains.

Now the murderous man who did him kill,
All on the ground his blood did spill,
Must wander far against his will,
And find no resting place.
Destructive things, his conscience stings,
He must wander through the world forlorn,
And ever feel the smarting thorn,
And pointed at with finger scorn,
And die in sore disgrace.

With its extended stanza form and complex rhyming scheme, 'The Gallant Poacher' looks to have been shaped by its distinctive melody. Unlike 'The Death of Poor Bill Brown', the song is not known to have been based on any identifiable historical incident. It is, however, notable for its poetic treatment of the figure of the keeper, who is again implicitly branded with the mark of Cain which is explicit in 'The Death of Bill Brown'.

'The Gallant Poacher' has been quite widely collected in England, with the odd record from the USA. The broadside record, with imprints including Jackson, Russell, Wright (Birmingham), Stewart (Carlisle), Beaumont (Leeds), Disley, Fortey, Paul, Ryle, Such, Taylor (London), Bebbington (Manchester), Ross, Walker (Newcastle), Plant (Nottingham), Harkness (Preston), Wilson (Whitehaven), Sefton (Worcester), tends to suggest an origin in mid 19th century, although Roy Palmer has argued for a rather earlier date on the basis of textual similarities with a song from the Luddite period (*Everyman's Book of English Country Songs*).

This version was collected by Henry Hammond from Henry Adams at Sturminster Newton, Dorset, in August 1905. In bar ten, we have split a single quaver in Hammond's notation into two semi-quavers (sixteenth-notes) to accommodate he words "he will". Adams's version has not preserved the rhyme scheme of the broadside versions, but it is easily restored. In the broadsides, "His case it makes our hearts to mourn" was "His case it makes our hearts lament"; "And bid those ponderous doors adieu" was "Those creaking doors we bade farewell".

**Recordings** Albion Country Band *Battle Of The Field*; Harry Cox *The Bonny Labouring Boy*; John Doyle *The Wayward Son*; George Dunn *Chainmaker*; Walter Pardon *Voice of the People, Vol. 18*.

A broadside of 'The Gallant Poacher', printed by Birt of London in the early part of the 19th century.

## The Gallant Poacher.

BIRT, Printer, 39, Great St. Andrew Street, 7 Dials

Come all you lads of high renown,
That love to drink strong ale that's brown,
And bring those lofty pheasents down,
   With powder, shot, and gun ;
     He is a gallant youth,
     He will tell the truth,
He has cross'd all life's temptations ways,
No mortal man his life could save,
He now lies sleeping in his grave,
   His deeds on earth are done.

Me and five more a poaching went,
To kill some game was our intent,
Our money being all gone and spent,
   We had nothing else to try,
     For the moon shone brigh,
     Not a cloud appeared in sight.
The keeper heard us fire the gun,
And to the spot he quickly ran,
And swore, before the rising sun,
   That one of us should die.

Now, the bravest youth among the lot,
It was his misfortune to be shot,
His deeds shall never be forgot,
   By all his friends below,
     For help he cri'd,
     But was deni'd,
His memory ever shall be blest,
He rose again to stand the test,
While down upon his gallant breast,
   His crimson blood did flow.

Now, the youth fell upon the ground,
And in his breast a mortal wound,
While through the woods the gun did sound,
   That took his life away ;
     In the midst of life he fell,
     His sufferings were full well,
Deep was the wound the keeper gave,
No mortal man his life could save,
He now lies sleeping in his grave,
   Untill the judgement day.

It makes our hearts to mourn,
Our comrades were to prison sent,
It being our enemy's intent,
   That there they should remain :
     But fortune chang'd their mind,
     And unto us did prove kind,
No more lock'd up in the midnight cells,
Here the turnkeys ring their bells,
And bid those ponderous doors adieu,
   And the rattling of their chains.

Now, the murderous man who did him kill,
All on the ground his blood did spill,
Must wander far against his will,
   And find no resting place,
     Destructive things,
     His conscience stings,
He must wander through the world forlorn,
Aud ever feet the smarting thorn,
And pointed at with fingers scorn,
   And die in sad disgrace.

# THE HUSBANDMAN AND THE SERVINGMAN
## (SERVINGMAN AND HUSBANDMAN) (ROUD 873)

"Well met, well met, my friend, all on the high-way, Whilst we here to-geth-er do stand. Pray tell un-to me, Oh who that you may be? Are you not some serv-ing-man?"

"O-ho! my broth-er dear, what makes you for to en-quire, Of a-ny such thing at my hand? For I will not re-frain to tell to you quite plain I am a down-right hus-band-man."

"Well met, well met, my friend, all on the highway,
Whilst we here together do stand,
Pray tell unto me, Oh who that you may be?
Are you not some serving-man?"

"O ho, my brother dear, what makes you for to enquire,
Of any such thing at my hand?
For I will not refrain to tell you quite plain,
I'm a downright husbandman."

"If a husbandman you be, then come along with me,
Within a little space of land,
Within a little space I could help you to a place
Where you may be some serving-man."

"As for our 'telligence, I return you many thanks,
I require no such thing at your hand,
But something to make sure where further I may know
The pleasures of a serving-man."

"Why sir, it is a fine thing to ride out with a King,
Lord, Duke or Squire or any such a one,
To hear the horn to blow, the hounds all in a row,
Such pleasure's for the serving-man."

"My joys be more than that, for to see my horses fat
And a good stack of hay by them stand
My reaping and my mowing, my ploughing and my sowing,
That's pleasures for a husbandman."

This dialogue concerning the respective merits of these two ways of making a living looks as if it may have begun its life in print. An apparently unique text in the *Roxburghe Ballads* (I, 299–305), which can probably be dated to the early 17th century, was printed by F. Coles and carries the initials 'R.C.' which may indicate the authorship of Richard Climsell. The record in print continues with London broadsides from the 18th and 19th centuries, with imprints including Catnach, Jennings, and Pitts. The dialogue form was common on early broadsides and another example from the mid 17th century is 'God Speed The Plow, And Bless The Corn Mow. A Dialogue Between The Husbandman And Servingman'.

Nevertheless, 'The Husbandman And The Servingman' has also been collected from rural singers in England. Cecil Sharp, Alfred Williams, and the Hammond brothers all collected versions. Williams stated that it was popular at harvest-homes, and *Ancient Poems, Ballads And Songs Of The Peasantry* (1846 and later editions) has the following description: "At a harvest-home feast at Selborne, in Hampshire, in 1836, we heard it recited by two countrymen, who gave it with considerable humour, and dramatic effect. It was delivered in a sort of chant, or recitative."

'We Servingmen Get Pleasure', which Cecil Sharp collected from Frederick Crossman in Somerset in 1906, seems to be a reduced version of the same song, but stands perfectly well on its own.

This version was collected by Henry Hammond from William Miller at Wootton Fitzpaine in Dorset, in April 1906. This is a very economical version of a song that can run to 16 verses or more in some of the printed versions. The husbandman's part is in the bass, to emphasise the contrast. Hammond also provides a chorus (below) which he says comes after the final verse, adding "but there was a bass part too, which I could not get". We don't know how this worked: perhaps the two characters sang the chorus in harmony.

**Recordings** Magpie Lane *The Oxford Ramble*; The Young Tradition *Galleries*.

This is Cecil Sharp's notebook entry for another version of 'The Husbandman And The Servingman', taken down from John Fry, at Tormarton, Gloucestershire, on April 3rd, 1907.

# THE PAINFUL PLOUGH (ROUD 355)

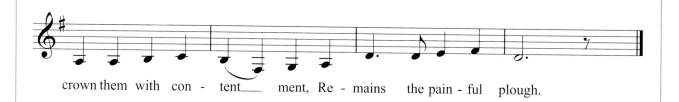

Come all you jolly ploughmen,
With courage stout and bold,
They'll labour all the winter,
Through stormy winds and cold.
To clothe your fields with plenty,
Your farm-yards to renew,
To crown them with contentment,
Remains the painful plough.

Adam was a ploughman,
When ploughing first began,
The next that did succeed him
Was Cain his eldest son.
Some of their generation,
Their calling doth pursue,
That head may not be wanted,
Remains the painful plough.

"Oh ploughman," says the gardener,
"Don't count your trade with ours.
There's walking in the garden,
To view those early flowers.
There's all those curious borders,
And pleasant walks to view.
There's no such peace and contentment,
Promoted by the plough."

"Oh gardener," says the ploughman,
"Our calling don't despise.
Every man for his living,
Doth on his trades relies.
Were it not for the ploughman,
Both rich and poor must rue,
For we're all depending,
Upon the painful plough.

"Behold the wealthy merchants,
That trades upon the seas,
That brings the golden treasures,
To those that lives at ease,
That brings the fruit and spices,
And silks too also,
They are brought from the Indies,
By virtue of the plough.

"And the men that do bring them,
We've only to be true,
They could not sail the ocean,
Without the painful plough.
For they must have bread biscuits,
Flour, pudding, beef and peas,
To feed the jolly sailors,
As they sail upon the seas."

"I hope no one's offended,
With me for singing this,
For I never was intended,
For anything amiss.
If you consider it rightly,
You'll find what I say is true,
Not a man that you can mention,
Can live without the plough."

Widely collected in England and Scotland from rural singers and often described as a very old agricultural song, the earliest records in fact are 19th-century broadsides. Imprints include Wilson (Bideford), Bloomer, Wright (Birmingham), Bennett, Boyes (Brighton), Marshall (Bristol), Ford (Chesterfield), Hoggett, Walker (Durham), Ringham (Lincoln), Batchelar, Catnach, Disley, Fortey, Such (London), Harkness (Preston), Angus, Fordyce (Newcastle), Harris (Salisbury), and Croshaw (York).

Samson, Solomon, Alexander, and King David are often mentioned in the course of the song, but just occasionally a King Henry intrudes.

This version was collected by Cecil Sharp from Thomas Mitchell at Merriott, in Somerset, on August 25th and September 3rd, 1905. Sharp comments, "Low notes on Mr Mitchell's voice not very distinct", and his notation includes a number of corrections and second thoughts. The typescript of the lyrics has a hand-written question mark against the word "head" in the second verse: "bread" would make better sense, taking the word "wanted" to mean "lacked". Mitchell's version omits the common verse about Samson, Solomon and so on. Here's an example, taken from Robert Bell's collection of *Ancient Poems, Ballads And Songs Of The Peasantry Of England*, published in 1854:

Samson was the strongest man, and Solomon was wise,
Alexander for to conquer 'twas all his daily prize;
King David was valiant, and many thousands slew,
Yet none of these brave heroes could live without the plough!

**Recordings** Bob Lewis *The Painful Plough*; Magpie Lane *Speed The Plough*; John Roberts & Tony Barrand *A Present From The Gentlemen*.

## THE RAMBLING BLADE (ROUD 490) As sung by Walter Pardon.

CD TRACK 14

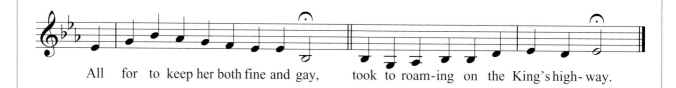

At Rambling Green where I was born,
A good broad sword I've always worn.
I was apprenticed to a trade,
But was always known as 'The Rambling Blade'.

At seventeen I took a wife,
I loved her as I love my life.
All for to keep her both fine and gay,
Took to robbing on the King's highway.

On this poor girl I based my choice,
For ever made my heart rejoice,
But that sad day she'll for ever rue,
Betrayed I was to Ned Fielding's crew.

I robbed Lord Golden in Leicester Square,
I robbed his wife, I do declare.
Tapping those shutters, bid them goodnight,
Taking the gold for my heart's delight.

To Covent Garden straight away,
My wife and I went to a play.
Ned Fielding's gang did then me pursue,
Taken I was by the gallows crew.

I never robbed a poor man yet,
Nor was I in a tradesman's debt,
But many a maiden will weep for me,
When my sad life ends on the gallows tree.

Then dig my grave both wide and deep,
Two tombstones at my head and feet,
And on them carve two pretty white doves,
To let the people know that I have died for love.

Let six bold robbers carry me,
Give them broad swords and sweet liberty.
Let six pretty fair maids hold up my pall,
Give them black gloves and white ribbons all.

And when I'm dead pray tell the truth,
Here lies a wild and wicked youth,
And on my tombstone pray let it be,
It was those bad girls that have ruined me.

Also known as 'Adieu, Adieu', 'Newry Town', 'In Newlyn Town', 'The Rambling Boy', 'The Wild And Wicked Youth', 'The Flash Lad', and by various other titles, 'The Rambling Blade' has been widely collected in England, Ireland and North America. It was also often printed, with imprints that included Bloomer, Pratt, Russell (Birmingham); Collard (Bristol); Whinham (Carlisle); Walker (Durham); Fordyce (Hull); Birt, Catnach, Disley, Edwards, Fortey, Goode, Paul, Pitts (London); Fordyce (Newcastle); Harkness (Preston).

Although the story is often less than explicit, the gist of this archetypal execution ballad is clear enough. It describes the career of a young man that begins with an early marriage to a wife with expensive tastes, and descends into highway robbery and burglary, ending eventually with his capture and execution. The song in its various incarnations is rich with social resonances, lending themselves to different readings in different contexts, and it has an impressive historical depth, beginning in the mid 18th century with the advent of London's police force.

Although the ballad is not known to recount a specific historic case, several of the versions make explicit reference to Tyburn and to "Fielding's Gang". Tyburn was the place of execution near Marble Arch in the West End of London, where public executions were staged, attracting substantial crowds. Fielding's Gang refers to the Bow Street Runners, the first police force, which was established in London in 1751 by the novelist Henry Fielding and his brother John, who were both magistrates in the mid 18th century.

**Recordings** Jumbo Brightwell *The Voice Of The People, Vol. 4*, as 'Newry Town'; Martin Carthy With Dave Swarbrick *Second Album*, as 'Newlyn Town'; The Johnstons *The Barley Corn*, as 'The Newry Highwayman'; Tommy Makem & Liam Clancy *Two For The Early Dew*, as 'The Newry Highwayman'; Walter Pardon *A World Without Horses*; Bob Scarce *Folk Songs Of Britain, Vol. 7*, as 'Newlyn Town'; Peggy, Barbara & Penny Seeger *Three Sisters*, as 'Newlyn Town'; Waterson:Carthy *Fishes & Fine Yellow Sand*, as 'Newry Town'; John Wright & Catherine Perrier *John Wright And Catherine Perrier*, as 'Newlyn Town'.

Walter Pardon

# VAN DIEMAN'S LAND (ROUD 519)

Come all you gallant poachers that rambles devoid of care,
That walketh out on a moonlight night with dog and gun and snare.
Here's the hares and the lofty pheasants, they stands at your command,
But you don't think on the dangers, all on Van Dieman's Land.

Here's poor Tom Brown from Nottingham, Jack Williams and poor Joe,
They was three of the daring poachers the country did well know.
One night they was trap-handed by the keepers hid in sand,
And for fourteen years transported, all on Van Dieman's Land.

The very first day we landed all on that fatal shore,
The planters they come round us, about three score and more.
So they harnessed up like horses and fit us out of hand,
And they yoked us to the plough, my boys, to plough Van Dieman's Land.

Oh those wretched huts that we live in is built with clods and clay,
And rotten straw for bedding, we dare not say nay.
Our cottages they're all fenced with fire, we slumber while we can,
To drive all wolf and tiger, all from Van Dieman's Land.

One night all in my slumbers I had a pleasant dream,
I dreamed I was with my dear wife down by some purling stream.
With the children's prattling stories all around me they did stand,
But I awoke quite broken hearted, all on Van Dieman's Land.

Here is a girl from Nottingham, Susan Somers is her name,
She got fourteen years transported for selling of our game.
But the planters bought her freedom and married her out of hand,
And she proved true and kind to us, all on Van Dieman's Land.

'Van Dieman's Land' (correctly 'Van Diemen's' but regularly spelled with an 'a' in broadside print) was the old name for Tasmania, first colonised by the British in 1803 and used for transportation from 1804 to 1853. The "wolf and tiger" quite possibly refers to the Tasmanian wolf (now probably extinct) and the Tasmanian devil (a carnivorous and on occasion quite fierce marsupial). Roy Palmer (*The Sound of History*, pp149–51) suggests that the ballad may have been written in response to an Act of 1828 specifying transportation only for a third conviction for poaching, except where violence was involved. It is possible that no more than around 300 convicted poachers were actually transported to Australia, but the threat of transportation remained real.

This is probably the most widely collected of transportation songs, turning up in England, Scotland, Ireland, and North America, and possibly also Australia. There are numerous broadside imprints from the 19th century. Most of these texts name the towns of Nottingham and Birmingham, suggesting a Midlands origin for the song, but there are Scottish versions that have Glasgow and Dundee, and an Irish text has Nenagh, showing some degree of localisation.

Two further songs appear to have followed on from 'Van Dieman's Land'. 'Young Henry the Poacher' (Roud 221) and 'The Female Transport'. 'Young Henry' may be connected with the transportation of 11 poachers for shooting at gamekeepers on the estate of D.S. Dugdale, MP, in Warwickshire in 1829, and/or with another similar case that took place on the Earl of Denbigh's estate near Coventry around the same time. This song, which has been collected several times from singers in England, appears under numerous broadside imprints. Place names from the Midlands are found in the earlier texts, with the consoling female hailing from Wolverhampton, while later instances situate the action in Lancashire. 'The Female Transport' tells the story of one Sarah Collins (or O'Brien) who is transported to Van Diemen's Land for 14 years for an unspecified crime. Although not collected from singers, this song appeared in a number of broadside printings.

Roy Palmer sums up the mood of these transportation ballads: "The transports are shocked, resentful, deeply unhappy, but seldom indignant; they speak more in sorrow than anger, and their gloom is relieved only by flashes of spirit or humour" (*The Sound of History*, p152).

This version was collected by Cecil Sharp from Robert Parish, at Exford, Somerset, on September 6th, 1906. "Trap-handed" seems to mean entrapped or caught.

**Recordings** The Bushwackers *Bushfire*; Harry Cox *What Will Become of England?*, as 'Henry The Poacher'; The Demon Barbers *Uncut*; The Dubliners *Irish Rebel Ballads*; Christy Moore *Whatever Tickles Your Fancy*; Walter Pardon *The Voice Of The People, Vol. 4*; The Young Tradition *The Young Tradition*.

# VIRGINIA (ROUD 1488)

Come all you young fellows, wheresoever you might be,
Come listen a while and I'll tell you,
There's many a young fellow myself I have seen,
More fitting to serve Victoria, our Queen,
But those hard-hearted judges so cruelly has been
For to send us poor lads to Virginia.

When we arrived in Virginia, that old, ancient place,
Which now I renown in my story,
Our captain he stands with a rod in his hand
To bargain for us like slaves out of bond.
When he saw those young fellows a-ploughing the main,
How hard was my fate in Virginia!

Old England, old England, I shall never see no more,
If I do, it's ten thousand to twenty,
For my fingers are rotting and my bones they are sore,
I wander about, I'm brought down to death's door,
But if I only live to see seven years more,
I will then bid adieu to Virginia.

'The Lads of Virginia' appears on broadsides with imprints including Collard (Bristol), Birt, Jennings, Pitts, NS Such (London). These are all of the 19th or the end of the 18th century, but the ballad, with its American destination, must date from before 1776 and the American War of Independence. Once convicts began to be sent to Australia instead, the song was readily adapted as 'Australia', although it does not appear to have been printed under that name. Both forms have been collected from English singers.

The song is not especially widespread, but it does appear to have been popular in Suffolk. Unlike other surviving transportation songs, such as 'Van Dieman's Land' (Roud 519), this one, in the broadside versions, specifies that the convict's crime was not poaching but highway robbery (although he blames his downfall on a woman's malign influence!). The sense of injustice at the hard treatment meted out to the convicts remains as strong as ever.

As a further example of the adaptation of such songs, Roy Palmer (*FMJ*, 3.2 (1976), 161) has drawn attention to 18th-century broadsides which purport to relate events that occurred in the 17th century, under the title 'The Poor Unhappy Transported Felon's Sorrowful Account Of His Fourteen Years Transportation, At Virginia, In America', supposedly written by the convict himself, one James Revel ('The Unhappy Sufferer', as the broadsides describe him). Subsequently, the 19th-century printer Bloomer of Birmingham issued the same song but with a few verbal alterations changing the scene to Botany Bay, New South Wales, while retaining the name James Revel and giving the date of his transportation as February 1806 and that of his return to London as March 1st 1821.

This version was collected by George Gardiner from Mrs Goodyear, at Axford, near Basingstoke, Hampshire, in July 1907. Mrs Goodyear was 74 years old at the time. The tune was taken down by George Gamblin of Winchester. The unusual six-line verse structure is found in the broadside versions, which mix six and four-line verses. A note on the typescript tells us that Virginia is pronounced "Virginny". Mrs Goodyear's version omits any detail of the crime or the criminal's motivation. Here's an extra verse from a broadside printed by Jennings in London at the end of the 18th century:

In the city of London I served my time,
Many hours serv'd duly and truly,
Till those buxom young lasses led me astray,
My work I neglected more and more every day
And for to maintain it went on the highway,
By that I got lagg'd to Virginia.

**Recordings** Martin Carthy *Crown Of Horn*, as 'Virginny'; Bob Fox *Borrowed Moments*; Bob Hart *Hidden English*, as 'Australia'; Geoff Ling *Songs Sung In Suffolk*, as 'Australia'; Cyril Poacher *Plenty Of Thyme*, as 'Australia'.

# Contributors

**Vic Gammon** is senior lecturer in folk and traditional music at Newcastle University. He has written the music for more than 20 stage and radio plays and features. He sings, plays melodeon, concertina, and banjo, and has performed in Britain, Europe, and the US.

**David Atkinson** is the author of *The English Traditional Ballad: Theory, Method, and Practice* and co-editor, with Ian Russell, of *Folk Song: Tradition, Revival, and Re-Creation*. As a research fellow at the University of Aberdeen, he is working on the critical edition of the James Madison Carpenter Collection. He is editor of *Folk Music Journal*.

**Malcolm Taylor** has been in charge of the Vaughan Williams Memorial Library at the EFDSS for more than 25 years and was awarded the Order of the British Empire for services to music librarianship and heritage in 2002. He was awarded the Gold Badge of the EFDSS in 2004.

**John Morrish** is commissioning editor for Backbeat Books in the UK. A former editor of the London magazine *Time Out*, he has contributed extensively to the national press in the UK as well as writing books on magazine editing and the English language.

**Mark Brend** is a writer and a musician. His books include *American Troubadours: Groundbreaking Singer Songwriters Of The Sixties* and *Strange Sounds: Offbeat Instruments And Sonic Experiments In Pop*. He has been releasing records on British independent labels for the past 20 years.

**Rikky Rooksby** is a songwriter, composer, guitar teacher and writer on music. He is the author of a series of successful guides to songwriting. He is a member of the Guild of International Songwriters & Composers and the Ralph Vaughan Williams Society.

**Stephanie Smith** is an archivist at the Center for Folklife and Cultural Heritage, Smithsonian Institution. She holds the M.Litt. and Ph.D. degrees in Scottish Studies from the University of Edinburgh. Her research specialties are British and Appalachian folk music and dance traditions, the British folk revival, and English country dance. She currently co-directs the English Country Dance Video Documentation Project.

**Nigel Williamson** is a leading British music journalist. He is author of *The Rough Guide To Bob Dylan*, *The Rough Guide To The Blues* and *Journey Through The Past: The Stories Behind The Classic Songs Of Neil Young*.

**David Sheppard** has written regularly for *MOJO*, *Q*, and *Uncut* magazines. He has written short biographies of Leonard Cohen and Elvis Costello, and is currently working on a book about Brian Eno. As a musician, he has worked with several critically-acclaimed ensembles including State River Widening and Ellis Island Sound.

**Martin Carthy**, sometimes called the "father of the English folk revival", is a guitarist, singer, songwriter, and arranger. His career began in the 1960s and continues today with his group Waterson:Carthy, which includes his wife Norma Waterson and daughter Eliza Carthy. He is recognised as an influence on both Bob Dylan and Paul Simon.

# What's on the CD

## CD TRACK 1
### The Barley Mow (PAGE 94)
Sung by HARRY CHAMBERS
Harry Chambers was born in 1908 and lived in the parish of Dennington, Suffolk, for more than 50 years. A farmhand before retirement, he learned 'The Barley Mow', a classic drinking toast, at a farmworker's union meeting in nearby Saxmundham, and would often use it to round off an evening at the Dennington Bell pub.
**Recorded at the singer's home in Dennington, Suffolk, by John Howson on August 1st, 1985.**
*Published on VTC2CD 'Songs Sung in Suffolk' (2000).*
*IRSC GB SNY 07 00040*

## CD TRACK 2
### Drink Old England Dry (PAGE 97)
Sung by WILL NOBLE & JOHN COCKING
Will Noble and John Cocking have been singing together for more than 20 years in the South Pennines area of Yorkshire. A builder and a drystone waller respectively, they learned their songs from family sources and from older traditional singers, developing their craft at shepherds' meetings and hunt suppers, particularly those of the Holme Valley Beagles, for whom John Cocking was kennelman.
**Recorded live at the Three Horseshoes, Dutton Hill, Essex, by Simon Ritchie and John Howson, on April 21st, 2004.**
*Published on VT147CD 'Yon Green Banks' (2004).*
*ISRC GB SNY 07 00635*

## CD TRACK 3
### John Barleycorn (PAGE 103)
Sung by TOM SMITH
Tom Smith, born in 1918, spent 25 years working on the land and 26 for Suffolk County Council. He learned most of his songs from his father, who used to lead a singing session at the Bull in Thorpe Morieux. Tom never considered himself a singer, preferring to concentrate on the piano accordion. He died in 2002.
**Recorded at the singer's home in Thorpe Morieux, Suffolk, by John Howson, on August 4th, 1985.**
*Published on VTC2CD 'Songs Sung in Suffolk' (2000).*
*ISRC GB SNY 07 00033*

## CD TRACK 4
### Banks of Sweet Primroses (PAGE 110)
Sung by VIC LEGG
Vic Legg was born into a well-known West Country travelling family, the Orchards, in 1941. He learned most of his songs from his aunts, Charlotte and Betsy Renals, and his mother, Sophie Legg. He learned more while serving as an apprentice in Devonport dockyard. A lifelong resident of Bodmin in Cornwall, and a stalwart of the local folk club, he has an infectious style that has made him popular on his rare trips outside the region.
**Recorded at the singer's home in Bodmin, Cornwall, by John Howson, on February 16th, 1993.**
*Published on VT129CD 'I've Come to Sing a Song' (2000).*
*IRSC GB SNY 07 00356*

## CD TRACK 5
### Barbara Allan (PAGE 112)
Sung by VIC LEGG
**Recorded at the singer's home in Bodmin, Cornwall, by John Howson, on February 16th, 1993.**
*Published on VT129CD 'I've Come to Sing a Song' (2000).*
*IRSC GB SNY 07 00354*

## CD TRACK 6
### Pleasant and Delightful (PAGE 142)
*(Hear the Nightingale Sing)*
Sung by TOMMY MORRISSEY & CHARLIE PITMAN
Tommy Morrissey and Charlie Pitman were from Padstow in north Cornwall. Tommy Morrissey, born in 1915, was a lifelong fisherman who teamed up with Pitman, born in 1914, a farmworker and golf course green keeper, to sing in local pubs. Pitman, especially, was a master of the comic song. They died in 1996 and 2003.
**Recorded at the Ship Inn, Wadebridge, Cornwall, by John Howson, on February 21st, 1991.**
*Published on VTC9CD 'Uncle Tom Cobleigh and All' (2004).*
*ISRC GB SNY 07 00207*

## CD TRACK 7 (PAGE 145)
### Sixteen Come Sunday *(Seventeen Come Sunday)*
Sung by JEAN ORCHARD
Jean Orchard is a member of the Orchards, a prominent West Country travelling family, and she sings in true

gypsy style. Her songs mostly came from family sources – though she also sings country and western on occasions – and have delighted audiences far from her north Devon home. She has usually recorded and performed with her husband, Tom, and son, Ashley, who are melodeon players.

**Recorded in Holsworthy, Devon, by John Howson, on March 5th, 2005.**
*Published on VT151CD 'Holsworthy Fair' (2005).*
*ISRC GB SNY 07 00732*

## CD TRACK 8

**Tommy Doddler** (*The Crabfish*)  (PAGE 194)
Sung by CHARLIE STRINGER

Charlie Stringer was born in Wickham Skeith, Suffolk, in 1900. He spent his entire life there, working on the land. He learned his songs from his father, Wag Stringer, who was the village blacksmith and a regular singer in the local pub, The Swan. Charlie first sang with him there at the age of five. He died in 1992.

**Recorded at the singer's home in Wickham Skeith, Suffolk by John Howson, on July 18th, 1983.**
*Published on VT130CD 'Who Owns the Game?' (2001).*
*ISRC GB SNY 07 00376*

## CD TRACK 9 (PAGE 216)

**Broomfield Hill** (*The Broomfield Wager*)
Sung by GORDON HALL

Gordon Hall, born in 1932, was the son of Mabs Hall, a noted singer who was first recorded in her eighties. He lived most of his life in Horsham, in Sussex, and it was there, in 1984, that he met Bob Copper, who first persuaded him (and his mother) to sing in public. A powerful musical story-teller, he had a distinctive style, with a pronounced 'kick' at the end of every line. He died in 2000.

**Recorded at the singer's home in Pease Pottage, Sussex, by John Howson on February 8th, 1995.**
*Published on VT131CD 'When the May is all in Bloom' (1995).*
*ISRC GB SNY 07 00398*

## CD TRACK 10

**Outlandish Knight** (PAGE 228)
Sung by VIC LEGG

**Recorded at the singer's home in Bodmin, Cornwall, by John Howson, on February 16th, 1993.**
*Published on VT129CD 'I've Come to Sing a Song' (2000).*
*ISRC GB SNY 07 00358*

## CD TRACK 11 (PAGE 234)

**'Cleverly Done,' Said He** (*The Poor Old Couple*)
Sung by MANNY ALDOUS

Manny Aldous was born in Offton, Suffolk, in 1906. He had many jobs after starting work at 12, including farm work, road-mending, factory work and finally working in the kitchens at a nearby RAF station. A singer all his life, he collected songs from the old men he encountered in local pubs. He died in 1988.

**Recorded at the singer's daughter-in-law's home in Needham Market, Suffolk, by John Howson, on October 13th, 1987.**
*Published on VTC1CD 'Stepping it Out!' (1993).*
*ISRC GB SNY 07 00010*

## CD TRACK 12 (PAGE 251)

**The Grand Conversation on Napoleon**
Sung by GORDON HALL

**Recorded at the singer's home in Pease Pottage, Sussex, by John Howson, on February 8th, 1995.**
*Published on VT131CD 'When the May is all in Bloom' (1995).*
*ISRC GB SNY 07 00389*

## CD TRACK 13 (PAGE 254)

**Bungay Roger** (*Muddley Barracks*)
Sung by CHARLIE HANCY

Charlie Hancy was born in Bungay, Suffolk, in 1899 and lived there all his life. A hay trader and horseman, he travelled the country in pursuit of his trade and learned many of his songs from the gypsies he met on his travels.

**Recorded at the singer's home in Bungay, Suffolk, by John Howson, on February 27th, 1986.**
*Published on VTC2CD 'Songs Sung in Suffolk' (2000).*
*ISRC GB SNY 07 00029*

## CD TRACK 14

**The Rambling Blade** (PAGE 270)
Sung by WALTER PARDON

Walter Pardon, born in 1914, was one of the most celebrated traditional singers of the 20th century (see p90). He spent his entire life in the same village, singing mostly for his own enjoyment. He had a repertoire of 180 songs but said this was his favourite. He died in 1996.

**Recorded at the singer's home in Knapton, Norfolk, by John Howson, on April 19th, 1981.**
*(Unpublished)*
*ISRC GB SNY 07 99990*

# Bibliography and web directory

This select bibliography includes references for books and articles mentioned in the song notes and essays, as well as some of the original collections of songs. More comprehensive bibliographies are available on the Resources page at the English Folk Dance and Song Society's website (http://www.efdss.org/resind.htm). The web directory is intended to showcase some of the more useful and interesting internet sites devoted to folk and traditional music.

Flemming G. Andersen and Thomas Pettitt, '"The Murder Of Maria Marten": The Birth Of A Ballad?', in *Narrative Folksong: New Directions: Essays In Appreciation Of W. Edson Richmond*, ed. by Carol L. Edwards and Kathleen E. B. Manley (Boulder, CO: Westview Press, 1985), pp. 132–78.

S. Baring-Gould and Cecil J. Sharp, *English Folk-Songs For Schools* (London: Curwen, 1906).

S. Baring-Gould and H. Fleetwood Sheppard, *Songs And Ballads Of The West*, 4 parts (London: Methuen; Patey & Willis, 1889–92).

S. Baring Gould, H. Fleetwood Sheppard, and F. W. Bussell, *Songs Of The West: Folk Songs Of Devon & Cornwall Collected From The Mouths Of The People*, new and rev. edn under the musical editorship of Cecil J. Sharp [3rd edn] (London: Methuen, 1905).

Robert Bell, ed., *Ancient Poems, Ballads And Songs Of The Peasantry Of England* (London: John W. Parker, 1857).

Lucy E. Broadwood and J. A. Fuller Maitland, eds, *English County Songs: Words And Music* (London: Leadenhall Press; J. B. Cramer; Simpkin, Marshall, Hamilton, Kent, 1893).

Bertrand Harris Bronson, *The Traditional Tunes Of The Child Ballads, With Their Texts*, 4 vols (Princeton: Princeton University Press, 1959–72).

J. Collingwood Bruce and John Stokoe, eds, *Northumbrian Minstrelsy: A Collection Of The Ballads, Melodies, And Small-Pipe Tunes Of Northumbria* (Newcastle-upon-Tyne: Society of Antiquaries of Newcastle-upon-Tyne, 1882; repr. Felinfach: Llanerch, 1998).

David Buchan, 'The Wit-Combat Ballads', in *Narrative Folksong: New Directions: Essays In Appreciation Of W. Edson Richmond*, ed. by Carol L. Edwards and Kathleen E. B. Manley (Boulder, CO: Westview Press, 1985), pp. 380–400.

William Chappell, *Popular Music Of The Olden Time: A Collection Of Ancient Songs, Ballads, And Dance Tunes, Illustrative Of The National Music Of England*, 2 vols (London: Cramer, Beale and Chappell, [1855–59]; repr. New York: Dover, 1965).

William Chappell and J. Woodfall Ebsworth, eds, *The Roxburghe Ballads*, 9 vols (London; Hertford: Ballad Society, 1869–97).

Francis James Child, ed. *The English and Scottish Popular Ballads*, 5 vols (Boston: Houghton, Mifflin, 1882–98; rpt New York: Dover, 1965; digital edn, New York: ESPB Publishing and Heritage Muse, 2003).

Tristram P. Coffin, 'The Murder Motive In "Edward"', *Western Folklore*, 8 (1949), 314–19.

Bob Copper, *A Song For Every Season: A Hundred Years Of A Sussex Farming Family* (London: Heinemann, 1971; repr. [new edition] Peacehaven: Coppersongs, 1997).

W. G. Day, ed., *The Pepys Ballads*, 5 vols, Catalogue of the Pepys Library at Magdalene College, Cambridge, Facsimile Volumes I–V (Cambridge: D. S. Brewer, 1987); http://emc.english.ucsb.edu/ballad_project/index.asp

Vivian de Sola Pinto and Allan Edwin Rodway, eds, *The Common Muse: An Anthology Of Popular British Ballad Poetry, XVth–XXth Century* London: Chatto & Windus, 1957.

Dianne Dugaw, *Warrior Women And Popular Balladry, 1650–1850* (Cambridge: Cambridge University Press, 1989; repr. Chicago and London: University of Chicago Press, 1996).

T. D'Urfey, *Wit And Mirth: Or Pills To Purge Melancholy; Being A Collection Of The Best Merry Ballads And Songs, Old And New*, 6 vols (London, 1719–20).

David C. Fowler, '"The Gosport Tragedy": Story Of A Ballad', *Southern Folklore Quarterly*, 43 (1979), 157–96.

A. H. Fox Strangways, in collaboration with Maud Karpeles, *Cecil Sharp* (London: Oxford University Press, 1933).

Vic Gammon, 'Folk Song Collecting In Sussex And Surrey, 1843-1914', *History Workshop Journal*, no. 10 (1980), 61–89.

Vic Gammon, 'The Grand Conversation: Napoleon And British Popular Balladry', *RSA Journal*, 137 (1989), 665–74; repr. http://www.mustrad.org.uk/articles/boney.htm

Steve Gardham, *An East Riding Songster: A Selection Of Folk-Song From The East Riding* (Lincoln and Hull: Lincolnshire and Humberside Arts, 1982).

Alice E. Gillington, *Songs Of The Open Road: Didakei Ditties And Gypsy Dances* (London: Williams, 1911).

Maud Karpeles, ed., *Cecil Sharp's Collection Of English Folk Songs*, 2 vols (London: Oxford University Press, 1974).

Maud Karpeles, ed., *The Crystal Spring: English Folk Songs Collected By Cecil Sharp*, 2 vols (also in one vol.) (London: Oxford University Press, 1975).

Maud Karpeles, *An Introduction To English Folk Song* (London: Oxford University Press, 1973; repr. with a new foreword by Peter Kennedy, Oxford: Oxford University Press, 1987).

Peter Kennedy, ed., *Folksongs Of Britain And Ireland: A Guidebook To The Living Tradition Of Folksinging In The British Isles And Ireland* (London: Cassell, 1975).

Frank Kidson, ed., *Traditional Tunes: A Collection Of Ballad Airs, Chiefly Obtained In Yorkshire And The South Of Scotland; Together With Their Appropriate Words From Broadsides And From Oral Tradition* (Oxford: Chas. Taphouse, 1891; repr. East Ardsley: S. R. Publishers, 1970).

A. L. Lloyd, *Folk Song In England* (London: Lawrence and Wishart, 1967).

A. L. Lloyd, *The Singing Englishman: An Introduction To Folk Song* (London: Workers' Music Association, 1944).

E. B. Lyle, ed., *Andrew Crawfurd's Collection Of Ballads And Songs*, 2 vols (Edinburgh: Scottish Text Society, 1975, 1996).

Ewan MacColl and Peggy Seeger, eds, *Travellers' Songs From England And Scotland* (London: Routledge & Kegan Paul, 1977).

Iona and Peter Opie, *The Oxford Dictionary Of Nursery Rhymes* (Oxford: Clarendon Press, 1951).

Roy Palmer, ed., *Everyman's Book Of British Ballads* (London: Dent, 1980; repr. as *A Book Of British Ballads*, Felinfach: Llanerch, 1998).

Roy Palmer, ed., *Everyman's Book Of English Country Songs* (London: Dent, 1979; repr. as *English Country Songbook*, London: Omnibus Press, 1986).

Roy Palmer, *The Sound Of History: Songs And Social Comment* (Oxford: Oxford University Press, 1988; repr. London: Pimlico, 1996).

Frank Purslow, ed., *Marrow Bones: English Folk Songs From The Hammond And Gardiner Mss.* (London: E.F.D.S. Publications, 1965).

Frank Purslow, ed., *The Wanton Seed: More English Folk Songs From The Hammond & Gardiner Mss.* (London: E.F.D.S. Publications, 1968).

Frank Purslow, ed., *The Constant Lovers: More English Folk Songs From The Hammond & Gardiner Mss.* (London: E.F.D.S. Publications, 1972).

Frank Purslow, ed., *The Foggy Dew: More English Folk Songs From The Hammond & Gardiner Mss.* (London: E.F.D.S. Publications, 1974).

James Reeves, ed., *The Everlasting Circle: English Traditional Verse, Edited With An Introduction And Notes From The Manuscripts Of S. Baring-Gould, H. E. D. Hammond And George B. Gardiner* (London: Heinemann, 1960).

James Reeves, ed., *The Idiom Of The People: English Traditional Verse Edited With An Introduction And Notes From The Manuscripts Of Cecil J. Sharp* (London: Heinemann, 1958).

Roger deV. Renwick, *English Folk Poetry: Structure And Meaning* (Philadelphia: University of Pennsylvania Press, 1980).

Roger deV. Renwick, *Recentering Anglo/American Folksong: Sea Crabs And Wicked Youths* (Jackson: University Press of Mississippi, 2001).

Steve Roud, Eddie Upton, and Malcolm Taylor, eds, *Still Growing: English Traditional Songs And Singers From The Cecil Sharp Collection* (London: English Folk Dance & Song Society in association with Folk South West, 2003).

Cecil J. Sharp, *English Folk Songs*, Selected Edition, 2 vols (London: Novello, 1920; Taunton: Barnicott & Pearce, 1907) repr. in one vol., 1959).

Cecil J. Sharp, *English Folk Songs From The Southern Appalachians*, ed. by Maud Karpeles, 2 vols (London: Oxford University Press, 1932).

Cecil J. Sharp, *English Folk-Song: Some Conclusions* (London: Simpkin; Novello; Taunton: Barnicott & Pearce, 1907).

Cecil J. Sharp, and Charles L. Marson, eds, *Folk Songs From Somerset*, 5 series [4th and 5th Series ed. by Cecil J. Sharp] (London: Simpkin, Marshall, Hamilton, Kent; London: Simpkin; Schott; Taunton: Barnicott and Pearce, 1904–09).

Cecil J. Sharp, ed. *One Hundred English Folksongs* (Boston: Oliver Ditson, 1916; repr. New York: Dover, 1975).

Hugh Shields, '"The Grey Cock": Dawn Song Or Revenant Ballad?', in *Ballad Studies*, ed. by E. B. Lyle, Mistletoe Series (Cambridge and Totowa, NJ: D. S. Brewer; Rowman and Littlefield for the Folklore Society, 1976), pp. 67–92.

Hugh Shields, *Narrative Singing In Ireland: Lays, Ballads, Come-All-Yes And Other Songs* (Blackrock: Irish Academic Press, 1993).

Barre Toelken, *Morning Dew And Roses: Nuance, Metaphor, And Meaning In Folksongs* (Urbana and Chicago: University of Illinois Press, 1995), chapter 6.

Lajos Vargyas, *Researches Into The Mediaeval History Of Folk Ballad*, trans. by Arthur H. Whitney (Budapest: Akadémiaia Kiadó, 1967), chapter 2.

Ralph Vaughan Williams and A. L. Lloyd, eds, *The Penguin Book Of English Folk Songs: From The Journal Of The Folk Song Society And The Journal Of The English Folk Dance And Song Society* (Harmondsworth: Penguin, 1959); revised as *Classic English Folk Songs*, rev. by Malcolm Douglas (London: English Folk Dance & Song Society in association with the South Riding Folk Network, 2003).

Tessa Watt, *Cheap Print And Popular Piety, 1550–1640* (Cambridge: Cambridge University Press, 1991).

Alfred Williams, ed., *Folk-Songs Of The Upper Thames* (London: Duckworth, 1923).

Mike Yates, 'A Note on the Ballad "Edward" (Child 13)', *Folk Song Research*, 1 (1983), 26–28.

# Web directory

## SONG TEXTS AND BROADSIDES

*Ancient Poems, Ballads And Songs Of The Peasantry Of England*, edited by Robert Bell (1857). http://theotherpages.org/poems/ballads.html

**Bodleian Library Broadside Ballads** Huge and invaluable online collection of facsimiles of broadsides, with basic publishing information. www.bodley.ox.ac.uk/ballads/

*The English And Scottish Popular Ballads* (1884–1898), edited by Francis J. Child, placed online by Cathy Lynn Preston and David Stampe of the University of Hawaii. http://ling.lll.hawaii.edu/faculty/stampe/Oral-Lit/English/Child-Ballads/child.html

**Glasgow Broadside Ballads** A collection of more than 350 19th-century broadside ballads published in Glasgow. Page images without transcriptions. www.broadsideballads.gallowayfolk.co.uk

*The Oxford Book Of Ballads* (1910), edited by Arthur Quiller-Couch. www.bartleby.com/243/

**The Pepys Ballads** The Early Modern Center at the University of California at Santa Barbara has catalogued and placed online the 1,800 printed ballads collected by Samuel Pepys. They are available as page images and transcriptions and there are also commentaries on the material. http://emc.english.ucsb.edu/ballad_project

*Popular Music Of The Olden Times*, edited by William Chappell. Online edition of Dover Publications' 1965 facsimile of the 1859 original. Requires free DjVu browser plug-in. More manageable if downloaded. www.archive.org/details/PopularMusicOfTheOldenTime

**The Word On The Street** A collection of 1,800 broadsides placed online by the Library of Scotland as page images with transcriptions and commentary. www.nls.uk/broadsides

## INTERNET DIRECTORIES

**English folk and traditional music on the Internet** Martin Nail's comprehensive guide to English folk resources online. http://web.ukonline.co.uk/Members/martin.nail/Folkmus.htm

**Folk Network Internet Resources Guide** Useful directory compiled by Malcolm Douglas of the South Riding Folk Network. www.folk-network.com/directory/links.html

**Song resources on the web.** Compiled by the Traditional Song Forum www.tradsong.org/link.html

## INDEXES

**Folk Music Index: An Index to Recorded Releases** A discography of 55,000 songs and 22,000 performers, compiled by Jane Keefer in Portland, Oregon. Includes

British, Irish, and (mostly) American recordings. www.ibiblio.org/folkindex/

**The Traditional Ballad Index** Index of ballads and traditional songs of the English-speaking world. Includes basic reference information but no texts. www.csufresno.edu/folklore/BalladSearch.html

**Vaughan Williams Memorial Library Online** Includes the Roud Folk Song Index and individual collectors' indexes. http://library.efdss.org

## ORGANISATIONS

**English Folk Dance And Song Society** The home of English traditional music for more than a century. www.efdss.org

**Folk Archive Resource North East** Impressive site for an organisation dedicated to Northumbrian traditional music. http://www.asaplive.com/FARNE/Home.cfm

**Traditional Song Forum** UK organisation fostering study, collection, and performance of traditional song. Site includes useful texts and resources. www.tradsong.org

## TEXTS AND TUNES

**The Contemplator's Folk Music Site** Texts and MIDIs for a wide range of songs from Britain, Ireland, and America. www.contemplator.com/folk.html

**Digital Tradition** Includes a database of 9,000 songs, with texts and MIDI tunes, and a lively discussion forum. Many of the songs are not from traditional singers. www.mudcat.org

**Folksongs Of Various Countries** Site by Frank Petersohn, including texts of many songs, not all of them traditional. Some MIDI tunes. No commentary or sources. http://ingeb.org/folksong.html

## MAGAZINES

*Dirty Linen* Website for US print magazine dealing with traditional music. www.dirtylinen.com

*English Dance And Song* Quarterly magazine first published in 1936. http://eds.efdss.org

*Folk And Roots* Online magazine published in UK. www.folkandroots.co.uk

*Folking.com* Online magazine and discussion forum. www.folking.com

*Folk Music Journal* Scholarly journal of the English Folk Dance and Song Society. Published annually. http://fmj.efdss.org

*FolkWorld* Online traditional music magazine published in Germany. www.folkworld.de

*fRoots* magazine (formerly Folk Roots) Site for print magazine and online discussion forum. www.frootsmag.com

*Musical Traditions* Rod Stradling's excellent online traditional music magazine, with news, reviews, and scholarly articles. www.mustrad.org.uk

## RECORD COMPANIES

**Beautiful Jo** www.bejo.co.uk
**Fellside** www.fellside.com

**Fledg'ling** www.thebeesknees.com
**Folktrax** www.folktrax.pwp.blueyonder.co.uk
**Folkwit** www.folkwit.biz
**Harbourtown** www.harbourtownrecords.com
**Market Square** www.marketsquarerecords.co.uk
**Mrs Casey** www.mrscasey.co.uk
**Musical Traditions** www.mustrad.org.uk
**No Masters** www.nomasters.co.uk
**Park** www.parkrecords.com
**Talking Elephant** www.talkingelephant.co.uk
**Topic** www.topicrecords.co.uk
**Veteran** www.veteran.co.uk
**WildGoose** www.wildgoose.co.uk

## MISCELLANEOUS

**The Copper Family** Official site of The Copper Family. www.thecopperfamily.com

**The Folk Map** Innovative visual guide to UK and Ireland folk scene. www.folkmap.co.uk

**International Percy Grainger Society** http://www.percygrainger.org

**Sabine Baring-Gould** Martin Graebe's site about the pioneering song collector. www.greenjack.btinternet.co.uk

**Ralph Vaughan Williams Society** www.rvwsociety.com

**UK folk music usenet group** uk.music.folk or http://groups.google.com/group/uk.music.folk/

# Discography

This selected discography is designed to provide more details of the recordings noted in each song entry in the body of the book. More details of each of those references will be found here under the name of the artist, or under the name of the album in the Various Artists section, which comes at the end of the listing. Where possible we have shown the original recording in the country of origin, although some are inevitably later releases, compilations, or reissues.

**Albion Country Band**, *Battle Of The Field*, 1976, Island HELP25

**Heather Alexander**, *Festival Wind*, 2003, Sea Fire Productions SFP-0308-2

**Peck Allmond**, *Kalimba Collage*, 2004, SoniCulture 3901

**The Almanac Singers** (including Woody Guthrie, Pete Seeger), *Deep Sea Chanteys And Whaling Ballads*, 1941, General G-20

**Altan**, *Local Ground*, 2005, Vertical VERTCD069

**Frankie Armstrong**, *And The Music Plays So Grand*, 1980, Sierra/Briar SBR-4211

**Frankie Armstrong**, *Out Of Love, Hope And Suffering*, 1973, Bay 206

**Louis Armstrong**, *The Complete Hot Five And Hot Seven Recordings*, 2003, Sony 63527

**Dave & Toni Arthur**, *The Lark In The Morning*, 1969, Topic 190

**Joan Baez**, *The First 10 Years*, 1970, Vanguard 5005
**Joan Baez**, *In Concert*, 1962, Vanguard 9112
**Joan Baez**, *Joan Baez*, 1961, Vanguard VRS 9078
**Joan Baez**, *Joan Baez 5*, 1964, Vanguard VRS-9160

**Joan Baez**, *Volume 2*, 1961, Vanguard VSD 2097
**Damien Barber**, *The Furrowed Field*, 2000, DJC 011
**Horton Barker**, *Anglo-American Ballads, Vol. 1*, 1999 (1940s recordings), Rounder 1511
**Battlefield Band**, *Out For The Night*, 2004, Temple COMD 2094
**Peter Bellamy**, *Wake The Vaulted Echoes*, 2000, Free Reed 14
**Bellowhead**, *Burlesque*, 2006, West Park 97132
**Emily Bishop**, *Country Songs & Carols*, 1975 (1952 recording) Folktrax Cassettes FTX-129

Blowzabella, *A Richer Dust*, 1988, Plant Life PLCD 080

Blue Epitaph, *Ode By...*, 1974, Holyground HG117

Blue Murder, *No One Stands Alone*, 2002, Topic 537

Ian Bostridge, *The English Songbook*, 1999, EMI Classics CDC 5 56830 2

The Bothy Band, *After Hours (Live In Paris)*, 1979, Polydor 2383530

Boys Of The Lough, *Lonesome Blues And Dancing Shoes*, 2002, Lough 008

Brass Monkey, *Flame Of Fire*, 2004, Topic 550

Jumbo Brightwell, *Songs From The Eel's Foot*, 1973, Topic 261

Kate Bush, *This Woman's Work*, 1990, EMI CDKBBX1

The Bushwackers, *Bushfire*, 1979, Image 806

Packie Byrne, *Donegal & Back! Songs, Ballads And Whistle Tunes*, 2002, Veteran VT132CD

Alex Campbell, *Yours Aye, Alex*, 1966, Transatlantic XTRA 1041

The Ian Campbell Folk Group, *Across The Hills*, 1964, Transatlantic 118

The Carter Family, *In The Shadow Of Clinch Mountain*, 2001, Bear Family BCD-15865

Eliza Carthy, *Anglicana*, 2002, Topic 539

Martin Carthy, *Crown Of Horn*, 1976, Topic 300

Martin Carthy, *Martin Carthy*, 1965, Fontana STL 5269

Martin Carthy, *Shearwater*, 1972, Pegasus PEG 12

Martin Carthy, *Signs Of Life*, 1999, Topic 503

Martin Carthy, *Sweet Wivelsfield*, 1974, Deram 1111

Martin Carthy, *Waiting For Angels*, 2004, Topic TSCD527

Martin Carthy & Dave Swarbrick, *But Two Came By*, 1968, Fontana STL 5477

Martin Carthy & Dave Swarbrick, *Straws In The Wind*, 2006, Topic 556

Martin Carthy With Dave Swarbrick, *Second Album*, 1966, Fontana STL 5362

Pete Castle, *False Waters*, 1995, Steel Carpet MATS012

Nick Cave & The Bad Seeds, *B-Sides And Rarities*, 2005, Mute CDMUTEL11

The Cecil Sharp Centenary Collective: Simon Care, Ashley Hutchings, Emily Slade, Roger Wilson, *As I Cycled Out On A May Morning*, 2004, Talking Elephant TECD053

Daisy Chapman, *Ythanside*, 2000, Musical Traditons MTCD308

Cherish The Ladies, *Threads Of Time*, 1998, BMG 09026 63131-2

The Clancy Brothers & Tommy Makem, *The First Hurrah!*, 1964, Columbia CS 8965

The Clancy Brothers & Tommy Makem, *Greatest Hits*, 1973, Vanguard VSD-53/54

Judy Collins & Theodore Bikel, *Live At Newport 1959-1966*, 1994, Vanguard 1570 77013 2

Shirley Collins, *Adieu To Old England*, 1974, Topic 238

Shirley Collins, *Amaranth*, 1976, Harvest 2008

Shirley Collins, *False True Lovers*, 1960, Folkways FG 3564

Shirley Collins, *No Roses*, 1971, Pegasus PEG7

Shirley Collins, *The Power Of The True Love Knot*, 1968, Polydor 583025

Shirley Collins, *Snapshots*, 2006, Fledg'ling 3057

Shirley Collins, *Sweet England*, 1959, Argo RG 150

Shirley Collins, *The Sweet Primeroses*, 1967, Topic 170

Shirley & Dolly Collins, *Anthems in Eden*, 1969, Harvest SHVL 771

Shirley & Dolly Collins, *Love, Death & The Lady*, 1970, Harvest 771

Bob & Ron Copper, *Twankydillo*, Folktrax 082, 1975

The Copper Family, *Come Write Me Down: Early Recordings*, 2001, Topic 534

The Copper Family, *Coppersongs: A Living Tradition*, 1987, EFDSS VWML004

The Copper Family, *Coppersongs 2*, 1995, Coppersongs CD2

The Copper Family, *Coppersongs 3: The Legacy Continues*, 1998, Coppersongs CSCD3

The Copper Family, *A Song For Every Season*, 1971, Leader LEAB 404/LEA 047

Cordelia's Dad, *Road Kill*, 1996, Scenescof 1004

Harry Cox, *The Bonny Labouring Boy: Traditional Songs & Tunes From A Norfolk Farm Worker*, 2000, Topic 512

Harry Cox, *What Will Become of England?*, 2000, Rounder 1839

Crooked Jades, *The Unfortunate Rake, Vol. 2*, 2003, Copper Creek CCCD-2005

Doris Day, *Best Of Big Bands*, 1990 (1940-1946 recordings), Columbia CK-46224

The Demon Barbers, *Uncut*, 2003, DJC 019

Johnny Doherty, *Johnny Doherty*, 1975, CCÉ CL 10

Lonnie Donegan, 'My Old Man's A Dustman' / 'The Golden Vanity' single, 1960, Pye 7N15256

Donovan, *HMS Donovan*, 1971, Dawn DNLD 4001

Johnny Doughty, *Round Rye Bay For More*, 1977, Topic 324

John Doyle, *The Wayward Son*, 2005, Compass Records 4408

Barry Dransfield, *Unruly*, 2005, Violin Workshop VW1CD

Robin & Barry Dransfield, *Lord Of All I Behold*, 1971, Trailer LER 2026

The Dubliners, *At Home With*, 1969, EMI SCX 6380

The Dubliners, *Irish Rebel Ballads*, 1995, Chyme CHCD1055

The Dubliners, *36 Irish Favourites*, 2005, Prism Leisure 7120

The Dubliners, *Wild Rover*, 1998, Double Classics 31011

George Dunn, *Chainmaker*, 2002, Musical Traditions MTCD317-8

Bob Dylan, *The Bootleg Series Volumes 1-3*, 1991, Columbia C3K 47382

Bob Dylan, *Live At The Gaslight 1962*, 2005, Columbia 96016

Seamus Ennis, *The Bonny Bunch Of Roses*, 1959, Tradition TLP1013

The Etchingham Steam Band (includes Shirley Collins), *The Etchingham Steam Band*, 1995 (1974–5 recordings), Fledg'ling 3002

E2K, *Shift*, 2001, Topic 522

Fairport Convention, *The Bonny Bunch Of Roses*, 1977, Vertigo 9102015

Fairport Convention, *Cropredy Box*, 1998, Woodworm 3CD026

Fairport Convention, *Five Seasons*, 1991, Rough Trade 005

Fairport Convention, *Liege & Lief*, 1969, Island ILPS 9115

Fairport Convention, *Tipplers Tales*, 1978, Vertigo 9102 022

Marianne Faithfull, *Go Away From My World*, 1965, London 452

Cilla Fisher & Artie Tresize, *Cilla And Artie*, 1979, Topic 12TS405

John Fleagle, *World's Bliss*, 2000, Archetype 60103

Chris Foster, *Jewels*, 2004, Living Tradition LTCD1102

Bob Fox, *Borrowed Moments*, 2003, Topic 544

Sam Friend, Alf Peachey & Jimmy Knights, *The Contented Countryman*, 1995, Neil Lanham NL02

Jerry Garcia & David Grisman, *Shady Grove*, 1996, Acoustic Disc 21

Steve Gillette & Cindy Mangsen, *The Light Of The Day*, 1996, Compass Rose CRM-7

Texas Gladden, *Ballad Legacy*, 2001 (1940s recordings), Rounder 1800

Cynthia Gooding, *Queen Of Hearts: Early English Folk Songs*, 1958, Elektra EKL-131

Davy Graham, *Large As Life And Twice As Natural*, 1968, Decca SKL4969

The Green House Band, *Mirage*, 2004, Market Square 126

Gryphon, *Gryphon*, 1973, Transatlantic TRA 262

Woody Guthrie, *Anglo-American Ballads, Vol. 1*, 1999 (1940s recordings), Rounder 1511

Hair Of The Dog, *Release The Hounds*, 1997, October Eve 262

Gordon Hall, *Good Things Enough*, 2001, Country Branch CBCD095

Gordon Hall, *In Horsham Town*, 1988, Veteran VT115

Herbie Hancock, *New Standard*, 1996, Verve 529584

John Wesley Harding, *Trad. Arr. Jones*, 1999, Zero Hour 2210

Roy Harris, *The Rambling Soldier*, 1979, Fellside FE017

Bob Hart, *A Broadside*, 1998, Musical Traditions MTCD301–2

Tim Hart & Maddy Prior, *Folk Songs Of Olde England, Vol.1*, 1968, Teepee TPR 102

Tim Hart and Maddy Prior, *Folk Songs Of Olde England, Vol. 2*, 1976, Mooncrest 26

Frank Harte & Dónal Lunny, *My Name Is Napoleon Bonaparte*, 2001, Hummingbird HDCD0027

Cliff Haslam & John Millar, *Colonial And Revolutionary War Sea Songs And Chanteys*, 1975, Folkways FW05275

Justin Hayward With Mike Batt And The London Philharmonic Orchestra, *Classic Blue*, 1993, Castle Music CLA385

Joe Heaney, *The Road From Connemara: Songs And Stories Told And Sung To Ewan MacColl & Peggy Seeger*, 2000, Topic 518D

Harry Holman, *Just Another Saturday Night: Sussex 1960* (various artists), 2001, Musical Traditions MTCD309-10

Home Service, *Alright Jack*, 1986, Makingwaves SPIN 119

Arthur Howard, *Merry Mountain Child*, 1981, Hill & Dale HD 006

Carolyne Hughes, *Blackdog & Sheepcrook*, c.1968, Folktrax FRX-043

Burl Ives, *Ballads*, 1959, United Artists UAL 3060

Burl Ives, *Sings His Favourites*, 1996 (rec. 1941/2), Magnum 007

Bert Jansch, *Jack Orion*, 1966, Transatlantic TRA 143

Bert Jansch, *Rosemary Lane*, 1971, Transatlantic TRA 235

The Johnstons, *The Barley Corn*, 1969, Transatlantic TRA 185

Nic Jones, *Ballads And Songs*, 1970, Trailer 2014

Nic Jones, *Nic Jones*, 1971, Trailer 2027

Fred Jordan, *In Course Of Time…*, 1991, EFDSS VWML006,

Fred Jordan, *A Shropshire Lad*, 2003, Veteran VTD148CD

Kathy And Carol, *Kathy And Carol*, 1965, Elektra EKS 7289

Lou Killen, *Sea Chanteys*, 1968, ESP 1085

Lou & Sally Killen, *Bright Shining Morning*, 1975, Front Hall FHR 006

John Kirkpatrick, *Shreds And Patches*, 1977, Topic 12TS355

Knot Fibb'n, *Knot Loitering*, 2000, Knot Fibb'n Music CD 7728

Spider John Koerner, *Raised By Humans*, 1992, Red House 44

Sam Larner, *Now Is The Time For Fishing: Songs And Speech*, 1999, Topic TSCD511

Vic Legg, *I've Come To Sing A Song: Cornish Family Songs*, 2000, Veteran VT129CD

Lehto & Wright, *The Thrashing Machine And Other Stories*, 2006, New Folk 8832

The Lemonheads, *Car Button Cloth*, 1996, Atlantic 92726

Bob Lewis, *The Painful Plough*, 2002, Foxide RUST105

A.L. Lloyd, *Leviathan! Ballads And Songs Of The Whaling Trade*, 1967, Topic 174

The Louvin Brothers, *Tragic Songs Of Life*, 1956, Capitol 769

The Love Hall Tryst, *Songs Of Misfortune*, 2005, Appleseed 1089

Bascom Lamar Lunsford, *Ballads, Banjo Tunes, And Sacred Songs Of Western North Carolina*, 1996, Smithsonian Folkways 40082

Ewan MacColl, *The Manchester Angel*, 1966, Topic 147

Ewan MacColl, *Scots Street Songs*, 1956, Riverside RLP 12-612

Ewan MacColl, *Solo Flight*, 1972, Topic

Ewan MacColl, *The Wanton Muse*, 1968, Argo ZDA 85

Ewan MacColl & A.L. Lloyd, *The Singing Sailor*, 1956, Topic TRL3

Ewan MacColl & Peggy Seeger, *Classic Scots Ballads*, 1961, Tradition 1015

Ewan MacColl & Peggy Seeger, *Popular Scottish Songs*, 1960, Folkways FW 8757

Magpie Lane, *English Songs And Dances*, 1994, Beautiful Jo BEJO-6

Magpie Lane, *The Oxford Ramble: Songs And Tunes Of Oxfordshire*, 1993, Beautiful Jo BEJO-3

Magpie Lane, *Speed The Plough: Songs & Tunes Of Rural England*, 1994, Beautiful Jo BEJO-4

Tommy Makem & Liam Clancy, *Two For The Early Dew*, 1992 (1970s recordings), Shanachie 52004

Roger McGuinn, *McGuinn's Folk Den Vol.1*, 2000, mp3.com 2720

Bob Mills, *An English Folk Music Anthology*, 1981, Folkways FW38553

Miranda Sex Garden, *Iris EP*, 1992, Elektra 61277

Christy Moore, *Prosperous*, 1972, Tara 2008

Christy Moore, *Whatever Tickles Your Fancy*, 1975, Polydor Super 2383 344

Morris On, *Morris On*, 1972, Island HELP5

Maggy Murphy, *Linkin' O'er The Lea: Traditional Folk Songs And Ballads From Tempo, Co. Fermanagh*, 1996, Veteran VT134CD

John Jacob Niles, *American Folk Lore Vol. 3*, 1941, RCA Red Seal M-824

John Jacob Niles, *Folk Balladeer*, 1965, RCA LPV-513

Will Noble, *In That Beautiful Dale: South West Yorkshire Songs*, 1992, Veteran VT 124

Tim O'Brien & The O'Boys, *Oh Boy! O'Boy!*, 1993, Sugar Hill 3808

Old Blind Dogs, *The World's Room*, 1999, Green Linnet 1201

The Old Hat Dance Band, *Old Hat Dance Band*, 1992, OH2CD

The Outlaws, *The Outlaws*, 1975, Arista AL 4042

Papa M, *Whatever, Mortal*, 2001, Drag City 194

Walter Pardon, *Put a Bit of Powder On It, Father*, 2000, Musical Traditions MTCD305-6

Walter Pardon, *A World Without Horses*, 2000, Topic 514

Patterson Jordan Dipper, *Flat Earth*, 2002, WildGoose WGS309CD

Pentangle, *One More Road*, 1993, Permanent SPV 084-92962

Pentangle, *Sweet Child*, 1968, Transatlantic TRA 178

Planxty, *After The Break*, 1979, Tara 3001

Cyril Poacher, *Plenty Of Thyme*, 1999, Musical Traditions MTCD303

The Pogues, *Red Roses For Me*, 1984, Stiff SEEZ55

Maddy Prior, *Arthur The King*, 2004, Park 58

Maddy Prior & June Tabor, *Silly Sisters*, 1976, Chrysalis 1101

The Prodigals, *Dreaming In Hell's Kitchen*, 2001, Grab 1103

James Raynard, *Strange Histories*, 2005, One Little Indian 487

Esma Redzepova & Usnija Jasarova, *Songs Of A Macedonian Gypsy*, 1994, Monitor 71496

John Renbourn, *A Maid In Bedlam*, 1977, Shanachie 79004

Revel Players, *The Wild Mountain Thyme*, 1993, Revels CD-1094

Jean Ritchie, *Ballads From Her Appalachian Family Tradition*, 1961, Smithsonian Folkways SFW40145

John Roberts & Tony Barrand, *Dark Ships In The Forest: Ballads Of The Supernatural*, 1977, Folk-Legacy 65

John Roberts & Tony Barrand, *A Present From The Gentlemen*, 1992, Golden Hind GHM-101

Jeannie Robertson, *The Queen Among The Heather*, Rounder 1720

Tony Rose, *On Banks Of Green Willow*, 1976, Trailer LER 2101

Tony Rose, *Young Hunting*, 1970, Trailer LER 2013

Kate Rusby, *The Girl Who Couldn't Fly*, 2005, Compass 4420

Kate Rusby, *Sleepless*, 1999, Compass 4277

Kate Rusby And Kathryn Roberts, *Kate Rusby And Kathryn Roberts*, 1995, Pure 01

Mick Ryan & Pete Harris, *The Widow's Promise*, 2002, Terra Nova UK 11

Scafell Pike, *The Month Of Maying*, 1974, Epic 65761

Buffy Sainte-Marie, *Fire & Fleet & Candlelight*, 1968, Vanguard 79250

Peggy Seeger, *Folksongs And Ballads*, 1958, Riverside RLP-12-655

Peggy, Barbara & Penny Seeger, *Three Sisters*, 1957, Prestige 13029

Pete Seeger, *American Ballads*, 1957, Folkways FA 2319

Simon & Garfunkel, *Parsley Sage Rosemary & Thyme*, 1966, Columbia 9363

Martin Simpson, *The Bramble Briar*, 2001, Topic 513

Martin Simpson, *Kind Letters*, 2005, Topic 553

Jasper Smith, *Here's Luck To A Man: Gypsy Songs & Music From South-East England* (various artists) 2003, Musical Traditions MTCD320

Levi Smith, *The Voice Of The People, Vol. 1* (various artists), 1998, Topic TSCD651

Phoebe Smith, *The Yellow Handkerchief: Traditional Songs And Ballads From England's Greatest Gypsy Singer*, 1998, Veteran VT136CD

Wiggy Smith, *Band Of Gold*, 1994, Ossian 96

The Spinners, *Folk At The Phil!*, 1964, Fontana STL 5219

Spriguns (of Tolgus), *Revel Weird & Wild*, 1976, Decca 5262

Joan Sprung, *Pictures To My Mind*, 1980, Folk Legacy FSI-073

Ralph Stanley & The Clinch Mountain Boys, *Featuring Keith Whitley And Ricky Skaggs*, 1971, Jalyn 129

Steeleye Span, *Back In Line*, 1986, Flutterby FLUT2

Steeleye Span, *Below The Salt*, 1972, Chrysalis CHR-1008

Steeleye Span, *The Best Of British Folk Rock*, 1997, Park B335

Steeleye Span, *Commoner's Crown*, 1975, Chrysalis CHR 1071

Steeleye Span, *Hark! The Village Wait*, 1970, RCA BF8113

Steeleye Span, *Storm Force Ten*, 1978, Chrysalis CHR-1151

Steeleye Span, *Ten Man Mop, Or Mr Reservoir Butler Rides Again*, 1971, Pegasus PEG9

Alex, Belle, Cathie and Sheila Stewart, *The Stewarts Of Blair*, 1994, Ossian OSS CD 96

June Tabor, *At The Wood's Heart*, 2005, Topic 557
June Tabor And The Oyster Band, *Freedom And Rain*, 1990, Rykodisc 194
June Tabor With Martin Simpson, *A Cut Above*, 1980, Topic 410
Phil Tanner, *The Gower Nightingale: Ballads, Songs And Mouth Music From South Glamorgan recorded in the 1930s & 40s,* Veteran VT145CD
Danny Thompson, *Whatever*, 1974, Hannibal HNBL 1326
Lisa Theriot, *A Turning Of Seasons*, 2001, Orchard 800669
Jane & Amanda Threlfall, *Gown Of Green*, 2002, Beehive Music 233
George Townshend, *Come Hand To Me The Glass*, 2000, Musical Traditions MT CD 304
Traffic, *John Barleycorn Must Die*, 1970, Island ILPS 9116
Trees, *On The Shore*, 1970, CBS 64168
Trian, *Trian II*, 1995, Green Linnet GLCD1159

Dave Van Ronk, *Inside*, 1962, Prestige 14025

Doug & Jack Wallin, *Family Songs And Stories From The North Carolina Mountains*, 1995, Smithsonian Folkways SF CD 40013
Lal & Norma Waterson, *A True Hearted Girl*, 1977, Topic 331
Mike Waterson, *Mike Waterson*, 1977, Topic 332
Norma Waterson, *Bright Shiny Morning*, 2000, Topic 520
Waterson:Carthy, *Common Tongue*, 1997, Topic 488
Waterson:Carthy, *A Dark Light*, 2002, Topic 536
Waterson:Carthy, *Fishes & Fine Yellow Sand*, 2004, Topic 542
Waterson:Carthy, *Waterson:Carthy*, 1994, Topic 475
The Watersons, *Early Days*, 1994, Topic 472
The Weavers, *Traveling On With*, 1958, Vanguard VRS 9043
Roisin White, *The First Of My Rambles: Folk Songs From Ulster*, 2000, Veteran VT126CD
The White Stripes, *The White Stripes*, 1999, Sympathy For The Record Industry 577
Duncan Williamson, *Put Another Log On The Fire: Songs And Tunes From A Scots Traveller*, 1994, Veteran VT128
John Wright & Catherine Perrier, *John Wright And Catherine Perrier*, 1978, Green Linnet SIF 1011

The Yetties, *Our Friends*, 1971, Argo 32
The Young Tradition, *Galleries*, 1969, Transatlantic 172
The Young Tradition, *The Young Tradition*, 1966, Transatlantic TRA 142

Frank Zappa, *The Lost Episodes*, 1996 (1960s recordings), Rykodisc 40573

## VARIOUS ARTISTS

*Anthology Of American Folk Music*, 1997, Smithsonian Folkways SFW40090
*Bad Man Ballads: Songs Of Outlaws And Desperadoes, Southern Journey, Vol. 7*, 1997, Rounder CD 1705
*The Birds Upon The Tree And Other Traditional Songs And Tunes: More Songs And Tunes From The Mike Yates Collection*, 2004, Musical Traditions MTCD333
*Catch Me If You Can: Songs From Cornish Travellers*, 2003, Veteran VT119CD
*A Century Of Song: A Celebration Of Traditional Singers Since 1898*, 1998, EFDSS CD02
*Classic Ballads Of Britain And Ireland: Folk Songs Of England, Ireland, Scotland & Wales, The Alan Lomax Collection, Vol. 1*, 2000, Rounder 1775
*Classic Ballads Of Britain And Ireland: Folk Songs Of England, Ireland, Scotland & Wales, The Alan Lomax Collection, Vol. 2*, 2000, Rounder 1776
*Deep River Of Song: Black Texicans*, 1999, Rounder 1821
*Down In The Fields: An Anthology Of Traditional Folk Music From Rural England*, 2001, Veteran VTC4CD
*Field Trip – England: Collected by Jean Ritchie and George Pickow. Edited by Jean Ritchie*, 1959, Folkways FW 08871
*Far In The Mountains: Songs, Tunes And Stories From Mike Yates's Appalachian Collections 1979–1983, Vol. 3*, 2002, Musical Traditions MTCD323
*The Folk Songs Of Britain*, 1961/1968–71, Caedmon (US) 10 volumes TC 1141–45, 1162–1166 / Topic (UK) 10 volumes 12T157–61, 194–98
*From Puck To Appleby: Songs Of Irish Travellers In England*, 2003, Musical Traditions MTCD325-6
*Garners Gay*, 1971, EFDSS 1006
*Good Order! Ladies And Gentlemen Please: Traditional Singing & Music From The Eel's Foot, Eastbridge, Suffolk, Recorded In The 1930s & 40s*, 2000, Veteran VT140CD
*The Hardy Sons Of Dan: Football, Hunting And Other Traditional Songs From Around Loch Erne's Shore*, 2004, Musical Traditions MTCD329-0
*Her Bright Smile Haunts Me Still, Vol. 2*, 2000, Appleseed APR CD 1036,
*Here's Luck To A Man: Gypsy Songs & Music From South-East England*, 2003, Musical Traditions MTCD320
*Hidden English: A Celebration Of English Traditional Music*, 1994, Topic TSCD600
*It Was On A Market Day, Vol. 1*, 2005, Veteran VTC6CD
*It Was On A Market Day, Vol. 2*, 2006, Veteran VTC7CD
*Just Another Saturday Night: Sussex 1960*, 2001, Musical Traditions MTCD309-10
*The Leaves Of Life: The Field Recordings Of Fred Hamer*, 1989, EFDSS VWML003
*Man Of Constant Sorrow And Other Timeless Mountain Ballads*, 2000, Yazoo 3001
*Nothing Seems Better to Me: The Music Of Frank Proffit And North Carolina*, 2000, Appleseed APR CD 1036
*O Love Is Teasin' – Anglo-American Mountain Balladry*, 1985, Elektra 60402-1
*Old Uncle Tom Cobleigh And All: Folk Songs Sung In The West Country*, 2004, Veteran VTC9CD
*Ozark Folksongs*, 2001, Rounder 1108
*Ozark Frontier: Ballads And Old-Timey Music From*

*Arkansas, Vol. 7*, 1997, Rounder CD 1707
*Rogue's Gallery: Pirate Ballads, Sea Songs, & Chanteys*, 2006, Anti 86817
*Sea Songs And Shanties: Traditional English Sea Songs & Shanties From The Last Days Of Sail*, 1994, Saydisc CD-SDL 405
*Sea Songs & Shanties*, 1964, Topic 205
*Songs And Stories From East Coast Fishermen, Voice Of Suffolk, No. 6*, undated, Helions Bumpstead NLCD6
*Songs From The Company Of The Butley Oyster, 1967/68*, 1999, Helions Bumpstead NLCD3
*Songs Of Seduction*, 2000, Rounder 1778
*Songs Of The Travelling People: Music Of The Tinkers, Gipsies And Other Travelling People Of England, Scotland And Ireland*, 1994, Saydisc CD-SDL 407
*Songs Sung In Suffolk: Popular Folk Songs, Old Songs And Ballads*, 2000, Veteran VTC2CD
*Southern Journey, Vol 6: Sheep Sheep Don'tcha Know The Road*, 1997, Rounder 1706
*Traditional Songs Of England*, 2005, Saydisc 402
*Traditional Songs Of Ireland*, 1995, Saydisc 411
*Travellers' Tales Vol. 2*, 2002, Kyloe 101
*Unto Brigg Fair: Joseph Taylor And Other Traditional Lincolnshire Singers Recorded In 1908 By Percy Grainger*, 1972, Leader LEA 4050
*Up In The North And Down In The South: Songs And Music From The Mike Yates Collection 1964–2000*, 2001, Musical Traditions MTCD311-2
*The Voice Of The People*, 1998, Topic, 20 volumes, TSCD651–670
*Voices: English Traditional Song*, 1997, Musica Pangaea 10004
*When The May Is All In Bloom: Traditional Singing From The South East Of England*, 1995, Veteran VT131CD
*When The Wind Blows: An Anthology Of Traditional Folk Music From Coastal England*, 2001, Veteran VTC5CD
*Who Owns The Game?: Traditional Songs And Melodeon Tunes From Central Suffolk*, 2001, Veteran VT130CD

# Index

Song titles are shown in 'Single Quotes'. Titles beginning with 'The' or 'A/An' appear under the initial letter of the second word.

# Acknowledgements

Many thanks to John Howson of Veteran, Elaine Bradtke and Peta Webb at the Vaughan Williams Memorial LIbrary, Lisa Knapp, Rod Fogg, Julian Elloway, Robert Ashton and Peter Muir. This book would not have been possible without Steve Roud's indexes.

MIDI files for the tunes are available at www.folkhandbook.com.

**Picture credits**
Cecil Sharp Collection/EFDSS: pp 5, 6, 8, 23, 66, 123, 131, 133, 137, 139, 166, 209.
Eddis Thomas/EFDSS: pp 21, 24, 26 (Grainger), 30 (Kennedy), 5, 9, 62, 65, 116, 210, 259.

EFDSS Collection: pp 25 (Gardiner), 26 (Baring-Gould), 26 (Williams), 27 (Hammonds, RVW, Karpeles), 28 (Broadwood), 29 (Kidson, Gilchrist), 30 (Butterworth), 55, 62.

Collections Picture Library: pp 22, 28 (Cox), 31 (Jordan), 35 (Seeger), 39, 40, 41 (Jansch), 42 (Swarbrick).

Redfern's: cover (Rusby), pp 30 (Lomax), 31 (MacColl), 35 (Weavers), 37, 41 (Simon), 42 (Denny), 44, 46, 47, 49, 51, 52, 53, 54, 126, 238.

Veteran: pp 96, 98, 104, 110, 144, 145, 195, 219, 235, 255, 271.

All the broadsides, notebooks, and woodcuts are from the Vaughan Williams Memorial Library.

'Old Wine, New Skins' is a compilation CD of contemporary versions of some of the songs in the book. Released by Market Square, the UK independent record label, it is intended to demonstrate the way artists continue to reinterpret the English tradition and use it to inspire their own work. The artists represented include such titans as Tom Paxton and Joan Baez, established names like Barry Dransfield and Pentangle, and comparative newcomers such as Lisa Knapp and Serafina Steer. Unexpected guests include singer/actor Noel Harrison, celebrated for his international hit 'Windmills Of Your Mind'. The album is a reminder of how far and wide these songs have travelled since their rediscovery in at the turn of the 20th century.